Nile Style

Hippocrene Cookbook Library

Afghan Food & Cookery
Alps, Cuisines of the
Aprovecho: A Mexican-American
   Border Cookbook
Argentina Cooks!, *Exp. Ed.*
Austrian Cuisine, Best of, *Exp. Ed.*
Belarusian Cookbook, The
Bolivian Kitchen, My Mother's
Brazil: A Culinary Journey
Burma, Flavors of
Cajun Cuisine, Stir the Pot: The
   History of
Cajun Women, Cooking with
Calabria, Cucina di
Caucasus Mountains, Cuisines of the
Chile, Tasting
China's Fujian Province, Cooking from
Colombian Cooking, Secrets of
Croatian Cooking, Best of, *Exp. Ed.*
Czech Cooking, Best of, *Exp. Ed.*
Danube, All Along The, *Exp. Ed.*
Egyptian Cooking
Egyptian Cuisine and Culture, Nile Style:
English Country Kitchen, The
Estonian Tastes and Traditions
Filipino Food, Fine
Finnish Cooking, Best of
French Fashion, Cooking in the
   (*Bilingual*)
Germany, Spoonfuls of
Greek Cooking, Regional
Greek Cuisine, The Best of, *Exp. Ed.*
Gypsy Feast
Haiti, Taste of
Havana Cookbook, Old (*Bilingual*)
Hungarian Cookbook, *Exp. Ed.*
India, Flavorful
Indian Spice Kitchen, The, *Exp. Ed.*
International Dictionary of Gastronomy
Irish-Style, Feasting Galore
Jewish-Iraqi Cuisine, Mama Nazima's
Kerala Kitchen
Korean Cuisine, Best of
Laotian Cooking, Simple
Lebanese Cookbook, The
Ligurian Kitchen, A

Macau, Taste of
Mexican Culinary Treasures
Middle Eastern Kitchen, The
Naples, My Love for
Nepal, Taste of
New Hampshire: from Farm to Kitchen
New Jersey Cookbook, Farms and
   Foods of the Garden State:
Norway, Tastes and Tales of
Ohio, Farms and Foods of
Persian Cooking, Art of
Pied Noir Cookbook: French Sephardic
   Cuisine
Piemontese, Cucina: Cooking from
   Italy's Piedmont
Poland's Gourmet Cuisine
Polish Cooking, Best of, Exp. Ed.
Polish Country Kitchen Cookbook
Polish Heritage Cookery, *Ill. Ed.*
Polish Holiday Cookery
Polish Traditions, Old
Portuguese Encounters, Cuisines of
Pyrenees, Tastes of
Punjab, Menus and Memories from
Rhine, All Along The
Romania, Taste of, *Exp. Ed.*
Russian Cooking, Best of, *Exp. Ed.*
Scottish-Irish Pub and Hearth Cookbook
Sephardic Israeli Cuisine
Sicilian Feasts
Slovenia, Flavors of
South Indian Cooking, Healthy
Spanish Family Cookbook, *Rev. Ed.*
Sri Lanka, Exotic Tastes of
Swedish Kitchen, A
Taiwanese Cuisine, Best of
Thai Cuisine, Best of, Regional
Trinidad and Tobago, Sweet Hands:
   Island Cooking from
Turkish Cuisine, Taste of
Tuscan Kitchen, Tastes from a
Ukrainian Cuisine, Best of, *Exp. Ed.*
Uzbek Cooking, Art of
Vietnamese Kitchen, A
Wales, Good Food from
Warsaw Cookbook, Old

Nile Style

EGYPTIAN CUISINE AND CULTURE

Ancient Festivals, Significant Ceremonies, and Modern Celebrations

Amy Riolo

Hippocrene Books, Inc.
New York

Book and jacket design by Wee Design, Inc.
Interior color photography by Michael Stewart Photography, Inc.
Interior black and white photos by Amy Riolo.

For more information, address:
HIPPOCRENE BOOKS, INC.
171 Madison Avenue
New York, NY 10016
www.hippocrenebooks.com

Library of Congress Cataloging-in-Publication Data

Riolo, Amy.
 Nile style : Egyptian cuisine and culture : ancient festivals, significant
ceremonies, and modern celebrations / Amy Riolo.
      p. cm.
 Includes bibliographical references and index.
 ISBN 978-0-7818-1221-4 (alk. paper)
 ISBN 10: 0-7818-1221-6
 1. Cookery, Egyptian. 2. Cookery--Egypt. 3. Egypt--Social life and
customs. I. Title.
 TX725.E35R56 2009
 641.5962--dc22

                                                          2008043166

Printed in the United States of America.

To my mother-in-law, Fathiya Al Zayat, and my sister-in-law, Soad El Tanbedawy, for their unconditional love and support.

Amy Riolo with her mother-in-law

Acknowledgments

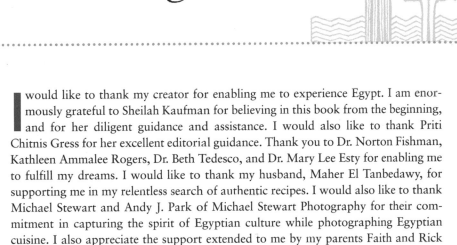

I would like to thank my creator for enabling me to experience Egypt. I am enormously grateful to Sheilah Kaufman for believing in this book from the beginning, and for her diligent guidance and assistance. I would also like to thank Priti Chitnis Gress for her excellent editorial guidance. Thank you to Dr. Norton Fishman, Kathleen Ammalee Rogers, Dr. Beth Tedesco, and Dr. Mary Lee Esty for enabling me to fulfill my dreams. I would like to thank my husband, Maher El Tanbedawy, for supporting me in my relentless search of authentic recipes. I would also like to thank Michael Stewart and Andy J. Park of Michael Stewart Photography for their commitment in capturing the spirit of Egyptian culture while photographing Egyptian cuisine. I also appreciate the support extended to me by my parents Faith and Rick Riolo, Nonna Angela Foti, the staff at the Embassy of Egypt in Washington, D.C., Dr. Mohamed Hamza and Dr. Maha Kamel of the Egyptian Cultural and Education Bureau, and Dr. Regine Schulz and Abdelwahab El Abd of the Baltimore-Luxor-Alexandria Sister City Committee; as well as the suggestions of Paul Trattner, Gail Forman, Enas Elhanafi, Joan Nathan, and Todd Kliman.

In Egypt, I am extremely grateful to my sister-in-law, Soad El Tanbedawy, my brothers-in-law, Abdu and Nabil El Tanbedawy, Chef Nasser Saiyd, Amira Mohsen, Saadeya Osman U'aah, and Kareema Mohamed Abdu for their culinary guidance and inspiration.

Thank you to Osman Shaheen, Mohamed Shaban, Mohamed Salah, Vivian Farook Yosif, Ali El Tanbedawy, Ayman and Rasha El Tanbedawy, Samy and Azza El Tanbedawy, and archeologist Elham Ali. In Luxor, I would like to thank my "brothers" Ahmed, Mahmoud, and Mohammed Edris and Mahmoud Fathy for treating me like one of the family. I would also like to thank Dr. Samier Farag, Bahaa Elden Aboelhamd Osman, General Mohamed El Metwali, Gerges Samael Azes, Hosny Hussein, Essam Ramadan, the staff of the Nubian Village in Luxor, the Nubian Community in Aswan, and the staff at the Egyptian Agricultural Museum in Cairo for sharing important cultural and historical information with me.

At the Tut Hotel in Luxor, I would like to thank Helmy Salah, Selem Mohamed, Chef Faisal, Chef Heggag, and Chef Ahmed Hashem for sharing their ideas and recipes. In addition, I would like to thank every shopkeeper, taxi driver, chef, and restauranteur who answered my questions and provided me with additional insight.

Contents

Foreword

Egyptian cuisine reflects the rich and varied cultural development of the country. Egyptians were typically open to foreign ideas and able to adapt or modify outside influences without giving up their main traditions. This principle also holds true for Egyptian food. Some of the recipes in this book date back to Pharaonic times, and others have their roots in Christian, Jewish, and Arabic traditions. There were influences from Mediterranean, Lebanese, Syrian, and Turkish cuisines, and also from Nubia. However, the Egyptian culinary tradition is not just a mixture of different influences—it is a highly advanced cuisine which developed its own characteristics over time. It reflects the needs of the Egyptians and their available food resources, as well as their cultural and religious customs.

Amy Riolo is an internationally recognized food historian and culinary expert with a special focus on oriental cuisines. When I first met her a couple of years ago in Baltimore, I was very impressed by her excellent knowledge and enthusiasm. I not only had the chance to taste her culinary art, but also to observe her talent for fascinating people with oriental food traditions. She is an outstanding instructor who combines seriousness and passion. During the last couple of years she has focused on researching and experimenting with Egyptian cuisine. Her main goal is to raise awareness about Egyptian culinary heritage, particularly in the U.S., and to help preserve the traditions in Egypt.

Nile Style presents Egyptian recipes as they relate to ancient and modern festivals and ceremonies. This kind of presentation is very helpful for a better understanding of the cultural and religious contexts for the development of Egyptian culinary art. More than just an excellent cookbook, *Nile Style* also gives the reader a chance to learn something about the history of and different types of people in Egypt. Short introductory paragraphs focus on historical facts, describing when and why changes occurred and how foreign influences became part of Egyptian life (for example, learn how Arabic merchants introduced coffee to Egypt on page 183).

Amy Riolo also focuses on how particular foods and meals are characteristic of special festivals and ceremonies. She offers excellent information, always keeping the prospective cook in mind—the introductory material to each menu is entertaining, and the recipe instructions are easy to follow. In addition, at the end of her book she offers a bibliography, a buyer's guide to finding special ingredients in the U.S., and a list of restaurants which serve the best Egyptian food in Egypt.

I congratulate Amy Riolo for this excellent introduction to Egyptian cuisine!

Regine Schulz, Ph.D.
*Curator of Ancient Art at The Walters Art Museum, Baltimore and
Professor of Egyptology, Ludwig-Maximilians-University, Munich*

Introduction

When I tasted true Egyptian food for the first time, I was delighted at how delicious it was. I was also astounded that such wonderful food could exist without my knowing about it! Before traveling to Egypt, I had only experienced Egyptian food prepared by Egyptian emigrants in Italy and the United States, who needed to substitute what was available for authentic Egyptian ingredients. Although the food was prepared by good cooks, it tasted like it was missing something. To make matters worse, the travel guide books that I read about Egypt stated that "Egypt has many things to offer … food is not one of them."

By the time I first traveled to Egypt I was scared to eat anything that wasn't familiar. So I stuck with my "safe" diet of white rice, chicken, and mangoes. After a while, my husband's cousin's wife said to me, "Amy, my daughters look up to you and copy everything you do. If you keep eating only white rice and mangoes, that's all they will eat, and they will get sick. Please, try to eat something else. Egyptian food is good, you will love it." Needless to say, she was right. After my culinary wake-up call, I made it a point to seek out true Egyptian cuisine. To my pleasant surprise, I found three common denominators at the heart of the Egyptian table: the freshest ingredients possible, ample amounts of spices and herbs, and a unique hospitality and graciousness.

By the time I returned to America, I was sad to leave my newfound friends and family behind. Creating Egyptian meals became my way of connecting with them from abroad. That is when my obsession with Egyptian food began. The fresh fruit stands offering the most addictively sweet nectars I'd ever tasted became a distant memory. The ubiquitous short-grain Egyptian rice and vermicelli was nowhere to be found. I had no idea how to re-create the sultry meat stews simmered in smoky spice mixtures that are integral to family meals. Where would I find the right vegetables to make the imaginative Egyptian salads whose flavors are so bright they barely need dressing? And although Turkish coffee is available in America, it is rarely brewed with the compliment of cool, crisp cardamom the way it is in Egypt. I longed for the typically Egyptian pastries that none of our local Middle Eastern markets prepared.

Since I couldn't find Egyptian restaurants offering all of the Egyptian foods I'd grown to love, I knew that if I wanted to relive my culinary memories, I would have to learn how to prepare them at home. Everyone, from my husband's relatives, friends, and professional chefs, to shopkeepers and taxi drivers, gladly shared their knowledge, recipes, and opinions with me. At the same time, I began researching everything I could about the cuisine, culture, and history of Egypt.

My research showed that Egyptian cuisine combines twenty-thousand years of insight, the traditions of three major world religions, and culinary ingredients and expertise from Asia, Africa, the Americas, and Europe. Despite its rich and lengthy history, however, Egyptian cooking is relatively unknown on the international culinary scene. A lack of Egyptian restaurants in major foreign cities makes Egyptian cuisine unfamiliar for people who have never traveled to Egypt. Tourists traveling to Egypt for the first time will often frequent establishments that cater exclusively to tourists by offering western dishes alongside only a few Egyptian dishes. As a result, most tourists don't experience the best cuisine Egypt has to offer. Today, Egyptian home cooks, street vendors, and authentic restaurants and cafes all serve delicious dishes whose flavors represent Egypt's international influences.

Over the years, I've found that Egyptian food is especially well adapted to family-style dining and parties. A notable distinction between Egyptian menus and those found in North America are the times of day that certain foods are eaten and the types of courses offered. In Egypt, breakfast and lunch consist of very large meals while dinner tends to be lighter. Lunch is not usually served until around 3:00 pm, reinforcing the significance of a large breakfast and a light dinner. At a true Egyptian table, everyone is welcome. Even in the most formal of settings, a familial spirit prevails. Hosts pay special attention to their guests' preferences. If one person doesn't eat a particular dish, it is not served. The notion of everyone eating together means that, in addition to sitting down together, they all consume the same foods.

While outlining Egyptian recipes and culinary history, I utilized research from ancient Egyptian tomb findings, archeological research, religious texts, artwork, museum displays, films, oral histories from farmers, and proverbs. When I began teaching Egyptian recipes to American audiences, I discovered ways to stream-line the recipes, making them easier to enjoy without sacrificing any flavor. Now when I return to Egypt, the roles are reversed. Egyptian friends and family members come to my home, or ask me to come to theirs, to prepare traditional Egyptian cuisine and learn its history. I am now the one who is responsible for passing down the culinary heritage to the next generation.

This book contains menus for the most historically, culturally, and religiously significant events in Egypt. Through these menus, you will learn to make the most popular Egyptian recipes. The menus are meant to provide inspiration for entertaining Egyptian-style, as well as to show the Egyptian way of pairing foods together. Any of the recipes may be prepared on their own, or they can be paired with recipes from other menus, if desired.

Note: Transliterations of the names of recipes in this book are written in the Egyptian spoken dialect of the Arabic language.

The Nafes Theory:
The Breath of a Good Cook

Nafes is the Arabic word for breath. In Egypt, a person who possesses good nafes is believed to be a good cook. Egyptians and other North Africans believe that a cook's intention and mood influence the overall taste of the food. A good person, for example, will have a good attitude and good intentions when they cook. Therefore, the breath that they breathe into the actual recipes as they are preparing them will enhance the food, making it exceptionally delicious. A guest who comes to your home and enjoys food that you have prepared will believe that you have good nafes. Their relationship with you will deepen, and they will trust you more. More than just evaluating your cooking skills, your guests will judge your actual character through the food you make.

Mother of the World Statue, Agricultural Museum, Cairo

It is also believed that the nafes of the food exudes into the air with its steam and aroma. If someone has bad nafes, the food will not smell appetizing to their guests, and people will not eat it. I have seen very hungry people forgo elaborate meals and expensive dishes offered to them because they did not have good nafes. I have also seen the most simple and least expensive dishes enjoyed immensely because the nafes of the cook was good. Traditionally, grandmothers and older people are seen as having the best nafes because of the love they feel for their family and the joy they experience when offering them good food. The highest compliment an Egyptian can give to your culinary skills is to say that your nafes made the meal exceptional. They will then tell you *"tislam edeeki,"* which means "bless your hands." I hope that this book increases your nafes and leads to many happy hours in the kitchen and at the table.

Part 1
Ancient Festivals

Egyptians have always loved to celebrate. In antiquity, they held festivals to celebrate the seasons and for religious reasons. During those ancient times, Egypt enjoyed agricultural, industrial, and military supremacy and its cuisine was considered to be luxurious. Grain was used as currency in ancient Egypt, and in fact the abundance of grain is what inspired the Greeks and the Romans to eventually conquer Egypt.

A particular ancient grain that is an ancestor of modern durum wheat, known as Kamut in the United States, is consistently gaining popularity with culinary and medical professionals alike. The president of the Kamut Association, Bob Quinn, is an organic founder who began growing and promoting the ancient grain in the late 1970s. Mr. Quinn told me that the legend surrounding the grain was that it was found in a tomb in Egypt—but analysis proved this theory to be false. His curiosity led him to further research the grain and to begin growing it on his farm. In 1990 he registered the Kamut trademark. The name comes from the ancient Egyptian term for "Soul of the Earth." Mr. Quinn says that the "high energy grain" was kept alive by small peasant farmers in Upper Egypt. He now uses the grain to produce Kamut brand cereal, pasta, grains, flour, and bulgur, a parboiled and dried wheat that is processed into grains.

Egypt's famous *fuul medammes* dish features a variety of fava bean known to be the world's oldest agricultural crop. Date crops have been religiously significant for more than five thousand years in Egypt. Figs grew three thousand five hundred years ago and have always been an important part of the Egyptian diet.

Papyri from 2800 BC described extensive spice usage only two hundred years after the first-ever accounts of spices were recorded in China. Old Kingdom (2700–2600 BC) tomb scenes depict bread being shaped and produced in mass quantities. Ramses II's tomb revealed pictures of elegant pastries, cakes, and pies being made in bakeries that catered specifically to royalty. Sweets were also prepared in communal ovens and sweetened with honey and molasses instead of sugar, which was extremely expensive at the time because it was just introduced by the Persians.

Ancient Festivals includes:

▶ Ancient Egyptian Nile Festival
▶ The "Smell of the Fresh Breeze" Celebration
▶ A Night in Nubia
▶ Bedouin Tent Party

Ancient Egyptian Nile Festival

The biggest Egyptian festival of all was dedicated to the Nile. Each year the Nile would begin to rise in June and eventually flood by July 19. For this reason, July 19 is the New Year on the ancient Egyptian calendar. On this date each year, there were huge celebrations honoring the rising of the river. To give thanks to what the ancient Egyptians referred to as a Nile god named Hapi, they would place a roll of papyrus containing a prayer in the Nile. Osiri was the name of the agrarian god who was cast into the Nile and returned to life. The ancient Egyptians drew a parallel between his resurrection and the growth of wheat that was sown into the ground previously flooded by the Nile. The Egyptians would also make offerings of fruits, vegetables, and flowers to show their appreciation for the Nile's rising. Dancing and singing would take place all night long, and people would drink water from the Nile. The joyous occasion of the Nile's rising in antiquity meant that fields of crops would be irrigated all year round, and that the citizens of Egypt would have enough to eat.

Agricultural crops grew abundantly in the Nile Valley during ancient times, thanks to the rising of the Nile. Peas, beans, cucumbers, leeks, lemons, lentils, grapes, garlic, mint, juniper, plums, figs, dates, and pomegranates all flourished. The ancient Egyptians ate a wide variety of meats, poultry, and fish. Ancient Egyptians used food to nourish their minds, bodies, and spirits. Many of the foods used by ancient Egyptians are now popular not only in modern-day Egypt but in the entire world. In addition to using them for culinary purposes, the ancient Egyptians also extracted essential oils from floral and food sources to make incense, perfume, ointments, and cosmetics.

The Egyptian love of food was even transported into the afterlife. Amulets of the son of the god Horus, named Duamutef, were created to protect the stomach of the deceased in the afterlife. From 1550–1070 BC, special *faience* (pottery) bowls were created to offer food to the goddess Hathor who was believed to nourish and protect the dead. The Egyptian museum in Cairo displays "food mummies" of poultry and meat that were preserved with salt and natron and placed in tombs to nourish the dead.

Ancient Egyptian pottery and utensils were very elaborate and symbolic. Different animal motifs would be used for serving corresponding foods. A fish motif, for example, would be painted onto platters used to serve fish. In the twelfth century BC, Ramses III was depicted using gold and silver plates, cutlery, and goblets while most of the people of Thebes (a portion of modern-day Luxor) went hungry. Outraged at his lack of empathy, the citizens of Thebes held what is known to be the first-ever recorded public strike in history.

When Christianity was introduced in Egypt via the preaching of Saint Mark in approximately 40 AD, the celebration of ancient festivals was discouraged by religious officials who viewed the pagan worship as a threat to the Christian church. The festivals were forgotten for centuries. Then, the ancient festival traditions enjoyed a resurgence in popularity during the tenth century when a North African Muslim dynasty known as the Fatimids declared Cairo as their capital. Prior to their arrival, Cairo was known as Fustat. They changed the name to "Al Qahara" meaning "the victorious." During their reign, they reinstated many of the ancient festivals, introduced the Egyptian *moulid* festivals (celebrations honoring the birth of prominent Jewish, Christian, and Muslim religious figures), and even encouraged cross-religious celebrations.

The Ancient Egyptian Nile Festival celebrates food with a spirit of gratitude, just as the ancient festival did. It is interesting that each recipe contains ingredients that were available in ancient Egypt, yet they are still popular today for their taste, nutritional properties, and widespread availability. There are some surprises as well. Who knew, for example, that foie gras was actually invented by the ancient Egyptians?

Ancient Egyptian Nile Festival Menu

▶ Egyptian Whole Wheat Pita Bread
▶ Pharaoh's Foie Gras
▶ Chicken Pita Bread Sandwiches
▶ Salad with Grapes & Fried Feta Balls
▶ Cleopatra's Kisses
▶ Licorice Drink

Egyptian Whole Wheat Pita Bread

[Aish Baladi]

The Egyptians give the same word to bread as they do to life, aish. Bread has been integral to the Egyptian diet since the twenty-fifth century BC. Pyramid laborers were rationed five pounds of it per person, per day. The ancient Egyptians were so fond of bread that the ancient Greeks referred to them as "the bread eaters."

As you walk through any market in Egypt, you'll see people carrying large stacks of bread on trays on top of their heads. Egyptians usually buy their bread directly from the baker. Because bread is so easily accessible in Egypt, it is not usually made at home. But if you're used to buying commercial varieties of pita bread, I urge you to try this recipe when time allows (it has been adapted for home kitchens). You can double it and freeze the leftovers. When needed, thaw the bread and heat it under the broiler until it is warmed.

Egyptian stores sell toasted, finely ground bran that has the same consistency as commercial bread crumbs. The addition of the bran gives Egyptian pita its characteristic crunchy texture. Since it is difficult to find this kind of bran outside of Egypt, I have substituted unprocessed bran that can be toasted to produce a similar texture.

MAKES 5 PITA BREADS

INGREDIENTS

1 cup unprocessed bran

3/4 cup unbleached all-purpose flour

3/4 cup whole-wheat pastry flour

2 teaspoons active dry yeast

1/2 teaspoon olive oil, plus extra for oiling bowl

3/4 cup tepid water

1/2 teaspoon sea salt or Kosher salt

Preparation:

Preheat oven to 350 degrees F. Place bran on a cookie sheet and crumble between fingers to make it finer. Bake for 5 to 10 minutes, or until bran granules are toasted. Remove from oven and set aside.

Mix together all-purpose flour, whole-wheat pastry flour, 1/2 cup of toasted bran, yeast, olive oil, water, and salt in a large bowl or one fitted to a standing mixer. Once the ingredients are incorporated, knead the dough for 20 minutes by hand or 3 minutes with a standing mixer using the dough hook on medium speed. Place dough in an oiled bowl and let rest for 45 minutes, uncovered.

Sprinkle a clean work surface and two large baking sheets with the additional 1/2 cup of bran. Shape the dough into an even log with your hands and cut it into 5 equal pieces. Form each piece into a flat 6-inch circle with your hands or roll out with a rolling pin to shape 5 round pita breads. Place 2 or 3 pitas on each baking sheet and allow to rest for 30 minutes before baking.

Preheat the broiler in your oven. Place bread under the broiler and bake for 2 to 3 minutes per side, until puffed and golden. Serve warm. Place extra bread in a plastic bag while still warm and seal to prevent it from drying out.

Pharaoh's Foie Gras

[Kibdet Firakh]

12 SERVINGS

INGREDIENTS

2 cups (4 sticks) unsalted butter, at room temperature, plus extra for buttering dish

2 pounds chicken livers, trimmed

1 medium onion, thinly sliced

5 cloves garlic, minced

2 cups chicken stock

Juice of 1 lemon

1 teaspoon salt, or to taste

GARNISHES

1/3 cup fresh whole cilantro leaves

1/3 cup fresh whole mint leaves

1/3 cup fresh whole parsley leaves

1/4 cup walnut halves

1 pint fresh figs, sliced in half if desired

A painting at the Louvre Museum in Paris, France, shows the ancient Egyptians developing the first form of foie gras. The painting was found in the funerary apt of Ti, who lived in the fifth century BC and was buried at Saqqara. The ancient Egyptians observed wild geese gorging themselves before their migration and realized that the extra fat was stored in their livers. The Egyptians then began "cramming" food into domesticated ducks and geese to produce the original versions of foie gras. Chicken, duck, and goose livers are still popular delicacies in Egypt today. This recipe makes an impressive pâté for entertaining.

Preparation:

Butter a 4-cup soufflé dish or loaf pan. Line dish with plastic wrap and butter the plastic wrap. Combine chicken livers, onion, garlic, and stock in a medium saucepan and bring to a boil over high heat. Reduce heat to low, cover, and simmer until livers are cooked through, approximately 10 minutes.

Drain cooking liquid and transfer livers, onion, and garlic to a food processor. Add butter, lemon juice, and salt and process until smooth and all ingredients are evenly distributed and butter is completely incorporated. Transfer to the prepared dish or pan, cover, and refrigerate overnight or until firm (a minimum of 4 hours).

To serve: Uncover the dish or pan and run a knife around the edges of the pâté to loosen it. Place a serving platter on top of the soufflé dish and turn upside down. Gently remove the plastic wrap. Arrange cilantro, mint, and parsley around the edges of the platter. Garnish top of pâté with walnuts and arrange fresh figs on top of and around pâté. Serve cold.

Chicken Pita Bread Sandwiches

[Shwarma bil Firakh]

Shwarma is the rotisserie-cooked meat that is "shaved" and piled high in sandwiches all over the Middle East. Traditionally, the meat is threaded with layers of fat, topped with tomatoes and/or peppers, and left to cook slowly for hours. The result is tender, succulent meat that is full of flavor. This recipe enables you to enjoy this popular street food at home, saving time and calories. Remember to marinate the chicken for 24 hours before proceeding with this recipe.

Preparation:

Combine chicken slices, salt, pepper, chili powder, nutmeg, allspice, cumin, lemon juice and peel, white vinegar, corn oil, garlic cloves, and onions in a large shallow bowl or dish. Stir to mix well and coat chicken. Cover with aluminum foil and place in refrigerator for 24 hours.

After chicken has marinated for 24 hours, preheat oven to 425 degrees F. Remove chicken from refrigerator and drain well. Spread chicken in a single layer on a baking sheet. Bake in the lower section of the oven for 25 minutes, turning once. Taste chicken and adjust seasonings if necessary.

Cut pita breads in half. Place on a baking sheet and warm in the oven for about 1 to 2 minutes. Remove from oven and top with the chicken meat.

Serve on a platter with small bowls of Egyptian Hot Sauce, Tahini Sauce, and pickles.

6 SERVINGS

INGREDIENTS

2 pounds skinless, boneless chicken breast, sliced into long 1/2-inch-wide pieces

1 teaspoon salt

1 teaspoon freshly ground black pepper

Dash of chili powder

1/4 teaspoon ground nutmeg

1 teaspoon ground allspice

1 teaspoon ground cumin

Juice and grated peel of 1 lemon

1/8 cup white vinegar

1/4 cup corn oil

5 cloves garlic, chopped

2 medium onions, chopped

FOR SERVING

6 pieces regular pita breads

Egyptian Hot Sauce, if desired (page 38–39)

Tahini Sauce (page 160)

Assorted pickles or preserved lemons

Salad with Grapes & Fried Feta Balls

[Salata bil Aghnib wa Gebna Makleyah]

8 SERVINGS

INGREDIENTS

1 head romaine lettuce

1 cup seedless red grapes

¼ cup extra-virgin olive oil

Juice of 1 lemon

1 teaspoon orange blossom water

Salt to taste

Freshly ground black pepper to taste

1 cup feta cheese, well-drained and crumbled

¼ cup plus 1 tablespoon all-purpose flour

1 large egg

2 cups vegetable or canola oil for frying

An ancient version of Egyptian white cheese, gebna baida, which is similar to feta, was found in First Dynasty (3200-2700 BC) tombs. In this modern recipe, the deep fried cheese provides the perfect complement to grapes and salad greens.

This salad makes an excellent first course. The feta balls can be formed into twelve large balls or thirty smaller ones. Use a melon baller to make small balls uniform in size. This entire salad, with the exception of the feta balls, can be made a day in advance and stored in the refrigerator. The next day, simply fry the feta balls, arrange them on top of the salad, and drizzle all with the dressing.

Preparation:

Chop lettuce into bite-size pieces and place in a large bowl or on a serving platter. Toss in grapes and set aside.

Make dressing by pouring olive oil into a small bowl. Whisk in lemon juice and orange blossom water and season with salt and pepper to taste.

In another small bowl, combine feta cheese, 1 tablespoon flour, egg, and some pepper. Mash together with a fork and then finish mixing ingredients with your hands. For large balls, break off 1-inch pieces of cheese mixture and roll into 12 balls the size of golf balls; to make smaller balls, use a melon baller.

Pour ¼ cup flour on a plate and roll cheese balls in flour to coat. Shake off excess and place on a platter. Heat the vegetable or canola oil in a large, deep saucepan. When the oil is approximately 375 degrees F it is ready. Carefully lower balls into the oil without crowding them. Do not allow them to touch each other. Turn the balls over when the bottom halves are brown, approximately 5 minutes. If they do not turn easily, wait a few more seconds. If they turn easily, that is a sign that they are ready to be turned. Fry the other sides until the balls are evenly colored. Remove from oil with a slotted spoon and drain on paper towels.

Arrange feta balls on top of salad. Drizzle dressing over salad and season with salt and freshly ground black pepper to taste. Serve warm.

Cleopatra's Kisses

[Cooblit Cleopatra]

It is said that Cleopatra used sugar extravagantly, even though it was extremely expensive in antiquity because Egyptians had just been introduced to the sugarcane crop via the Persians, whose victory over the Egyptian armies ended the Pharaonic era in 525 BC. Walnuts, which were another important agricultural crop for the Persians, are the other main ingredient in this recipe.

The original version of this recipe is said to have been deciphered from hieroglyphs, and it is believed that the nutritional benefits of the walnuts and the high sugar content were used to restore the spirits of both Caesar and Mark Anthony. It is interesting to note that in Egyptian culture, walnuts are considered important in stimulating mental activity, and sugar at the time was a status symbol. I believe that this recipe represented the sweetness of not only love, but intellect, strength, and power as well.

MAKES 1 POUND

INGREDIENTS

½ cup ground blanched almonds

1½ cups sugar

1 tablespoon orange blossom water

1 tablespoon orange juice

1 pound walnut halves

Preparation:

Mix ground almonds with ½ cup sugar, orange blossom water, and orange juice in a medium bowl to form a paste. Place a small amount of the paste over the flat inside of a walnut half. Press the flat side of a second walnut half on the top and press down lightly to seal. Place on a work surface covered with wax paper. Repeat until all the walnuts are used.

In a small saucepan, melt the remaining 1 cup sugar with 2 tablespoons water over low heat. Once it melts, increase the heat to medium high, stirring occasionally with a wooden spoon until the sugar turns amber colored, approximately 10 minutes. Remove from heat and stir well as caramel continues to darken in color. (Be very careful not to touch or splatter caramel at this point, as it can cause serious burns.)

Using a spoon, carefully drizzle caramel over the stuffed walnuts. Set aside to cool. Walnuts can be stored in an airtight container for up to 1 week.

Licorice Drink

[Ir'sus]

8 SERVINGS

INGREDIENTS

3 tablespoons ground licorice root

1/8 cup honey, or sugar to taste

Licorice root is known to be a digestive aid and liver cleanser in Egypt. It has been used as a general well-being tonic since ancient times. Nowadays, Licorice Drink vendors walk around crowded urban areas in Egypt with huge metal canteens full of the drink strapped to their backs. They also carry glasses to serve it to their customers. During the month of Ramadan, many sidewalk stands sell the Licorice Drink in plastic bags. People buy it and take it home where it is poured into a pitcher and served with the evening break-fast meal.

Licorice Drink is made with ground licorice root, which outside of Egypt can be bought at health food stores, organic markets, and Egyptian grocers. Some Egyptian grocers also sell pre-sweetened licorice powders, but many people find the drink to be more refreshing without the addition of sugar.

Preparation:

Put ground licorice root into a tea-ball strainer used for loose tea. Place strainer in a pitcher and fill with 1/2 gallon cold water. Allow this to sit for 1 hour and then remove the tea ball.

Strain liquid through a fine sieve into another pitcher and sweeten with honey or sugar, if desired. Cover the pitcher and shake vigorously or whirl in blender to create a frothy top. Serve ice cold.

Greco-Roman Museum, Alexandria, Egypt

The "Smell of the Fresh Breeze" Celebration

Springtime in Egypt is a world of sensory delights. The air is filled with freshness and picture-perfect weather becomes the norm. Fresh new vegetables and crops start to emerge from the banks of the Nile as Egypt gives birth to a new season. One of the most widely observed traditions of Spring originated in Egypt—the use of colored eggs to symbolize new life at Easter time. Since antiquity, colored eggs were seen as a symbol of new life in Egypt. They were originally decorated with natural dyes to celebrate the "Smell of the Fresh Breeze" or *Sham an Nassim* festival.

This celebration began during ancient times, and once Christianity became widespread, used to be held in the middle of the Coptic Lenten period. This meant that the Coptic Christians, who were abstaining from meat, fish, dairy products, and sweets for Lent, could not participate. Under Fatimid Muslim rule, the date was changed so that everyone could participate in the festivities. The Fatimids changed the date to Coptic Easter Monday, so that the festival would still be in springtime, but after the Lenten fasting period was over.

Since the holiday has no religious connotations, Egyptians of all faiths celebrate with picnics, outings, and family gatherings. Outdoor parks become crowded and everyone enjoys the most pleasant weather of the year. Each menu item is symbolically important. Fresh sardines and fish in general are symbols of fertility, and were available to commoners and pharaohs alike. Hard-boiled colored eggs symbolize rebirth and the children traditionally used the eggs to play games. Onions are constantly used in ancient Egyptian lore because of both their medicinal properties and ability to ward off the constant threat of the "evil eye." Green chickpeas are a symbol of the abundance that comes with new crops.

The menu presented here combines the traditional elements of the festival with modern interpretations in an easy-to-prepare manner perfect for a picnic anywhere. The naturally colored eggs add a nice touch to Easter luncheons. The Roasted Sardines with Arugula are an upscale treat with humble origins, while the Circassian Chicken is a noble ancestor of chicken salad. The Cherry-Topped Semolina Cookies are sweet and crunchy, and the homemade lemonade is infused with honey and orange blossom water.

The "Smell of the Fresh Breeze" Celebration Menu

▶ Colored Eggs

▶ Roasted Sardines with Arugula

▶ Mixed Herb and Spring Onion Salad

▶ Circassian Chicken

▶ Cherry-Topped Semolina Cookies

▶ Egyptian Lemonade

Colored Eggs
[Baid Mil'on]

It is amazing to think that a tradition integral to the Christian Easter holiday is actually rooted in pre-monotheistic festivities. During ancient times, Egyptians used onion peel, beets, and spices to color their eggs. In Europe, egg coloring did not become popular until the fourteenth century. The Easter bunny, another symbol of the Christian Easter, also has roots in ancient Egypt where rabbits and hares were viewed as symbols of fertility, new life, and the moon.

Try using this recipe instead of buying commercial coloring packages for your Easter luncheon. Or use them to add Egyptian flair to a breakfast table anytime. Yellow onion skins will add a peach colored hue to the eggs, while the red onion skins will produce a tan color.

6 SERVINGS

INGREDIENTS

6 white eggs
Skin of 2 yellow onions
Skin of 3 red onions

Preparation:

Place 3 eggs in a small pot, cover with water, and add yellow onion skins. Place the remaining 3 eggs in a separate pot, cover with water, and add red onion skins. Bring both pots to a boil over high heat, reduce heat to low, and simmer, uncovered, for 20 minutes. Let eggs stand in the water for 1 hour; drain, allow to cool, and serve or refrigerate.

Roasted Sardines with Arugula

[Sardeen Fee al Forn bi Gargheer]

4 SERVINGS

INGREDIENTS

5 tablespoons extra-virgin olive oil

1 pound whole sardines, cleaned and scaled (see Tip below)

4 cloves garlic

1 teaspoon ground coriander

1 teaspoon ground cumin

1 teaspoon *zataar,** dried thyme, or dried oregano

Pinch of chili powder

Juice of 1 lemon or lime

Salt

Freshly ground black pepper

Arugula

Egyptians usually buy their sardines from shops that marinate them in large quantities for their Sham an Nassim *picnics. This oven-roasted version is a quick way to prepare sardines; you can use fresh or frozen (thawed) for this recipe. Chances are if you don't like sardines, you've only tasted canned ones. All across the Mediterranean region sardines are served grilled, fried, cured, and roasted.*

Arugula grows abundantly in Egypt and is a traditional accompaniment to fish. Because of its availability, it is actually considered to be a peasant food throughout the country. Huge platters of arugula are piled high and served alongside the fish.

Preparation:

Preheat oven to 425 degrees F.

Oil a baking pan with 1 tablespoon of olive oil and place sardines in the pan. Blend remaining 4 tablespoons olive oil, garlic, coriander, cumin, *zataar*, thyme, or oregano, and chili powder in a blender or a food processor to form a dressing. Pour dressing over the sardines.

Bake sardines for 20 to 25 minutes until the edges are golden and the flesh is opaque. Squeeze lemon or lime juice over the sardines; season with salt and freshly ground pepper to taste. Serve hot or at room temperature with arugula.

* See Where to Buy Guide on page 203–205 for purchasing information.

TIP ▶ *To clean sardines, hold one end down on a work surface and run the blade of the knife against the pattern of scales on the fish to remove them. Next, slit the stomachs and remove the innards. Cut off the heads at the gills and cut off the tails. Rinse in cold water and dry well.*

Mixed Herb and Spring Onion Salad

[Salata Khadra bil Bassal]

Parsley, cilantro, and mint are a classic Egyptian herb mix that has been used since antiquity. Sometimes fresh dill is added in addition to or in place of one of the other herbs. The fresh herbs, spring onions, and citrus juices are loaded with vitamins and minerals, making this salad a nutritious addition to any meal.

Preparation:

Trim stems off of parsley, cilantro, and mint; immerse them in a large bowl and cover with water. Drain and continue immersing the herb leaves in clean water until they are clean and leave no residue on the bottom of the bowl (this may take as many as seven washings). Dry the leaves and lay them on a large serving platter.

Trim ends off of spring onions and lay them on top of the bed of herbs.

Mix lemon and lime juice in a small bowl. Whisk in olive oil to make a smooth dressing. Add salt, pepper, and cumin to dressing, mixing well to combine. Pour over salad and serve.

6 SERVINGS

INGREDIENTS

1 bunch fresh parsley
1 bunch fresh cilantro
1 bunch fresh mint
2 bunches spring onions
Juice of 1 lemon
Juice of 1 lime
1/4 cup extra-virgin olive oil
Pinch of salt
Pinch of freshly ground black pepper
Pinch of ground cumin

Circassian Chicken

[Shirkaseya]

6 SERVINGS

INGREDIENTS

3 whole boneless chicken breasts

5 cups chicken stock

Salt

Freshly ground black pepper

1 carrot, peeled and sliced in half

3 slices stale bread, cut into chunks

1 1/2 cups ground walnuts

1 clove garlic

1/2 cup whole milk

GARNISHES

1 tablespoon olive oil

1 teaspoon paprika

3 walnut halves

Circassian Chicken is one of the great dishes that Egypt inherited from Turkey. It had a reputation for being a sophisticated and elegant entertaining dish. Many of the Egyptians who learned how to make it were originally of Turkish ancestry and came to Egypt during Ottoman rule. Inviting someone to their home to eat Circassian Chicken let their guests know that they were of aristocratic origins.

Traditionally, Circassian Chicken is made with a whole chicken and the broth it produces. In this version, I've used boneless chicken breasts and ready-made chicken stock to cut down on the preparation time. If you have the time, see the variation below for the traditional method. This dish can be served at room temperature or cold. I like to make sandwiches out of the leftovers. They make a wonderful alternative to ordinary chicken salad sandwiches.

Preparation:

Place chicken breasts, 4 cups of stock, salt, pepper, and carrot in a large saucepan. Bring to boil over medium-high heat, uncovered. Skim the scum off the top of the liquid as it forms. Reduce heat to medium-low, and simmer, uncovered, for 45 minutes or until chicken is cooked through.

Puree remaining 1 cup of stock, bread, walnuts, garlic, and milk in a blender to form a smooth paste. Taste and adjust salt and pepper to taste. When chicken is finished cooking, drain and let cool slightly. Reserve the broth for another use. When it is cool enough to handle, shred the chicken into bite-size pieces with your fingers. Place the chicken pieces on a serving platter and top with walnut paste. Pour olive oil in a small bowl and whisk in paprika. Drizzle on top of the chicken and top with walnut halves.

Variation:

Place 1 whole chicken, cut into 8 pieces, in a large stock pot with a carrot, an onion, salt, and pepper. Cover with water and bring to a boil over high heat. Remove the scum that forms at the top of the pot. Reduce the heat to medium low and simmer 45 minutes, until the chicken is cooked through. Remove the chicken from the pot, let cool, and then debone it, tearing the meat into shreds. Strain the broth with a fine strainer and reserve 1 cup to make the walnut paste. Refrigerate remaining broth for another use. Proceed with the recipe above.

Cherry-Topped Semolina Cookies

[Biskoweet bil Smeed wa Kareez]

Semolina is a yellow-colored flour made from the heart of durham wheat. The very fine milled version is used for pastries. Coarser grinds and pellets are used for pasta and couscous. In Egypt, semolina is almost exclusively used in pastries.

These are delicious simple cookies that I first sampled on a dessert buffet on a Nile cruise. After learning how to make them, I began bringing them to picnics since they don't require refrigeration and everyone loves them. They also make a nice breakfast and teatime cookie because they are not too sweet. They can be stored in an airtight container and frozen for up to a month.

MAKES 20 COOKIES

INGREDIENTS

½ cup semolina

½ cup ground almonds

½ cup sugar

¼ teaspoon ground cinnamon

1 egg white

10 maraschino cherries, halved

2 tablespoons apricot jam

Preparation:

Line 2 cookie sheets with parchment paper or silicone liners. Mix semolina, almonds, sugar, and cinnamon in a bowl. In a separate bowl, whip the egg white until stiff peaks form; fold into flour mixture. Roll the dough into 1-inch balls and place at least 1 inch apart on cookie sheets. Place half of a cherry on top of each cookie and press down slightly. Refrigerate for 1 hour to chill.

Preheat oven to 475 degrees F. Bake cookies in center of oven, until lightly golden, 8 to 10 minutes. Place the jam in a small saucepan with a tablespoon of water and cook over medium heat until melted. Strain through a sieve and brush on hot cookies. Allow to cool on pans; serve at room temperature.

Cherry-Topped Semolina Cookies

Egyptian Lemonade

[Assir Limoon]

6 SERVINGS

INGREDIENTS

2 ripe lemons, quartered

5 tablespoons sugar

5 tablespoons honey

1 teaspoon orange blossom
water

6 mint sprigs, for garnish

This drink brings back many memories for me. I remember coming in from outside on a very hot day in Luxor. Someone offered me hot, unsweetened lemonade to drink as soon as I hit the air conditioning. He said that it would prevent me from getting sick because of the temperature difference. My brother-in-law, Abdu, also loves lemonade. He judges restaurants by how good, and how expensive, their lemonade is.

The Egyptian love of lemons dates back to ancient times. Lemon juice has a reputation for both preventing and curing a wide range of maladies, including indigestion, lethargy, food poisoning, and the common cold. It is used to preserve foods, enhance flavor, and also as a tonic. Egyptian lemonade is made by extracting the juice from hot lemons and mixing it with honey, sugar, and orange blossom water. It is a smooth and pleasing drink that can be enjoyed any time of year. Limes can be substituted for the lemons to make limeade. Egyptian lemons are actually very similar to what we know as key limes; key limes can be substituted any time a lemon or lime is called for in this book.

Preparation:

Place lemons and 6 cups water in a pot; cover and bring to a boil. Reduce heat and simmer for 20 minutes. Strain liquid into a pitcher and press the juice of the lemons through the strainer with a fork.

Add sugar, honey, and orange blossom water. Stir to mix well and then allow to cool. Refrigerate lemonade until cold.

Before serving, place the lemonade in a blender and whip until frothy. Serve in chilled glasses garnished with mint sprigs.

A Night in Nubia

Between 5500 BC and 350 AD, the land of Nubia stretched from Aswan in Upper Egypt to Khartoum in modern-day Sudan. The Nubians had twenty-seven kings who were of African descent and ruled Egypt and Nubia for nearly a century. Ancient Nubian royalty would be carried on ox-drawn carts in a procession to meet with members of the Egyptian royal court. The ancient Nubians spoke the Meroitic language, as do modern Nubians.

Today, many Nubians live in stucco homes with colorful motifs along the Nile in and around Aswan, Egypt, close to their ancestral homeland, while others have moved to the larger cities of Cairo and Alexandria or have gone to live abroad. The new Nubian Museum in Aswan, Egypt, and the new Nubian village in Luxor, Egypt, are testimonies to this group's impressive culture and civilization.

The Nubian Museum in Aswan displays stunning Nubian artifacts, such as pottery bowls with cattle and geometric motifs and antique coffee pots. The Nubians also used cosmetics, as can be witnessed by the 4,000-year-old palettes used for storing kohl, a natural eyeliner. Traditional aspects of modern Nubian culture are displayed along with those of the ancient Coptic and Islamic portions of Nubian history.

The new Nubian village in Luxor is a beautiful, brightly colored outdoor museum that displays all aspects of daily life in traditional Nubian culture. When I visited, a preschool class was being held in the classroom portion. At the Nubian village, one can see the way in which a typical Nubian whitewashed home was built around a courtyard with its bright motifs. Both functional necessities like wood-burning cooking stoves and water wells, along with beautiful Nubian contemporary artwork are showcased. Despite the fact that the temperature was well over 100 degrees Fahrenheit when I visited the Nubian village, the insides of the homes were comfortably cool due to the ancient, environmentally friendly architectural concepts developed by the Nubians.

One form of body art that the modern world is very familiar with—henna tattooing—is actually an ancient Nubian art. Nubian women are experts at creating exquisite henna designs. In antiquity, Nubian wedding celebrations would last for weeks. The night before the wedding reception was, and still is, known as the "*tur*," or "Henna Night" as it is called in English. The women of the community gather to pamper the bride-to-be, decorate her with henna, and anoint her with special blends of Nubian oils. After that, a large outdoor concert takes place. I once attended a Nubian Henna Night held near Karnak in Luxor, Egypt. The bride wore a beautiful red dress and sat at one end of the party with her female family members sitting around her. Couples danced nearby. At the opposite end of the party, three different Nubian singers sang traditional songs in the Nubian language while men danced together in circles. The whole community gathered for the Henna Night that lasted until the early morning.

Dining with Nubian singer Essam Karika at Kebabgy Restaurant in Luxor

Nubians are also known for their delicious food and for their generous nature. Ancient Nubian farmers grew grains, peas, lentils, and dates. They also raised livestock, with an emphasis on cattle. They traded with the Egyptians for other staples, like oil, which they did not produce themselves. The Nile also provided a constant supply of fish to the Nubians. Traditionally, Nubian men worked outside of the home and preparing food was the women's role. Whenever large festivities took place, however, they would join in on the preparations and demonstrate their culinary knowledge.

When I went to a Nubian village in Aswan, Egypt, I was invited to attend a wedding that week, offered a cup of hibiscus punch (a traditional Nubian drink), and invited into the homes of the locals. Wherever I went, I found people eager to share their history with me. I was told that Egypt's King Farouk chose to employ Nubians in his palace in Alexandria, Egypt, because he felt that they were not only great chefs but honest, trustworthy people who would not disturb any of his property.

The menu presented here highlights authentic Nubian ingredients that have been prepared the same way for more than two thousand years. This meal is meant to be shared, since Nubians eat communally. If you play traditional Nubian music, like that of Mohamed Mounir or Hamza el Din, you'll be able to imagine yourself drifting down the Nile. And if you happen to travel to Aswan, Egypt, remember to "dip your feet in the Nile" to ensure that you'll come back again, as my Nubian friends tell me.

A Night in Nubia Menu

▶ Nubian Bread

▶ Hibiscus Punch

▶ Egyptian Rice

▶ Stewed Okra and Tomatoes

▶ Fried Nile Perch

▶ Shepherd's Salad

▶ Aswan Date Cookies

Nubian Bread

[Aish Nubi / Maltoud]

The recipe for this traditional bread was kindly shared with me by Mohamed Salah, a Nubian friend who lives in Cairo and is very knowledgeable and proud of his culture. It is a recipe of his mother, Mrs. Kareema Mohamed Abdu. She tells me that any kind of flour can be used to make this large, round bread shaped like a volcano and golden in hue.

As with most indigenous cultures, cooking and baking Nubian-style is not measurement specific. Everything in Nubian culture is prepared "to the eye," "to the touch," or "to the smell." After being taught recipes at a young age along with other important daily life skills, Nubian cooks rely on their senses exclusively to tell them what their food needs. The original recipe for this bread, for example, is a simple list of ingredients, with no quantities. This method can be frustrating for the modern chef, who views baking as a chemical composition. However, to ancient cultures this method is actually more accurate because it allows for inconsistency in weather, altitude, and ingredients that can affect a recipe every bit as much (if not more) than the wrong measurements.

12 SERVINGS

INGREDIENTS

2 teaspoons expeller pressed corn oil

6 cups unbleached bread flour or any other kind of flour

2 teaspoons salt

1 tablespoon baking powder

1 tablespoon active dry yeast

Preparation:

Lightly grease a baking sheet with 1 teaspoon corn oil. Combine the flour, salt, and baking powder in a large bowl. Mix the yeast with ⅔ cup tepid water and stir until dissolved. Pour into the flour mixture and stir to combine. Stir in 1⅔ cups water and mix to a firm dough. (The humidity level in your home will affect the flour-to-water ratio. If dough seems too dry, add more water, a little at a time; if dough seems too loose, add more flour a little bit at a time until you get a firm dough.)

Lightly dust a work surface with flour and knead the dough for 10 minutes, or until smooth and elastic. Oil a large bowl with remaining teaspoon of oil, place dough inside, and turn to coat. Cover with lightly oiled clear plastic wrap, a lid, or a kitchen towel, and leave to rise in a warm, draft-free place for 1 hour, or until doubled in bulk.

After dough has risen, turn out onto a lightly floured work surface and form into a 7-inch-wide circle. Using your hand, grab the top of the dough in the center of the circle, pull up slightly, and twist to form a 3-inch knob on top of the center of the dough. Transfer to a baking sheet and cover with an inverted bowl. Allow to rise for another hour.

Preheat oven to 425 degrees F and bake the bread for approximately 35 to 40 minutes, or until it is lightly golden and sounds hollow when tapped. Cool on a wire rack.

Hibiscus Punch

[Karkade]

10 SERVINGS

INGREDIENTS

1 cup dried hibiscus leaves*

½ cup sugar, or to taste

1 teaspoon orange blossom
water

Hibiscus plants can be found growing in gigantic numbers in Southern Egypt. Dried hibiscus leaves are harvested and turned into this traditional ruby-colored Nubian drink. It contains a high amount of vitamin C, is said to act as a purifying tonic for the body, and is known to lower blood pressure when consumed in large quantities. Wherever you go in Aswan, you will be offered either cold or hot karkade, sweetened to your preference. Once I was in a traditional Nubian home in the Nubian village in Aswan, and I was offered karkade. I noticed that the owner's daughter was drinking Pepsi. Everyone laughed when I remarked that it was unusual that the American was drinking karkade, while the Nubian was drinking Pepsi.

In the summer, I freeze the drink in ice cube trays and popsicle molds. Kids love the popsicles and the sweet red ice makes even the simplest drink seem festive. Karkade can also be enjoyed hot, in place of tea. The orange blossom water in this recipe is my addition—I think it really enhances the rich, fruity tones of the drink. Interestingly, hibiscus flowers are becoming a gourmet ingredient in the United States, offered in syrups and drinks in gourmet markets.

Preparation:

Fill a large pot with a gallon of water. Add hibiscus leaves and bring to a boil over high heat. Let boil 5 minutes; remove from heat. Strain juice through a colander into a pitcher. Add sugar and orange blossom water and stir. Discard leaves or use them as a fertilizer in your garden. Serve the punch warm, room temperature, or cold.

* See Where to Buy Guide on pages 203–205 for purchasing information.

Dried hibiscus and dates

Egyptian Rice

[Roz]

It's no accident that Egyptian rice has a short-medium grain similar to Spanish calasparra and Italian arborio rice—they're related. During the eighth century, the Umayyad caliphate ruled Egypt and Islamic Spain. The Umayyad prince Abd al-Rahman began importing not only rice, but spices, fruits, sugar, okra, and hibiscus into Spain from Egypt. From Spain, the goods would be traded with other Mediterranean countries. When the Spanish colonized the Americas, they then introduced many of these plants there.

Egyptian Rice was the first Egyptian food I ever tasted, and the first food my husband ever prepared for me. Since then, it is often part of the family dinners I prepare. It is a simple, quick, and flavorful base for stews and a great accompaniment to poultry, meat, and seafood.

4 SERVINGS

INGREDIENTS

- 1 teaspoon clarified butter (*ghee*)
- 1 cup Egyptian or other short-grain rice
- 1¾ cups vegetable or chicken stock
- ¼ teaspoon salt, or to taste

Preparation:

Melt clarified butter over medium heat in a medium saucepan. Add half of rice, stir once, and continue to cook for 2 to 3 minutes, until rice is transluscent. Add the remaining rice, stock, and salt. Stir to mix well and bring to a boil. Lower heat to low and cover the pot with a tight-fitting lid. Simmer 15 to 20 minutes or until all of the liquid is absorbed. Let stand 5 minutes before serving.

Nubian Village, Aswan, Egypt

Stewed Okra and Tomatoes

[Bamya Matbukh]

6 SERVINGS

INGREDIENTS

2 teaspoons clarified butter (*ghee*) or expeller pressed corn oil

1 medium yellow onion, finely chopped

3 cups fresh or frozen okra (baby okra can be left whole, otherwise slice into ¼-inch rounds)

2 cups vegetable, chicken, or meat stock

½ cup chopped tomatoes

1 teaspoon dried wild thyme, *zataar,** or dried oregano

Salt

Freshly ground black pepper

Okra has been a popular Nubian ingredient since ancient times. The okra plant actually has flowers that resemble hibiscus because it is related to hibiscus. In addition to eating okra when it is in season, Nubians also dry it to preserve for when it isn't available fresh. At most spice shops in Aswan you will find dried okra, which can be soaked in water to reconstitute it and then be used in this or other recipes. If you prefer a heartier meat stew, see Beef and Okra Stew (page 167).

Preparation:

Melt the clarified butter in a medium saucepan over medium heat. Add onion, stir, and saute until translucent. Add okra and stir to combine. Add stock, tomatoes, wild thyme, and salt and pepper to taste.

Bring mixture to a boil over high heat and then reduce heat to low. Stir, cover, and let simmer for 20 minutes or until okra is tender. Taste and adjust seasonings if necessary. Serve hot.

* See Where to Buy Guide on pages 203–205 for purchasing information.

Nubian musicians

Fried Nile Perch

[Samak Bulti Ma'li]

Nile perch are prized fish all along the Nile, and especially so in the area of Lake Nasser, near the Nubian village in Aswan. The size of Nile perch can range from a few pounds to up to 400 pounds, and catching them is a dream of fishermen all around the world. Typically, the fish are fried and served whole. In this recipe, you can substitute any white fish fillets such as bass, tilapia, rockfish, or orange roughy for the Nile perch. If you have the opportunity to eat one in Egypt, however, don't miss it.

Preparation:

Rinse fish and lay in a large shallow bowl for marinating. In a small bowl, mix together lemon juice, garlic, some pepper, 2 tablespoons of corn oil, and cumin. Pour mixture over the fish, cover the bowl, and marinate for 30 minutes.

Pour flour onto a plate. Remove fish from marinade and dredge in the flour. Shake off excess and lay on a large platter. Season each side of fish with a sprinkling of salt.

Heat olive oil in a large, heavy skillet over medium heat. Add the fish to the fry pan and cook at least 5 minutes before turning. When underside is golden, turn over and cook on the other side for another 5 minutes, or until fish is cooked through. (Whole fish will take longer depending on their size.) When the fish is cooked through, transfer to a warm serving platter and garnish with lemon slices and parsley.

6 SERVINGS

INGREDIENTS

4 pounds Nile perch or other fresh white fish (small whole cleaned fish or de-boned fillets)

2 lemons, 1 juiced, 1 thinly sliced

8 cloves garlic, chopped

Freshly ground black pepper, to taste

4 tablespoons expeller pressed corn oil

1 tablespoon ground cumin

1/2 cup all-purpose flour

Salt to taste

2 tablespoons olive oil

1 bunch fresh parsley, chopped

Shepherd's Salad

[Salata bil Gebnit al Ma'iz]

4 SERVINGS

INGREDIENTS

1 bunch lettuce, arugula, or assorted herbs

4 ounces fresh goat cheese, crumbled

1/2 cup shredded carrots

2 small (about 5 inches long) cucumbers or 1/2 of 1 large cucumber, diced

Handful of dates, pitted and sliced in half

1/2 cup frozen corn, thawed

Salt

Freshly ground black pepper

4 teaspoons extra-virgin olive oil

Juice of 1 lemon

Shepherds in Egypt have a long history of raising goats in addition to or instead of sheep. The star of this salad is creamy goat cheese. Any combination of other vegetables and herbs can be used. Traditionally, shepherds would use what was fresh and in season to make this scrumptious salad.

Preparation:

Place lettuce, arugula, or assorted herbs on a large serving platter. Top with goat cheese, carrots, cucumber, dates, and corn. Sprinkle a pinch of salt and pepper on the top of the salad.

Make the dressing by whisking olive oil with the lemon juice in a small bowl. Drizzle over the salad and serve.

Philae Temple

Aswan Date Cookies

[Biskoweet bil Agwa min Aswan]

*When I saw these date-filled cookies piled high in bak-
eries all over Aswan, they immediately reminded me of a
rustic version of my grandmother's Calabrian (Southern
Italian) fig cookies that she makes every Christmas, and
the famous wild cherry stuffed Neapolitan cookies. They
look like plump, over-stuffed fig bars and make the perfect snack. The sweet date filling is a delicious surprise.
These cookies can be frozen in an airtight container for
up to a month.*

Preparation:

In the bowl of an electric mixer fitted with a pad-
dle attachment, cream the butter and sugar; add
the whole egg, egg yolks, and vanilla and mix well.
With the mixer running on low speed, slowly pour
in the semolina, flour, and salt. Continue mixing
until dough comes together. Wrap dough in plastic
wrap and chill for 1 hour.

Grease two baking sheets and preheat the oven to
375 degrees F. Make the filling by combining the
dates, cinnamon, and butter in a food processor.
Pulse on and off until a paste forms. If mixture
seems too thick, add a few tablespoons of water to
obtain a smooth paste.

After the dough has finished chilling, use a rolling
pin to roll it out into a 10x15-inch rectangle on a
lightly floured work surface. Make 4 equally spaced vertical lines down the rectangle. Make 3 horizontal lines going across the rectangle, making 12 equal-sized pieces.
Fill the center of each piece with 1 heaping tablespoon of the date mixture. Using a
bench scraper/pastry cutter, lift the edges of the dough squares around the top of the
filling and roll over to cover. Seal the edges leaving the ends exposed. After they have
all been filled, cut each one in half and place 1-inch apart on baking sheets.

Brush the tops of the cookies with egg wash and sprinkle with sesame seeds. Bake
for 25 to 30 minutes until golden brown. Let cool on the cookie sheets. Store the
cookies in an airtight container at room temperature for up to 2 days.

MAKES 24 COOKIES

INGREDIENTS

COOKIE DOUGH:

2 sticks (1 cup) unsalted butter,
room temperature (reserve
wrappers for greasing baking sheets)

1/2 cup sugar

1 large whole egg

2 large egg yolks

1 teaspoon pure vanilla extract

1 cup semolina

1 1/2 cups unbleached all-
purpose flour

Pinch of salt

DATE FILLING:

2 1/2 pounds dates, pitted

1 teaspoon ground cinnamon

2 tablespoons unsalted butter,
room temperature

TOPPING:

1 egg yolk mixed with a teaspoon of water

1/4 cup sesame seeds (optional)

Bedouin Tent Party

Egyptian desert tribes, known as Bedouins, live in the desert in Sinai, Egypt. The Bedouins have traditionally maintained a distinct heritage and a strong relationship with nature. For centuries, Bedouins lived off the land by making their homes in camel-hair or goat-hair tents, but nowadays they use more permanent structures. Bedouin tribes vary in size and can be as small as a very close-knit family or as large as thousands of people. Each tribe has an elder who is instrumental in teaching Bedouin traditions and maintaining harmony.

Nomadic desert tribes relied upon such staples as rice, dates, mutton, and lamb, which they would take with them when they traveled. Roasting lamb or mutton to honor a guest was the main event at Bedouin festivals. The Bedouins often bartered with people in settled communities for other food staples that they did not have. Those living along the shores of Sinai's Red Sea developed a love affair with seafood that is as strong today as it was in ancient times.

Today there are large Bedouin communities in the hills around St. Catherine's Monastery in Sinai, and in the stunning coastal city of Nuweiba in Eastern Sinai, as well as along Egypt's northern Mediterranean coast. They make their living from herding camels, sheep, and goats, as well as selling artesian crafts and traditional beaded jewelry to tourists. Some have opened restaurants that highlight Bedouin delicacies.

Bedouins have their own traditional foods, the recipes for which have remained guarded for centuries. No one other than the Bedouins knows how to prepare these dishes. When I was in Nuweiba, some wonderful restaurateurs and shopkeepers shared some of their favorites with me. Special breads, teas, and lamb dishes are unique to the Bedouins.

The Bedouins in Egypt are also the only part of the population who take advantage of *terfez*, the truffles that grow in the Egyptian desert near the Marsa Matruh resort area. Most other Egyptians have never heard of them. They are known as "the thunder plant" because desert storms are crucial to their formation. There are white, black, gray, and pinkish red truffles. The pink/red ones are the best quality and the most expensive. They are harvested during the fall and winter by the Bedouins. Unlike European truffles, which are shaved sparingly on top of other foods, desert truffles constitute whole dishes on their own.

Desert truffles are believed to improve the eyesight. According to the Prophet Mohammed,* "Truffles are the manna of manna, and their water contains a cure for the eyes." He believed that they were a gift that God bestowed upon the Children of Israel because they needed no planting, seeding, or cultivation to grow. In Arabic, the word *manna* also means "favor."

Egyptians believe that a mixture of truffle water and antinomy (a substance used as a constituent of alloys in medicine) helps the vision. There are also many culinary applications for desert truffles. Egyptian Bedouins eat truffles in season, not preserved. To prepare them, they bury them overnight in mud, soak them in fresh spring water, season them with salt and spices, and enjoy them raw. Some people toss them into salads with spices like cumin and ginger, which are known to aid digestion since it is believed that the desert truffles slow the digestive process down. Desert truffles can also be roasted over campfires and eaten sliced and fried or roasted in clarified butter.

For the Bedouin meal offered here, be sure to pick a remote location, or your own backyard, and enjoy getting back to nature with these simple, delicious recipes.

*Although it is not written in this book, according to Islamic tradition, the words "may peace be upon him" are to be mentioned every time the name of the Prophet Mohammed, or another prophet is mentioned.

Bedouin Tent Party Menu

▶ Bedouin Bread
▶ Bedouin Tea
▶ Bedouin Lamb Stew
▶ Fresh Dates (purchased)

Bedouin women in Nuweiba, Sinai

Bedouin Bread

[Aish Bedawi]

MAKES 5 DINNER-PLATE-SIZE BREADS

INGREDIENTS

1 cup whole-wheat pastry flour

1 cup unbleached, all-purpose flour, plus extra for dusting work surface

Pinch of salt

5 tablespoons extra-virgin olive oil or other cooking oil

I first tasted this bread in Nuweiba, a Red Sea village on Egypt's eastern Sinai shores. The restaurant we ate in had huge picture windows overlooking the Red Sea and a large buffet table filled with fresh fish and local specialties. I found this easy-to-prepare bread, which looks like a homemade tortilla, to be the most delicious dish of all. It is traditionally shaped into the size of "two-dinner plates" and cooked over an open flame or in a clay oven and served with Chickpea and Tahini Puree/Hommus bil Tahina (page 165). But I like to make it on the stovetop. It is quick and easy because it doesn't need to rise. Kids love to help with this recipe.

Preparation:

Pour whole wheat pastry flour and all-purpose flour into a large mixing bowl. Stir in salt. Slowly stir in 1 cup of lukewarm water, or enough to make a dough. Turn out onto a lightly floured surface and knead the dough for 5 minutes, until it is smooth and elastic. Let it rest for 10 minutes.

Divide the dough into 5 equal parts. On a lightly floured work surface, using a lightly floured rolling pin, roll each piece of dough out until it is the size of a dinner plate. Toss each one up in the air like a pizza crust and set on a lightly floured surface until ready to fry.

Heat a tablespoon of olive oil over medium heat in a frying pan large enough to accommodate the bread. Add one of the dough circles and fry for 4 to 5 minutes, until top of bread is bubbly and underneath is lightly golden. Carefully turn over and continue cooking for another 4 to 5 minutes. Transfer to a dinner plate. Heat another tablespoon of olive oil and continue frying the breads, adding a tablespoon of oil between cooking each bread, until finished. Serve warm. Wrap any leftovers in plastic wrap and freeze.

Bedouin Tea

[Shai Bedawi]

Bedouins have their own special blends of teas that they make from the dried leaves of various desert plants. On special occasions, they mix the leaves from those plants with other spices. This version was given to me by a spice vendor in Dahab, a resort in Sinai, and contains Bedouin tea, dried rosebuds, cinnamon, and black tea. In the Middle East, Bedouin tea is available at spice shops in areas that have a significant Bedouin population. Many tourists have tea with the Bedouins they meet and then buy the blends to take home as a reminder of their amazing experiences. It is quite expensive because it is scarce. In the United States, dried thyme or sage can be substituted for the Bedouin tea.

4 SERVINGS

INGREDIENTS

4 teaspoons Bedouin tea (or dried thyme or dried sage)

4 teaspoons dried organic rosebuds*

1 cinnamon stick

4 teaspoons loose black tea (regular or decaffeinated)

Sugar, if desired

Preparation:

Heat 4½ cups water, Bedouin tea, dried rosebuds, cinnamon stick, and loose black tea in a teapot or saucepan over high heat. Once the water boils, reduce heat to low and simmer for 5 minutes. Turn off heat, and steep the tea, covered, for 5 minutes. Strain into tea cups and sweeten with sugar, if desired.

* See Where to Buy Guide on pages 203–205 for purchasing information.

The Red Sea Ras Mohamed National Park

Bedouin Lamb Stew

[Tagin Lahma Dani]

6 SERVINGS

INGREDIENTS

1 tablespoon expeller pressed corn oil

3 yellow onions, thinly sliced

3 pounds lamb shoulder meat, cut into 3-inch pieces

1 teaspoon ground cinnamon

$\frac{1}{2}$ teaspoon ground nutmeg

$\frac{1}{2}$ teaspoon ground allspice

1 teaspoon salt or to taste

Freshly ground black pepper

Serving lamb has always been symbolic of Bedouin hospitality. Since sheep were expensive, they were often used to make milk, yogurt, and cheese. Only on special holidays and occasions would lambs be consumed—as part of a sacrifice for a religious occasion, or to honor a special guest. Whole lambs were often roasted on a spit over an open fire. This dish has been adapted for home kitchens. Serve it when you want to let your guests know how much you care about them. You may add potatoes or another vegetable to this stew after the first $1\frac{1}{3}$ hours of baking. Bedouins often add desert truffles to the stew when they are in season.

Preparation:

Preheat oven to 325 degrees F. Heat oil in a large, oven-proof saucepan. Add onions and sauté over medium heat until brown, 5 to 7 minutes. Add lamb and brown on all sides, about 10 minutes. Season lamb with cinnamon, nutmeg, allspice, salt, and a sprinkling of pepper. Toss meat to coat. Pour enough water over lamb to barely cover and place in the oven, uncovered. Braise for $2\frac{1}{2}$ hours, turning every half hour. Add more water to cover if no liquid remains and braise for another 30 minutes or until lamb is tender. Serve warm.

Full Dinner Spread: *Roasted Leg of Lamb (p. 79), Phyllo Triangles with Cheese (p. 46), Grilled Prawns (p. 148), Egyptian Rice with Vermicelli (p. 166), Pea, Carrot, and Tomato Stew (p. 158), Mixed Country Salad (p. 161)*

Egyptian Rice with Vermicelli (p.166) and Pea, Carrot, and Tomato Stew (p. 158)

Roasted Marinated Chicken (p. 78) with Jew's Mallow Soup (p. 77)

Lentils, Rice, and Pasta with Spicy Tomato Sauce (p. 47–48)

Beef Croquettes (p. 159)

Chicken and Spinach Matzo Pie with Egyptian Hot Sauce (p. 38)

Spice-Infused Lamb Shanks (p. 40)

Meat and Bulgur Wheat Fingers (p. 54–55)

Chicken Breasts Stuffed with Cheese, Tomato, and Hulled Grains (p. 187–188)

Roasted Leg of Lamb (p. 79)

Roasted Fish with Herbs and Tomatoes (p. 63) and Calamari with Tahini (p. 150)

Traditional Eid Cookies (p. 113–114)

Semolina Cake with Honey Syrup (p. 49)

Apricot Pudding (p. 42)

Mango Juice (p. 176)

Coffee with Cardamom (p. 183)

Black Tea with Mint (p. 67)

Part 2
Significant Ceremonies

Religion has always been an important aspect of Egyptian life. Egyptians believed in monotheism since antiquity. The country's three major religions—Judaism, Christianity, and Islam—all have deep-rooted traditions and customs surrounding their holidays. There are many monuments, tombs, and shrines dedicated to important religious figures in Egypt. Today, mosques, churches, and synagogues are an integral part of Egyptian life and constant reminders of the divine. Egyptian culture combines a spiritual zeal with a zest for life in its seasonal festivities.

It seems as if there is always a festival or holiday of some sort taking place in Egypt. Many of the holiday meals have special foods associated with them. Even when preparing food, religion plays an important role, and food constructs cultural bridges. One thing that has always struck me as unique in Egypt is that Egyptians do not assign certain foods to specific religions, the way that Americans and Europeans do. All foods are meant to be enjoyed by all religions. Many of the same dishes are prepared by people of different faiths, with traditional motives, for completely different religious holidays.

In Egypt, no one can guess one's religion by what he or she eats—instead, it is determined by the foods one *does not* eat. Judaism prohibits pork, shellfish, and the combination of meat and dairy products in the same meal. Coptic Christianity requires long periods of fasting where no meat, poultry, seafood, dairy, and egg products are consumed. During these fasting periods, such as Lent, Coptic Christians adhere to a completely vegan diet. Islam prohibits the consumption of pork and alcohol. Since the majority of the Egyptian population today is Muslim, these items do not play a role in the traditional diet, with the exception of the Christian community, who view wine as a religious sacrament to bring them closer to the divine in the churches.

Holiday and special occasion menus in Egypt usually feature larger quantities and varieties of food than what is consumed every day. Elaborate meals and exquisite, labor-intensive desserts are prepared. Each holiday in this section has a suggested menu. Depending upon the occasion, some families make up different holiday menus each year, while other holidays demand the presence of a particular food. Let taste preferences, local availability, and the theme and historical significance of the occasion dictate how to put your own Egyptian holiday meals together.

Significant Ceremonies includes:

► Passover
► Hanukkah
► Jewish New Year
► Christmas
► Lenten Vegetarian Dinner
► Easter
► Ramadan Pre-Dawn Breakfast
► Ramadan After-Sunset Dinner
► Eid al Fitr Celebration
► Eid al Adhu
► Ashoora
► The Prophet Mohammed's Birthday

Passover

"Moses received the Torah at Sinai, and handed it down to Joshua, and from Joshua to the Elders, and from the Elders to the Prophets, and the Prophets handed it down to the Men of the Great Assembly ..."

—Torah: Ethics of the Fathers 1.1

Jews have been present in Egypt since ancient times. According to the Bible, the Israelites came to Egypt in Joseph's time. While most people associate Judaism with the Exodus, Egyptian Jewish history after the Exodus is rarely discussed. Many of Egypt's historical landmarks offer a glimpse into this period.

One of Egypt's most well-preserved treasures is the Ben Ezra synagogue in Cairo, built during the ninth century on the papyrus reefs where Moses was found as a baby. It contains stunning specimens of ancient Torah scrolls, and is the world's oldest synagogue still in existence. Since Christians and Muslims also believe that Moses was a prophet, all three religions receive inspiration from this location, as well as Mt. Moses in Sinai.

After Arabic became the official language of Egypt, Egyptian Jews, like all other Egyptians, began to speak Arabic. As with other Sephardic Jews who used the language of the country they were living in, Jewish celebratory recipes were given Arabic names. Since Jewish history is so closely intertwined with Egypt's history at large, there are relatively few distinctly "Jewish" recipes in Egypt today. Many museums and historical centers provide evidence that Jewish recipes did play a role in Egypt's past. Places like the Agricultural Museum in Cairo, for example, provide evidence of ancient Jewish versions of bread from Sinai.

Passover is an eight-day holiday that has been celebrated by Jews since Biblical times in honor of the Jews being led out of slavery into freedom by Moses. The Ben Ezra synagogue in Coptic Cairo plays an important role in the Passover celebrations. Sinai is also a popular destination for both Egyptian and Israeli Jews, as well as people from around the word, for its historical significance as the site where Moses received the word of God.

Interestingly, there is a Muslim holiday that is also celebrated in honor of the same principle of Passover called Ashoora (page 127). Because Islam follows a lunar calendar, its date changes every year. It is recommended that Sunni Muslims follow the suggestion of the Prophet Mohammed and fast during this period.

Passover Menu

▶ Traditional Seder Plate

▶ Fried Eggplants with Garlic Dressing

▶ Chicken & Spinach Matzo Pie

▶ Egyptian Hot Sauce

▶ Spice-Infused Lamb Shanks

▶ Date Haroset

▶ Apricot Pudding

▶ Hot Cinnamon Drink

Traditional Seder Plate

Seder platters typically separate plates with religiously significant items. One of them includes three whole matzo or other unleavened loaves of bread on one platter, representing the haste with which the Jews had to leave Egypt. Although Jews typically ate leavened breads in Egypt, the usage of matzo at Passover is a reminder that they needed to flee their homes, so the bread did not have time to rise. During Passover, it is actually forbidden for Jews to eat any wheat, corn, or other leavened products. Kitchens are cleaned and all of those products are removed before Passover begins. For the eight-day period, matzo is the only form of bread eaten.

The main Seder platter consists of bitter herbs, a mixture called haroset, *a roasted lamb bone, and boiled eggs. The bitter herbs used in Egypt are called* maloukhiya *and are referred to as "Jew's Mallow" in English. During ancient times this plant was plentiful, as it is today, and was known for its nutritional properties. Its presence on the Seder platter represents the bitter memories of slavery and the Jews having to leave Egypt and the foods and land they loved.*

Haroset is a compote made to simulate the mortar that Jews made while the Pharaoh used them to build the "treasure cities" in Egypt.

The roasted lamb shank bone is used to symbolize the ancient Jew's sacrifices to God. The egg is a reminder (which started with other ancient festivities) of Spring and new life. It is traditional to hold a special ceremony while reading from a book called a Haggadah *to tell the Passover story before the meal begins. When the eating begins, it is customary to dine while reclining as a symbol of freedom.*

INGREDIENTS

1 bunch fresh *maloukhiya** or other bitter herbs

1 recipe Date *Haroset* (page 41)

1 roasted lamb bone

3 hard-boiled eggs

Preparation:

Place *maloukhiya*, date horoset, roasted lamb bone, and eggs in separate portions on a large platter. Place plate in middle of table and pass around during the ceremony to remember the Passovers significance.

* See Where to Buy Guide on pages 203–205 for purchasing information.

Fried Eggplants with Garlic Dressing

[Bittingan Ma'li bil Toum]

4 SERVINGS

INGREDIENTS

3 long, slender Japanese egg-plants (approximately 8-inches long, 3-inches thick)

Salt

3 cups expeller pressed corn oil

10 cloves garlic, minced

1/4 cup distilled white vinegar

1 tablespoon ground coriander

1 tablespoon fresh parsley, chopped

This delicious dish is popular with restaurant chefs and home cooks alike. Its simplicity allows the smooth, fleshy eggplant texture and assertive garlic flavor to shine through. Be sure to choose bright, shiny eggplants with no bruises. I like to use long Japanese eggplants, which are known as aroosa or brides in Egypt, because they are slender.

Preparation:

Slice off the tops of the eggplants, cut them in half lengthwise, and then in half widthwise. Place them in a colander, sprinkle with salt, and let stand for an hour. Rinse them off and dry well.

In a large frying pan or deep fryer, heat oil over medium-high heat until it reaches approximately 325 degrees F. Place eggplants in oil and fry 3 to 5 minutes per side or until golden. Remove with a slotted spoon and place onto a plate lined with paper towels to drain.

In the meantime, place garlic, white vinegar, and coriander in a small saucepan over medium heat. Bring to a boil and cook until almost all of the liquid is evaporated.

Transfer eggplant to a serving platter. Spoon garlic dressing over the top and sprinkle with fresh parsley. Taste and adjust salt if needed. Serve immediately.

Amy Riolo working with chefs at Tut Hotel in Luxor, Egypt

Chicken & Spinach Matzo Pie with Egyptian Hot Sauce

[Mayeena]

This is the Egyptian version of a popular Sephardic Passover dish, Mina. This dish can be made up to a day ahead of time, refrigerated, and reheated before serving. When I was testing the Chicken & Spinach Matzo Pie recipe, I had my cousin Matthew's friend Chris Haley taste it. He told me, "It is good … but it needs a condiment … maybe hot sauce." I knew that traditional ta'liya sauce full of garlic, tomatoes, vinegar, and coriander would do just the trick. Although this is not a typical Sephardic addition, the flavors and colors go well together.

Preparation:

Place chicken thighs in a medium saucepan and cover with water. Bring to a boil on medium-high heat, and then reduce heat to medium-low. Skim off scum from the top of the pot, and simmer uncovered for 30 minutes, or until chicken is cooked through. Drain and reserve 1 cup of broth.

Preheat the oven to 375 degrees F. When chicken is cool enough to handle, remove meat from bones and shred it into bite-size pieces.

Heat 2 tablespoons corn oil in a large frying pan over medium heat. Add half of the onions and sauté until tender and translucent. Stir in half of the garlic and cook uncovered for 1 minute.

Add spinach to the skillet; cook 1 minute, uncovered. Stir the chicken meat into the mixture; cook another minute. Season with a sprinkling of salt and pepper, the allspice, coriander, and cinnamon. Lower the heat to low and cook for 1 minute. Stir in parsley and cilantro.

Carefully pour the beaten eggs into the skillet, stirring vigorously, so that the eggs do not curdle. Cook for 2 minutes, stirring constantly, and then remove from the heat.

6 SERVINGS

INGREDIENTS

- 2 pounds chicken thighs
- 7 tablespoons expeller pressed corn oil
- 2 yellow onions, diced
- 10 cloves garlic, minced
- 2 pounds frozen spinach, thawed and drained
- Salt to taste
- Freshly ground black pepper
- 1 teaspoon ground allspice
- 1 teaspoon ground coriander
- 1 teaspoon ground cinnamon
- 1/2 cup chopped parsley
- 1/2 cup chopped cilantro
- 5 eggs, lightly beaten
- 1 cup chicken stock (reserved from cooking the chicken)
- 6½ organic, whole wheat matzo sheets
- 2 cups tomato puree
- 1 teaspoon ground cumin
- 1/4 teaspoon chili powder
- 1 tablespoon distilled white vinegar

Oil a 9 x 13-inch baking pan with 1 tablespoon corn oil. Pour the chicken stock into a large shallow pan or bowl. Dip a matzo sheet into the broth so that it is saturated and softened, yet still intact, and then lay in bottom of the oiled pan. Continue until the entire bottom of the baking pan is completely lined with matzo. (You may need to break some pieces up to make them fit.)

Spread half of the chicken/spinach mixture evenly over the layer of matzo. Pour 1/4 cup of chicken stock over the chicken/spinach mixture. Place another layer of wet matzo over the top of the chicken/spinach mixture. Pour remaining broth over the matzo. Carefully brush 3 tablespoons of corn oil over the top of the casserole. Bake for 30 minutes or until golden.

While the casserole is baking make the Egyptian Hot Sauce: Heat remaining 1 tablespoon corn oil in a medium saucepan over medium heat. Add remaining half of the onions and sauté until soft and golden. Add remaining half of garlic and sauté until it begins to turn color. Add tomato puree, stir, and season with salt and pepper to taste. Add cumin and chili powder and stir well; cover and simmer for 20 minutes. Add vinegar and simmer, covered, for an additional 5 minutes. Taste and adjust salt and pepper, if necessary. Remove from heat and keep covered until serving.

Serve the sauce hot in a bowl next to the hot matzo casserole.

Ben Ezra Synagogue, Cairo

Spice-Infused Lamb Shanks

[Kawara Lahma Dani]

Although braised lamb shanks are economical, they evoke a luxurious and festive note at the dinner table. Perhaps the scent of spices and broth slowly seeping into the air makes us associate this dish with special occasions. You'll find yourself turning to this recipe often. I sometimes add chopped root vegetables like rutabagas or potatoes to the pan an hour before the lamb is finished cooking.

Preparation:

In a large shallow fry pan, heat vegetable oil over medium heat. Add lamb shanks to pan and brown on all sides. Season each side of the lamb with a sprinkling of salt and pepper, the nutmeg, cinnamon, paprika, and cumin. Remove lamb from the pan and set aside.

Add celery, onions, carrots, and garlic to the pan and stir to mix well. Sauté until vegetables are translucent.

Add lamb back to the pan and pour stock over the shanks. Increase the heat to high and bring to a boil. Reduce heat to low, cover, and simmer for 1½ hours.

Add anise seeds and lemon or orange juice to the pan. If using root vegetables, add them to the pan at this time as well. Stir, cover, and continue braising the meat until it is tender and falling off the bone, approximately 1½ hours more.

Taste and adjust salt and pepper, if necessary. To serve, place lamb on a serving platter with edges. Strain the broth over the lamb. Allow meat to stand 10 minutes before serving.

4 SERVINGS

INGREDIENTS

2 tablespoons vegetable oil

4 lamb shanks

Salt

Freshly ground black pepper

½ teaspoon ground nutmeg

1 teaspoon ground cinnamon

1 teaspoon paprika

1 teaspoon ground cumin

2 celery stalks, diced

2 yellow onions, quartered

2 carrots, peeled and diced

2 cloves garlic, minced

4 cups vegetable, chicken, or beef stock

2 teaspoons anise seeds

Juice of 1 lemon or orange

Root vegetables (potatoes, rutabagas, etc.) to taste, chopped (optional)

Date Haroset

[Agwa]

MAKES APPROXIMATELY 1 CUP

INGREDIENTS

1 pound dates, pitted

3 tablespoons date or fig jam

In Egypt, as in other Sephardic countries, the Haroset *mixture often consists of dates. What is used in Egypt is very similar to the* agwa *date filling that is also used in traditional Egyptian breads and pastries. In some areas, the usage of dates as "mortar" is not only symbolic, but a literal representation. Up until the nineteenth century, some homes in the Middle East still used date paste as a mortar.*

Preparation:

Place the dates in a large bowl and cover with boiling water. Let stand until very soft, a minimum of 2 hours or overnight.

Drain the dates and place in a food processor with the fig or date jam. Pulse on and off until paste is smooth and dark. If paste seems too thick, add a few tablespoons of water, one at a time, to thin it out.

Date palm orchard, Montaza, Alexandria, Egypt

Apricot Pudding

[Mahallibayat Amr al Din]

Apricots are significant in both the Judaic and Islamic faiths. Fresh apricots, known as mish mish *in Arabic, bloom very early in the spring, around the time of Passover. Our English word "apricot" is a derivative of the Arabic word* al burquq *that means "precocious" and described the early-blooming apricots. Qamr al Din means "moon of faith" in Arabic, and is the word given to dried apricots. In the Egyptian dialect, the "Q" at the beginning of the word is silent. Traditionally, this pudding is made with cornstarch, but I've substituted potato starch for Passover. Keep in mind that dried apricots need to be soaked overnight before proceeding with the recipe. In a pinch, you can substitute 4 cups good quality apricot nectar for the dried apricots and omit the soaking time.*

8 SERVINGS

INGREDIENTS

1 pound dried apricots, cut into small pieces

1 cup sugar

4 tablespoons potato starch dissolved in ¹/₄ cup cold water

Handful of blanched almonds or other nuts, to decorate

Handful of raisins, to decorate

Preparation:

Place apricot pieces in a large bowl and cover them with 4 cups of boiling water. Allow to stand at room temperature overnight or until the apricot pieces absorb most of the water.

Add sugar to the apricots and stir. Puree the mixture in a blender.

Pour the apricot puree into a medium saucepan. Add the potato starch mixture and stir well with a wooden spoon to combine. Increase the heat to high and boil mixture for 2 minutes, stirring constantly. Reduce heat to medium-low and continue cooking the pudding, stirring slowly, until it thickens and pulls away from the sides of the saucepan.

Pour pudding into individual ramekins or a large decorative bowl. Sprinkle raisins and nuts on top in a pattern by laying cookie cutters on top and filling the insides of the shapes with nuts or raisins. Remove cookie cutters and refrigerate pudding approximately 2 hours or until set. Serve cold.

Hot Cinnamon Drink

[Irfa]

4 SERVINGS

INGREDIENTS

4 cinnamon sticks

4 teaspoons sugar, or to taste

4 teaspoons mixed unsalted nuts, chopped

This is a popular after-dinner and bedtime drink in Egypt that offers many health benefits. Cinnamon is very popular with Egyptians. Egyptian cinnamon is pure cinnamon, and tastes mellower than American cinnamon. Medical doctors in the United States have begun prescribing cinnamon as a therapy for type II diabetes patients because it has been proven to regulate blood sugar levels.

Keep in mind that when using cinnamon for medicinal reasons, it needs to be pure. Commercial brands of American ground cinnamon often contain high levels of cassia, which is another spice with separate medicinal properties. Its taste is often stronger than pure cinnamon. Many Egyptian and Middle Eastern markets sell Egyptian cinnamon in tea bags to make this drink instantly.

Preparation:

Combine cinnamon sticks with 4 cups water in a medium saucepan and bring to a boil. Cook until the cinnamon sticks open and release their aroma, approximately 10 minutes.

Remove cinnamon sticks from the liquid with a slotted spoon and discard them. Add sugar and stir well. Pour liquid into teacups and top each serving with a teaspoon of mixed nuts.

Fruit stand, Sharm el Sheikh, Egypt

Hanukkah

Hanukkah commemorates the legend that Judah and his followers could not find enough oil to keep their menorah lit in the Temple that they had just rededicated. A single day's worth of oil miraculously lit the menorah for eight continuous nights, until the new oil arrived. Nowadays, Jews celebrate Hanukkah with candle-lighting, gift exchanging, and parties. Some Egyptian Jews and foreign Jews of Egyptian ancestry celebrate Hanukkah on sailboats, called *felucca*, while cruising down the Nile with a lit menorah.

Foods fried in oil are popular Hanukkah treats. For this menu, I have included vegetarian kosher foods that are easy to transport. They are perfect for eating while sailing down the Nile, or to serve buffet-style in your home.

Hanukkah Menu

▶ Guava, Mango, and Coconut Cocktail
▶ Phyllo Triangles with Cheese
▶ Lentils, Rice, and Pasta with Spicy Tomato Sauce
▶ Semolina Cake with Honey Syrup

Guava, Mango, and Coconut Cocktail

[Cocktail bil Gooafa, Manga, wa Jowz al Hind]

4 SERVINGS

INGREDIENTS

1 cup cold mango nectar

1 cup cold sweetened coconut milk, well stirred

1 cup cold pink guava nectar

This is one of the many different fruit cocktails that I've come to love in Egypt. When guava and mangoes are in season, they are piled high on donkey-driven carts and sold at roadside stands. To me, these fruits are among the greatest culinary delights on the planet. Luckily, this drink can be easily reproduced with good quality import-ed juices. See the Where to Buy Guide on pages 203–205 for details, or look for brands like Mira and Best sold in the Latin food aisle at most major supermarkets.

Preparation:

Place four clear glasses in the refrigerator and chill for 15 minutes.

Pour ¼ cup mango nectar into each glass. Hold a spoon upside down over the top of the mango nectar and pour ¼ cup sweetened coconut milk over the top of it in each glass (this prevents the coconut milk from mixing with the mango juice). Hold a spoon upside down over the top of the coconut milk and pour ¼ cup of the pink guava nectar over the coconut milk in each glass. Serve immediately.

Phyllo Triangles with Cheese

[Sambousik bil Gebna]

Sambousik *are flaky pastries combined with a wide variety of fillings. Usually three separate types—meat, cheese, and spinach—are served for special occasions. If you have a Middle Eastern market in your area, it is worth looking for good quality feta cheese. Fresh Egyptian feta has a soft, smooth, and creamy consistency quite different from the variety sold in U.S. supermarkets. The* sambousik *may be made ahead of time, frozen, and thawed a few hours before serving. Once reheated, they will taste fresh again.* Sambousik *can be deep-fried or made with puff pastry instead of phyllo dough.*

In our family, I am the official sambousik *queen. I have taught my nieces from Cairo how to make them, and receive requests from friends and family everywhere to include them in my menus. My favorite place to eat Phyllo Triangles with Cheese is the El Tabei restaurant in the Mohandiseen neighborhood of Cairo, which specializes in a wide variety of appetizers and Egyptian street foods. It has both a takeaway window and a spotlessly clean, efficient diner-style restaurant.*

8 SERVINGS – 15 PHYLLO TRIANGLES

INGREDIENTS

1 cup good-quality feta cheese, crumbled and whipped to a smooth consistency

1 medium onion, grated

Freshly ground pepper

Salt to taste

9 phyllo pastry sheets (18x14-inch), thawed according to package directions

1/3 cup clarified butter (*ghee*)

Dash of paprika

Preparation:

Preheat oven to 350 degrees F. Line 2 baking sheets with parchment paper or silicone liners.

Make filling by combining feta cheese and onion in a medium bowl. Season with a few dashes of pepper. Stir well and taste the mixture. Due to the salt content in the cheese, the mixture may not need salt at all. If it does, add salt to taste and set aside.

Open the phyllo sheets and spread them out onto a work surface in a rectangular position. Layer three sheets on top of each other, brushing the top one with clarified butter to cover. Cut 5 equal strips (from top to bottom) going down the length of the rectangle. Place one teaspoon of cheese mixture at the top of each strip. Fold the phyllo over the filling on the diagonal and continue to fold the phyllo in a flag-folding (or paper-football-making) fashion into a triangle. Continue with remaining phyllo and filling. Brush clarified butter over the tops of each triangle. Sprinkle with paprika and bake for 20 to 25 minutes or until golden. Serve warm or at room temperature.

Lentils, Rice, and Pasta with Spicy Tomato Sauce

[Koushari]

6 SERVINGS

INGREDIENTS

- 1 cup brown or black lentils, rinsed
- 3 tablespoons expeller pressed corn oil
- 2 medium yellow onions, 1 diced, 1 thinly sliced
- 6 cloves garlic, minced
- 2 cups tomato puree
- Salt to taste
- Freshly ground black pepper to taste
- 1 teaspoon ground cumin
- 1/4 teaspoon chili powder
- 1 tablespoon distilled white vinegar
- 1 cup Egyptian or other short-grain rice
- 1/2 cup elbow macaroni or mini penne pasta
- 1 cup canned chickpeas, rinsed and drained well

I first sampled this Egyptian street delicacy when a taxi driver in Cairo offered my husband and me a taste from a bowl. In Egypt, it is considered rude to eat in front of people who aren't eating. Not only was this an interesting cultural insight, I ended up experiencing the ultimate vegetarian meal.

Koushari shops are everywhere in Egypt. In their windows, they have large pots of lentils, pasta, rice, sauce, and fried onions piled high over a heating element. When people order it, the items are assembled in a certain order and handed to the customers. The best Koushari shops have long lines outside of them at meal times and late at night, when Egyptians like to stroll the urban areas. Although I've tried many different versions of Koushari, my favorite is my sister-in-law Soad's. Koushari (which is the Egyptian version of Indian kitchiri) is very simple to make, but keep in mind that it takes four separate pots on the stove at the same time.

Serve Koushari with Mixed Country Salad (page 161) and Tahini Sauce (page 160) for a complete vegetarian meal.

Preparation:

Place lentils in a medium saucepan and cover with water. Bring to a boil on high heat and then reduce heat to medium. Simmer, uncovered, until tender, approximately 20 minutes. Drain and reserve lentils until needed.

Heat 1 tablespoon corn oil in a medium saucepan over medium heat. Add diced onion and sauté until soft and golden. Add garlic and sauté until it begins to turn color. Add tomato puree, stir, and season with salt and pepper to taste. Add cumin, and chili powder, stir well. Cover and simmer for 20 minutes. Add vinegar and simmer, covered for another 5 minutes. Taste and adjust salt and pepper, if necessary. Remove from heat and keep covered until serving.

Fill a medium saucepan three-quarters full of water and bring to a boil over high heat. Add Egyptian rice and reduce heat to medium. Cook until rice is tender and then drain. Place rice back in saucepan and cover to keep warm until serving.

continued on next page

Lentils, Rice, and Pasta with Spicy Tomato Sauce

continued from previous page

Meanwhile, fill another medium saucepan three-quarter full of water and bring to a boil over high heat. Season with salt and reduce heat to medium. Add pasta and cook until done. Drain well, place pasta back in saucepan, and cover to keep warm until serving.

Heat remaining 2 tablespoons corn oil in a large, wide, frying pan over medium heat. Add sliced onion and sauté until dark golden brown. Take off heat and stir in chickpeas.

Assemble the *Koushari* by spooning the rice evenly into the bottom of a large, shallow serving bowl. Scatter pasta on top of rice, and lentils on top of the pasta. Pour sauce evenly over the top of rice and pasta. Arrange onions and chickpeas in a pattern around the center of the dish. Serve hot.

TIP ▶ *Cook the lentils and make the tomato sauce one day in advance and store in the refrigerator. On the day of serving cook rice and pasta, fry onions, assemble, and serve.*

Detail, Ben Ezra Synagogue, Cairo, Egypt

Semolina Cake with Honey Syrup

[Basboosa]

10 SERVINGS

INGREDIENTS

SYRUP:
1 lemon
1 cup sugar
2 teaspoons honey

SEMOLINA CAKE:
Unsalted butter, for greasing pan
1½ cups semolina
½ cup unbleached all-purpose flour
½ cup sugar
1 teaspoon baking powder
¾ cup (1½ sticks) unsalted butter, at room temperature
½ cup plain, full-fat yogurt
Handful of blanched almonds, to decorate

Basboosa is my all-time favorite Egyptian dessert. On short trips to Egypt, I like to indulge, and I take the opportunity to eat as much as I can. During long stays, however, I need to exercise great self-restraint. In addition to being delicious, Basboosa is a breeze to prepare. Basboosa vendors in old Cairo used to entice passersby with the phrase "Come and taste the basboosa … it's sweeter than a bride's kiss!" (it rhymes in Arabic!). In Alexandria, Egypt, basboosa is sometimes called harissa.

Preparation:

For the syrup: Peel 2 to 3 strips of lemon peel off of the lemon and place into a medium saucepan. Juice the lemon and pour into the same saucepan. Add sugar and 1 cup water and stir. Bring to a gentle boil over medium heat, stirring occasionally. Stop stirring once the mixture begins to boil and allow mixture to simmer for a few minutes. Take syrup off heat, add honey, and stir. Allow to cool some and then discard lemon peel. Set aside to cool completely while making the cake.

Preheat oven to 350 degrees F. Grease an 11x17-inch baking pan with some unsalted butter. Mix semolina, flour, sugar, and baking powder together in a large bowl. Add butter, blend well, and then stir in the yogurt. Spread the mixture into the prepared pan. With wet hands, press down evenly, making sure that the surface is smooth and level. Place almonds on top approximately 2 inches apart from one another making 6 rows of 4 evenly spaced almonds. Bake for 30 to 40 minutes, or until golden.

Remove cake from oven and cut about halfway through the thickness of the cake into 2x2-inch squares or diamonds (with an almond in the center of each), being careful not to cut all the way down to the bottom of the pan (this would cause the syrup to immediately sink to the bottom when poured on top). Pour syrup evenly over the hot cake and allow the cake to sit for awhile until it is cool and the syrup has been absorbed.

Jewish New Year
Ras a Sana Yehudi / Rosh Hashanah

Jews have been spiritually linked to Egypt since the days of Moses, and Egypt's synagogues are a testament to the role that Jews have played in Egypt's history. Even after leaving Egypt during the Exodus in 70 AD, many Jews eventually immigrated back into Egypt to avoid Roman persecution. At one time, there were as many as forty synagogues in Egypt. Today, the Ben Ezra, Gates of Heaven, and Adly Street Synagogues in Cairo, as well as the Nabi Danial Street Synagogue in Alexandria, are excellent examples of an illustrious Jewish history in Egypt.

The earliest Jewish settlements in Egypt were around the areas of the West Bank of the Nile (in Giza) and in Fustat, which is what Cairo was called prior to 969 AD. It is believed that there was a Jewish temple located on the breathtaking Elephantine Island in modern-day Aswan. There was also a temple at Giza where Moses was born and lived. A rock from this area, where Moses used to sit and pray, was placed at the entrance of the Ben Ezra Synagogue.

Jewish Square in Muski became a very prominent Jewish neighborhood during the ninth through the twelfth centuries. As the Egyptian Jewish population grew, Jews became increasingly more dispersed throughout the country. They settled not only in Cairo, but in the beautiful oasis of El Fayoum, and in other cities such as Alexandria and Aswan as well. Many Jews chose to live in the Jewish neighborhood in Cairo though, for both religious and practical reasons. Living in a close-knit community provided the benefits of being near synagogues, religious schools, and kosher butchers. This type of lifestyle promoted a strong sense of community, which in turn strengthened the faith of the people who lived there.

In the tenth century AD, the Al Azhar Mosque (which to this day is the authority on Sunni Muslim religious affairs) was built near the Jewish Square. Al Azhar was built by the Fatimids (a Shiite Muslim dynasty) who, among other things, promoted cross-religious festivities as a means of cultural bridge building. During the Fatimid Era in Egypt, Jews enjoyed high social status, and the Fatimid government even paid the salary for the head of the Jewish community and funded some of its projects. This period became known as "The Golden Era" for Jews in Egypt. By the twelfth century, there were 80,000 Jews who called Egypt home.

During the fifteenth through the nineteenth centuries, many Jews (and Muslims) who escaped persecution in Southern Europe found a safe haven in Egypt. Sultan Hussein Kamel opened the doors of Alexandria to the mass Jewish immigration. There, the Jews set up a cultural center, hospitals, and synagogues. Many Jews earned their livings as merchants, artists, doctors, and politicians. A prominent Egyptian Jewish theologian, philosopher, and doctor of the period was Musa Bin Maymoun. There was even an Egyptian Jewish Pasha known as Yosef Catawi Pasha. "Pasha" was an honorific title given to prominent individuals during Turkish rule in Egypt.

Many of Egypt's Jews immigrated to France in the beginning of the twentieth century, and later to Israel. Today there are only a few hundred Egyptian Jews living in Egypt. Proud to be both Jewish and Egyptian, they feel that their history and culture are evident in Egypt's synagogues and soil. The location of their synagogues and communities are evidence that followers of the three monotheistic faiths coexisted peacefully in Egypt for many years. In 2003, the Egyptian Department of Antiquities began restoring Jewish Square in Muski. Although today this area is an extremely busy, densely populated area in downtown Cairo, everyone still refers to it by its original name, *Haret el Yahud*.

During Rosh Hashanah (Jewish New Year Festival), families hold gatherings at home and prepare special meals for the holiday. Presented here is a kosher menu with a sampling of old-fashioned, traditional dishes.

Jewish New Year Menu

▶ Chickpea Soup with Zataar Croutons
▶ Eggplant Salad with Pomegranate Molasses
▶ Meat and Bulgur Wheat Fingers
▶ Veal and Potato Tagin
▶ Tamarind Juice
▶ Creamy Orange Pudding

Al Azhar Mosque, Cairo, Egypt

Chickpea Soup
with Zataar Croutons
[Shurba bil Hommus]

This creamy soup can be served as a first course to a large meal or as part of a light supper with salad, bread, and cheeses. This recipe uses dried chickpeas that require soaking overnight before using. If you don't have time to soak dried peas, you may substitute rinsed canned chickpeas. Doing so will also cut the cooking time down significantly.

Preparation:

Place chickpeas in a large saucepan or stockpot with 6 cups water and onion slices. Cover pan and simmer on medium-low heat until chickpeas are tender, approximately 5 minutes for canned or 1 hour for dried chickpeas.

Take off heat and carefully pour mixture into a blender. Add lemon juice, cumin, and some salt and pepper. Blend well until a puree is formed. Return mixture to pot. Taste and adjust salt if necessary. If soup is too thick, stir in a few tablespoons of water. Simmer on low heat until ready to serve.

To make croutons: Preheat oven on broil. Place bread on a baking sheet. Brush bread pieces with olive oil and sprinkle with *zataar* or thyme. Place under broiler and toast until lightly golden on each side, about 2 minutes per side. Remove from oven and divide bread evenly into soup bowls. Ladle the soup over the croutons and serve.

* See Where to Buy Guide on pages 203–205 for purchasing information.

6 SERVINGS

INGREDIENTS

SOUP:

1 cup dried chickpeas, soaked overnight, or canned chickpeas, rinsed, and drained well

1 medium yellow onion, thinly sliced

Juice of 1 lemon

1 teaspoon ground cumin

Salt to taste

Freshly ground black pepper to taste

CROUTONS:

1 (6-inch) pita bread, chopped into 1-inch squares

2 tablespoons olive oil

1 teaspoon *zataar** or dried thyme

Eggplant Salad with Pomegranate Molasses

[Salata Ruman bil Dabs Ruman]

4 SERVINGS

INGREDIENTS

2 Japanese eggplants (approximately 8 inches long by 2 inches across)

Salt

2 large, ripe tomatoes

2 tablespoons olive oil

1 small yellow onion, chopped

2 cloves garlic, chopped

2 tablespoons fresh mint leaves, finely chopped

2 tablespoons fresh parsley, finely chopped

1 tablespoon sugar

1 tablespoon distilled white vinegar

3 tablespoons pomegranate molasses*

Freshly ground black pepper

When eggplants were first brought to the Middle East from eastern Asia, they were treated with fear and suspicion. Originally they were called "Bayd an Jinn," literally, "Jinn's (demon's) eggs." When Arabs introduced them into southern Europe, they were given the name "insane apples" in Italy and Greece. Fortunately, people adapted to their taste and versatility. The abundance of eggplants during their harvest led to hundreds of eggplant-based recipes throughout the Mediterranean and the Middle East. This tangy, sweet-and-sour forerunner to Sicilian Caponata can be used as a side dish or appetizer.

Preparation:

Cut off tops and bottoms of the eggplants, slice them in half lengthwise, and place in a colander in the sink. Sprinkle them with salt and let them sit for 1 hour. Rinse off the salt and pat dry. Cut the eggplants into cubes and set aside.

Fill a saucepan three-quarter full with water and bring to a boil over high heat. Add the tomatoes and boil for 1 to 2 minutes, until their skins split. Drain tomatoes and plunge into a bowl of cold water. When cool enough to handle, peel the skins of the tomatoes using your hands, and then cut them into cubes.

Heat olive oil in a large frying pan over medium heat. Add onion and garlic and sauté until onion is translucent. Add the eggplant, tomatoes, mint, parsley, sugar, and vinegar. Stir, reduce heat to medium-low, and simmer for 20 minutes. Stir in pomegranate molasses and cook for another two minutes, or until eggplant is tender. Taste and add salt and pepper as needed.

* See Where to Buy Guide on pages 203–205 for purchasing information.

Meat and Bulgur Wheat Fingers

[Kibbeeba]

These delicious croquettes consist of a shell made of ground meat and bulgur and a filling of ground meat, nuts, spices, and herbs. They are deep fried and eaten as a snack, appetizer, or as part of a meal. In Levantine countries, Kibbeeba are known as Kibbeh. They can be served with Cucumber and Yogurt Salad (page 123) or Tahini Sauce (page 160).

Preparation:

To make the shell: Place bulgur in a medium bowl and cover with 2 cups cold water. Soak for 15 minutes, drain well, and return to bowl. Put the bulgur, minced beef or lamb, red chili, onion, salt, and pepper into a food processor. Pulse on and off until mixture forms a paste.

To make the stuffing: Heat olive oil in a large frying pan over medium heat. Sauté onion until translucent, about 3 to 5 minutes. Add pine nuts, mix well, and cook for 5 minutes. Add the meat, nutmeg, cinnamon, paprika, and cumin and fry the meat until it is brown. Stir in cilantro or parsley and set aside until cool. Taste and adjust by adding salt if necessary.

Spoon the shell mixture from the food processor onto a work surface. With your hands, shape the mixture into a flat, round cake about 8 inches in diameter. Cut the cake into 13 equal-size wedges. Flatten each wedge with the palm of your hand (they should resemble pancakes). Place 1 teaspoon of stuffing mixture into the middle of a round. Next, bring the sides over to cover all of the stuffing mixture. Roll it into an egg shape, making sure the stuffing remains concealed. Repeat with the remaining 12 pieces.

Heat 2 inches of cooking oil over medium heat in a large, deep frying pan.

When oil is hot, carefully lower *kibbeeba* into the oil. Be careful not to crowd the pan—you may need to work in batches; there should be at least an inch of space

8 SERVINGS —
13 *KIBBEEBA*

INGREDIENTS

SHELL:

1¹/₃ cups fine bulgur*

¹/₂ pound minced lamb or beef

1 red chili, seeded and minced

1 medium yellow onion, coarsely chopped

Salt to taste

Freshly ground black pepper to taste

STUFFING:

2 tablespoons olive oil

1 medium yellow onion, finely chopped

¹/₄ cup pine nuts

¹/₂ pound minced lamb or beef

¹/₄ teaspoon ground nutmeg

¹/₂ teaspoon ground cinnamon

¹/₄ teaspoon paprika

1 teaspoon ground cumin

4 tablespoons fresh cilantro or parsley, finely chopped

Expeller pressed corn oil or safflower oil for frying

between each one. Fry the *kibbeeba* on one side for 3 to 5 minutes until golden brown. Turn them and cook for the same amount of time on the other side. Using a slotted spoon, remove the *kibbeeba* onto a platter lined with paper towels. Sprinkle with salt, if desired, and continue frying the rest of the *kibbeeba*. Serve warm or at room temperature.

*See Where to Buy Guide on pages 203–205 for purchasing information.

The Role of Clay Baking Dishes in Egypt

The word *tajin* (sometimes spelled *tajine*) is the word used to describe a clay baking dish in the Arabic-speaking world. In Egyptian dialect, the "j" sound is pronounced like a hard "g" so the word is pronounced *TAH-gin*. Clay baking dishes are a traditional way of baking and serving stews. Families serve meals in large ones, while restaurants serve individual portions in small ones. Keep in mind that only the *tajines* of northwestern Africa (namely Morocco and Tunisia) have conical-shaped lids.

Egyptians love stews baked in clay dishes. They always taste homey and delicious, and can be made from whatever produce is in season and whatever meat people have on hand. Before air conditioning and home ovens were commonplace in Egypt, housewives and cooks would send their stews to the bread baker to be dropped off by the children on their way to school to have them cooked in the cooler portions of the oven while the bread baked. On their way home from school, the children would stop at the bread shop and pick up their bread and stew for lunch. This method was very cost and energy efficient. In a hot climate like Egypt, it takes a lot of air conditioning to cool down a home after turning the oven on, so sometimes, in very densely populated urban areas in Egypt, I still see children navigating their way through the labyrinthine maze of *souk* shops to bring their *tagins* to the bread baker. It always puts a smile on my face, and reminds me that sometimes the old ways are the best ways.

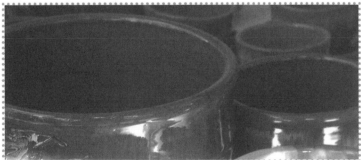

Artisan tagins, Luxor, Egypt

Veal and Potato Tagin

[Tagin Bitello wa Batatas]

Although this cooking method is ancient, it is still pre-ferred by many modern chefs (see page 55). Clay-pot cooking is one of the healthiest cooking methods avail-able because it requires hardly any fat, and the food retains its flavor, thereby enhancing the whole dish. Clay pots also "seal" the flavor inside and don't need to be checked on often during cooking.

Preparation:

Preheat oven to 300 degrees F. In an ovenproof saucepan, or regular saucepan if you will be using a clay baking dish, heat clarified butter over medi-um heat. Add onion and sauté until translucent. Add tomatoes, veal, garlic, and potatoes. Season with salt, pepper, red pepper flakes, nutmeg, cinna-mon, and paprika and stir well.

If using a clay baking dish, spoon stew into dish and cover. Otherwise cover saucepan and place in the oven. Bake for 1 hour and 15 minutes, or until meat and potatoes are tender and a "crust" forms on top. Remove from oven, taste, and adjust salt, if necessary. Garnish with parsley and serve in bak-ing dish.

4 SERVINGS

INGREDIENTS

- 1 tablespoon clarified butter (*ghee*)
- 1 medium yellow onion, chopped
- 3 cups chopped tomatoes with juice
- 1 pound boneless veal shoul-der, cut into 1-inch cubes
- 5 cloves garlic, sliced
- 3 large Yukon Gold potatoes, peeled and sliced into thin rounds
- 1 teaspoon salt
- 1/2 teaspoon freshly ground black pepper
- 1/8 teaspoon ground dried red pepper flakes
- 1/4 teaspoon ground nutmeg
- 1/2 teaspoon ground cinnamon
- 1/4 teaspoon paprika
- 2 tablespoons chopped fresh parsley

Tamarind Juice

[Assir Tamr Hindi]

12 SERVINGS

INGREDIENTS

2 cups tamarind syrup*
4 cups cold water

The Arabic word for tamarind, tamr hindi, *means Indian date because many people believe that tamarind originated in India. Tamarind, however, comes from the* tamarindus indica *tree, which is an evergreen tree native to Africa. It was present in Africa in prehistoric times and is believed to have spread to India and Asia in general long before recorded history. Its fruit grows in long, brown shell clusters. When the shells are opened, the sour beans are eaten, or pressed into juice.*

Today many international cuisines feature tamarind-based products. Using tamarind syrup is the easiest way to make this drink, and it also adds a wonderful flavor to marinades and glazes for fish and chicken dishes.

Preparation:

Pour tamarind syrup and water into a pitcher. Stir well to combine and refrigerate to chill until serving.

*Tamarind syrup can be found in Middle Eastern, Mediterranean, Caribbean, and Indian grocers. See Where to Buy Guide on pages 203–205 for purchasing information.

Creamy Orange Pudding
[Mahallabayat Bortu'an]

Northern Egypt is studded with beautiful orange orchards. When my husband and I drive from Cairo to my husband's hometown of Shiben El Khom, our senses become overwhelmed by the intoxicating scent of orange blossoms. During the mornings in March, the orange harvest is in full swing. Since orange blossoms open in the morning, that is when their smell is strongest. During the drive, I always know where we are by the smell, and the orange blossom aroma reaches my nose exactly one mile before my eyes spot the first orange tree. Farmers set up roadside stands all along the highway with oranges and lemons arranged in attractive pyramid shapes. They are so inexpensive that we often buy large boxes full of them. This is one of the recipes they inspired me to create. Serve it with ladyfingers or Egyptian Pound Cake (page 93).

4 SERVINGS

INGREDIENTS

3 cups freshly squeezed orange juice (approximately 15 to 20 oranges)

3 tablespoons rice flour*

3 tablespoons cornstarch, dissolved in $1/4$ cup water

$3/4$ cup sugar, or to taste

Grated peel of 1 orange

Preparation:

Place orange juice, rice flour, cornstarch mixture, sugar, and orange peel in a large saucepan and stir. Bring to a boil over medium heat and boil for two minutes, stirring constantly with a wooden spoon. Reduce heat to low and let simmer, stirring often, until pudding is half its original volume, between 10 and 20 minutes. Once pudding is thickened, allow to cool completely and then transfer to a large, clear serving bowl or individual pudding dishes.

* See Where to Buy Guide on pages 203–205 for purchasing information, or substitute additional cornstarch in its place.

Fruit stand, Alexandria, Egypt

Christmas

The abolishment of ancient Egyptian paranoiac religions by the Romans caused many Egyptians to adopt Christianity. The word Coptic was a word that originally was used to describe all Egyptians but now refers to Egyptians who practice the Eastern Orthodox religion. The Coptic alphabet is based largely upon the Greek one, with seven additional letters derived from hieroglyphs. By 190 AD the Coptic community began to flourish.

Egyptians accepted Christianity with fervor and their strong allegiance to the religion caused them to question their patriotism towards the Roman Empire. Eventually the Egyptian Christians were viewed as a threat to the ruling Romans, and the Roman Empire was divided into East and West in 395 AD. The Egyptian Christians became known as Coptic Christians. Today, Egypt is home to a sizeable Coptic community.

Christmas Menu

▶ Traditional Qurban Bread
▶ Pureed Zucchini Soup
▶ Beef-Filled Bread Triangles
▶ Roasted Fish with Herbs and Tomatoes
▶ Turkey Stuffed with Rice and Meat
▶ Sweet Fritters Topped with Syrup
▶ Black Tea with Mint

Church in Aswan, Egypt

Traditional Qurban Bread

[Aish Qurban]

Coptic Christians follow the Coptic calendar, according to which Christmas is celebrated on the 29th day of the month of Kiohk, which is January 7th on the Gregorian calendar. Coptic Christians attend midnight mass at churches and cathedrals all over Egypt. The mass held in St. Mark's Cathedral in Cairo is administered by the Coptic pope.

Golden Qurban bread, with its crunchy crust, plays a role in the church ceremonies. Special decorative molds for making this bread are sold in some Greek and Egyptian markets. The mold has a cross in the middle, and the twelve dots around it represent the twelve apostles of Jesus. If you don't have a mold, you can make your own designs freehand on top of the bread. This bread is made with yeast to make it more appropriate for the dinner table, and can be made in advance, frozen, and reheated before dinner.

MAKES 4 LOAVES

INGREDIENTS

2¹/₄ teaspoons active dry yeast

1 teaspoon sugar

Pinch of salt

3 cups bread flour

1 tablespoon extra-virgin olive oil

Preparation:

Line 2 baking sheets with parchment paper. Dilute yeast and sugar in ½ cup of lukewarm water. Sift the salt and flour together and make a well in the middle. Add the yeast and another ¹/₂ cup water (or enough to make a homogenous dough).

Divide the dough into 4 equal parts and shape into 4 (4½-inch) round flat loaves. Place 2 loaves on each pan, leaving them a few inches apart to allow room to rise. Cover the loaves with a kitchen cloth and let rise in a warm, draft-free area for 1 hour.

Preheat the oven to 400 degrees F. When bread has risen make desired design on top with a sharp knife, and brush the tops with olive oil. Bake for 20 minutes or until light golden. Allow to cool slightly but serve warm.

Pureed Zucchini Soup

[Shorbat Koosa]

4 SERVINGS

INGREDIENTS

2¼ pounds zucchini, ends removed and chopped

2 cups beef, chicken, or vegetable stock

1 cup whole milk

Salt to taste

Freshly ground black pepper to taste

There are many beautiful Coptic churches and museums in Egypt. According to archeologist Elham Aly, Old Cairo is home to "The Hanging Church" (called this because it is built on the southern tower of Babylon, an ancient Roman fortress) known as El Mouallaqa, *and the* Abou Serga *church (which is built above the place where the Holy Family is said to have rested during their stay in Egypt). In addition, old Cairo is also home to Egypt's first synagogue,* Ben Ezra, *and its first mosque,* Amr ibn al As.

This soup makes a tasty and nutritious first course. Its beautiful green color makes it a perfect choice for a Christmas meal. When choosing zucchini, look for small, dark green varieties with firm exteriors. This soup can be made in less than 20 minutes.

Preparation:

Place zucchini, stock, and milk in a large saucepan and bring to a boil over high heat. Reduce heat to medium-low and simmer, covered, until zucchini is tender, approximately 5 minutes. Remove from heat and puree the mixture with an immersion blender; or pour it into a blender, cover, remove the center spout of the middle of the lid, and hold a kitchen towel over the hole. Puree the soup until smooth.

Return the soup to the saucepan, and season with salt and freshly ground pepper to taste. Simmer over medium heat for 3 to 5 minutes or until soup is thoroughly heated. Serve warm.

Beef-Filled Bread Triangles

[Sambusak bil Lahma]

These delicious bread pockets can also be stuffed with lamb, spinach, leeks, or cheese. They can also be made with phyllo dough instead of bread dough. This version is wonderful when time permits. But keep in mind that this recipe can be made in advance and frozen. Thaw and reheat the triangles in a 350 degree F oven for 5 to 10 minutes before serving.

8 SERVINGS

INGREDIENTS

3 cups unbleached all-purpose flour, plus extra for dusting

1 tablespoon active dry yeast

1 teaspoon salt

4¹/₂ cups expeller pressed corn oil

1 pound ground beef

1 onion, peeled and diced

1 teaspoon ground cumin

Preparation:

Place the flour in a large bowl. Mix in yeast and salt. Add ¹/₂ cup of the corn oil and ¹/₂ cup lukewarm water and stir well to combine. Continue mixing until mixture forms a dough. If mixture seems too sticky, add more flour, tablespoon by tablespoon. If mixture seems too dry, add more water, tablespoon by tablespoon. Once dough is formed, divide into 8 equal pieces. Set on a lightly floured work surface in a warm, draft-free location. Cover with kitchen cloths and allow to rise for an hour.

Heat a large frying pan over medium heat. Add ground beef, onion, and cumin; cook, stirring occasionally, until meat is browned. Remove from heat and allow to cool. (This can be done a day in advance.)

Once dough has risen, remove kitchen cloths. Lightly dust a work surface and rolling pin. Roll the dough pieces out into 4- to 5-inch circles. Place 2 tablespoons of meat mixture in the center of each round. Fold dough rounds in half to cover the meat and using a fork press down around edges to seal.

Heat remaining 4 cups of corn oil in a large skillet. Fry the *sambusak* for 3 to 5 minutes per side or until golden. Remove from oil with a slotted spoon and transfer to a platter lined with paper towels. Serve hot.

TIP ▶ *If you don't have time to make fresh dough, you can use phyllo dough or puff pastry instead.*

Roasted Fish with Herbs and Tomatoes

[Samak Fee al Forn bi Tomatum]

12 SERVINGS

INGREDIENTS

2 teaspoons dried coriander

4 cloves garlic, chopped

Juice of 1 lemon

2 teaspoons ground cumin

1 whole (2 to 3 pound) sea bass or red mullet, scaled and cleaned

2 tablespoons olive oil

6 ripe tomatoes, sliced

1 yellow onion, thinly sliced

1 lemon, thinly sliced

1 tablespoon chopped fresh parsley

1 tablespoon chopped fresh cilantro

1 tablespoon chopped fresh mint

Salt

Freshly ground black pepper

During the Fatimid rule of Egypt in the tenth century AD, Muslim Caliphs would distribute mullet fish and doughnuts to the leaders of the Christian community. Since Coptic Christians traditionally abstained from meat, fish, dairy products, and sweets before holidays, the fish and doughnuts were considered celebratory foods at the time. This tradition became so popular that it spread throughout the Fatimid Empire into Sicily. Fish has been an important part of Southern Italian Christmas Eve menus ever since.

Nowadays, Egyptians tend to not mix seafood and meat and poultry in the same meal. I have included it in this chapter for its historical significance and great taste. You may choose to serve it with an array of seafoods and salads on Christmas Eve. If you cannot find fresh sea bass or red mullet for this recipe, use whatever fresh, whole white fish you can find. When purchasing fresh fish, check to make sure their eyes are clear. Next, ask to smell the fish. If the fish has an ammonia-like or "fishy" smell to it, it is not fresh. Fish should smell like the sea.

Preparation:

Preheat the oven to 425 degrees F. In a small bowl, mix coriander, garlic cloves, lemon juice, and cumin to combine.

Make 4 equally spaced diagonal slash marks on both sides of the fish. Spread the garlic mixture in the cavity and in the slits of the fish. Oil a baking dish with olive oil. Place fish in the dish and turn to coat in the oil. Scatter tomatoes and onion around the sides of the fish. Place lemon slices, parsley, cilantro, and mint inside the fish cavity. Season the fish with a sprinkling of salt and freshly ground pepper. Bake for 30 minutes, or until fish is opaque and cooked through; the fish is thoroughly cooked when it flakes easily. Serve warm with lemon slices.

Turkey Stuffed with Rice and Meat

[Deeq Rumi Meshi Ma Roz wa Lahma]

Turkey is a special occasion food in Egypt—often served at large wedding banquets and on holidays. Rice and hulled grains are popular stuffings. In this recipe, the classic stuffed turkey gets a flavor boost from rice, meat, spices, raisins, almonds, and a tomato puree.

Preparation:

Preheat oven to 375 degrees F.

Heat 1 tablespoon corn oil in a large saucepan over medium heat. Add almonds and raisins and fry for 1 minute or until almonds are golden and raisins are plumped up. Remove with a slotted spoon and set aside.

Add meat and onion to the same saucepan and cook until meat is brown. Stir in rice, fry for 1 minute or until opaque. Add 3½ cups water, stir, and increase heat to high. As soon as mixture begins to boil, reduce heat to low and season with salt and freshly ground pepper. Cover and simmer for approximately 15 minutes or until all of the water is absorbed.

Pour rice mixture into a large bowl and stir in almonds, raisins, cumin, coriander, and cinnamon.

8 SERVINGS

INGREDIENTS

3 tablespoons expeller pressed corn oil

⅛ cup slivered almonds

⅛ cup raisins

¼ pound ground beef or lamb

1 small onion, diced

2 cups Egyptian or other short grain rice

1 teaspoon salt

½ teaspoon freshly ground pepper

1 teaspoon ground cumin

1 teaspoon ground coriander

½ teaspoon ground cinnamon

1 carrot, coarsely chopped

1 leek, coarsely chopped

1 celery stalk, coarsely chopped

1 whole turkey (10 to 12 pounds), cleaned and rinsed well, giblets reserved for another use

1 cup tomato puree

Grease a 9 x 13-inch baking pan or a roasting pan with a lid with remaining 2 tablespoons corn oil. Place carrot, leek, and celery pieces in the bottom of the pan.

Place turkey breast side up in pan and turn to coat with oil. Place rice mixture in cavity and secure legs with butcher's twine. Pour tomato puree over turkey. Season with salt and freshly ground pepper. Cover with aluminum foil or lid and bake for 3½ to 4 hours or until turkey is done, basting turkey every 30 minutes. (Turkey is done when clear juices run from the thickest part of the thigh after it is pierced with a fork and it registers 170 degrees F on a meat thermometer.)

Sweet Fritters Topped with Syrup

[Lomut al Adi]

8 SERVINGS

INGREDIENTS

SYRUP:

3/4 cup sugar

Juice of 1 lemon

SWEET FRITTERS:

1 1/8 teaspoons active dry yeast mixed with 1 teaspoon sugar

2 1/4 cups unbleached all-purpose flour

1 tablespoon rice flour

1 large egg, beaten

1 tablespoon clarified butter (*ghee*)

4 cups expeller pressed corn oil for frying

The name of this dessert, Lomut al Adi, *means "Judge's Mouthfuls" in Arabic. They are a spin-off of the doughnuts that officials from the Fatimid Muslim palaces used to distribute to the Christian community at Christmas time. The tradition was so well-loved that the making of these fritters caught on in Fatimid-ruled areas all across the Mediterranean. Today, no Southern Italian street festival would be complete without "zeppole," nor would Greek festivals forget to incorporate "loukamadis," which are close cousins to these sweet fritters.*

Preparation:

Make the syrup by placing 1 cup water, sugar, and lemon juice in a large saucepan. Stir and bring to a boil, uncovered, over medium heat. Once syrup begins to boil, reduce heat to low, discontinue stirring, and simmer for 10 minutes. Remove from heat and set aside to cool.

Make the sweet fritters by dissolving yeast mixture in 1/4 cup lukewarm water in a small bowl. Allow to rest 15 minutes or until bubbly and doubled in volume (this is called proofing the yeast).

In a large bowl, combine all-purpose flour, rice flour, proofed yeast mixture, egg, and clarified butter with 1 3/4 cups of water. Mix well to combine, then whisk to remove lumps. Mixture should resemble a pancake batter. If batter seems too thick, add more water, tablespoon by tablespoon, until it is smooth. If batter seems too thin, add more flour, tablespoon by tablespoon, until it is smooth.

Cover batter with a clean kitchen cloth, and then wrap entire bowl in a clean towel. Set in a warm, draft-free place for 2 hours or until batter is bubbly and has doubled in volume.

When batter is ready, heat 4 cups of oil in a large, wide frying pan. Using two teaspoons shape a heaping teaspoonful of batter into an oval and push the oval off with one of the spoons. Repeat with remaining batter.

continued on next page

Sweet Fritters
Topped with Syrup
continued from previous page

When oil reaches 350 to 365 degrees F, carefully drop the small balls into the hot oil (you may choose to wear oven mitts while doing this). Fry 2 to 3 minutes per side, until golden brown. Remove with a slotted spoon onto a platter lined with paper towels. Repeat until all batter is used.

Carefully place fritters into reserved lemon syrup, turn gently to coat, and remove onto a serving platter. Repeat until all fritters are coated.

TIP ▶ *You can make the syrup up to 1 month in advance and store in an airtight container in the refrigerator.*

Black Tea with Mint

[Shai bil Na'na]

4 SERVINGS

INGREDIENTS

4 teaspoons high quality black, loose tea leaves

4 cups boiling water

Sugar, if desired

4 mint sprigs

Tea is more than a drink in Egypt, it is a national pastime. Tea is enjoyed morning, noon, and night. On average, Egyptians use 2.47 pounds of tea leaves per person each year. They prefer special blends of Ceylon teas that are renowned for their golden hue and strong flavor. For breakfast, glasses of half black tea and half warm milk are served.

Remember to ask your guests whether they would like one, two, or three teaspoons of sugar, and add it to the hot tea before serving. Black tea is usually served in short clear glasses in restaurants and coffee shops or fine porcelain in homes. Many Egyptian cafés decorate their tables with small vases or clear glasses filled with fresh mint. That way, people can break off a stem and place it in their tea. As the tea cools, the mint flavors it.

Preparation:

In a teapot, place tea leaves in boiling water. Cover and steep for 10 minutes for strong tea, or 5 minutes for regular strength. Stir in sugar, if desired. Place mint sprigs into glasses. Strain tea and pour over mint in glasses.

Tea sign

Lenten Vegetarian Dinner

Egyptian Coptic Christians fast for a period of fifty-five days before celebrating Coptic Easter. The Coptic Easter falls on the Sunday following the first full moon in Spring, which was a date agreed upon by Christians in 325 AD in what is present-day Turkey. Nowadays, this date differs from the date Easter is celebrated on the Gregorian calendar.

The Lenten fasting period includes many important holy days that are often celebrated in churches. Some of the most famous churches are located in Coptic Cairo. Although I had been to The Hanging Church before, I never was able to truly appreciate all of the significance of each icon and artifact until a young woman named Vivian Farook Yosif gave me a tour. She showed me the one hundred and fourteen icons on the property—some ancient and others made in the nineteenth century. Many reliefs of Egyptian saints are currently under restoration. Almost every inch of the church includes Christian symbolism, from the three columns representing the Holy Trinity, to the eight columns representing Noah and the other seven people saved from the flood. The church also contains many marvelous hand-fitted mosaics and Arabesque motifs that resemble what the West considers to be Islamic design motifs, including bold stars that are used because their points are actually crosses shooting out in all directions.

The church was purposely built high up to avoid attack from the Romans. It also has two doors in its floor that open up so that worshippers could escape underground if needed. According to Vivian, priests could not stop preaching during an attack, so they would head downstairs instead. In the 1980s, a small church dating back to the fourth century was found underneath the Hanging Church.

During their fasting period, Copts abstain from meat, seafood, poultry, dairy products, eggs, and sweets. Popular Egyptian restaurant chains and local shops often cater to the Christian community by offering special vegan versions of classic Egyptian dishes. They are differentiated from the rest of the menu with the phrase "for fasting Christians" written next to them. In addition to the Lenten fasting period, many Copts also observe fasting requirements a day or two each week throughout the year. Presented here is a vegan menu made up of typical Egyptian ingredients.

Lenten Vegetarian Dinner Menu

▶ Citrus Green Bean Salad

▶ White Pita Bread

▶ Egyptian Fava Falafel

▶ Chickpea, Tomato, and Tahini Salad

▶ Red Lentil Croquettes

▶ Caraway Tea

Citrus Green Bean Salad

[Fasoulea bi Limoon]

6 SERVINGS

INGREDIENTS

1 pound green beans, ends trimmed

2 tablespoons olive oil

Juice and grated peel of 1 lemon

1 tablespoon finely chopped fresh parsley

1 tablespoon finely chopped fresh mint

1 tablespoon finely chopped fresh oregano or thyme

Salt

Freshly ground black pepper

The Coptic Museum in Old Cairo provides us with a glimpse of what kitchens looked like during Egypt's Coptic era. Built in 1910 by Morkos Smeika Pasha, the Mediterranean-inspired building consists of white stone walls with high ceilings and marble floors and windows covered with traditional mashrabeya *screens. Among the museum's 14,000 display items are third- and fourth-century bronze jugs etched with angel and flower patterns, and bronze skillets with mother-of-pearl designs from the fifth and sixth centuries.*

Nowadays, just as in ancient times, Egyptian Christians are extremely adept at creating delicious and satisfying dishes for the Lenten fast. These beans are prepared in an age-old manner—they are blanched until tender and simply dressed. You may adjust the herbs to whatever is available. Serve warm or at room temperature.

Preparation:

Place green beans with water to cover in a large saucepan over medium heat. Bring to a boil, reduce heat to low, and simmer, uncovered, until tender, approximately 15 minutes. Remove from heat, drain, and place in a large bowl full of ice water. Let stand for 5 minutes.

Place olive oil, grated lemon peel, lemon juice, parsley, mint, oregano or thyme, and some salt and pepper to taste in a small bowl. Whisk well to combine. Drain green beans and toss with dressing. Pour onto a serving platter.

White Pita Bread

[Aish Shammi]

White pita bread is sold by most bread bakers in Egypt alongside the traditional Aish Baladi *(page 4). Restaurants in Egypt usually serve one or the other, but some serve both kinds of pita. The Agricultural Museum in Cairo displays hundreds of kinds of breads from various periods throughout history. It also demonstrates how traditional bread bakeries were operated (and in some places still do operate). The role of home baking in Egypt is also explained. Prior to the twentieth century, for example, wheat mills were as essential to a home as a stove and oven. Having a wheat mill gave the Egyptians the security of knowing that they would not have to rely on purchased wheat to provide beloved bread for their families.*

MAKES 13

INGREDIENTS

2 tablespoons active dry yeast

1 tablespoon salt

7 cups unbleached, all-purpose flour

2 tablespoons extra-virgin olive oil

Preparation:

Pour 2¼ cups warm water into a large bowl. Add yeast and stir until dissolved. Add salt and then gradually incorporate the flour to form a dough. Turn out onto a lightly floured work surface and knead for 10 minutes, until smooth and elastic, or place in the bowl of an electric mixer fitted with a hook attachment and knead on medium speed for 2 minutes. Pour oil into a large bowl and place dough inside bowl, turning to coat. Cover with a kitchen towel and let rise until doubled in bulk, about 1½ to 2 hours.

When dough has risen, punch down gently. Divide dough into 13 equal portions and shape into balls. Place on a lightly floured surface and cover with a dry kitchen towel. Let rest for 15 minutes.

Preheat oven to 475 degrees F. Place baking stone or sheet in lowest section of oven. Roll out each dough ball to form a 6-inch circle. Place 3 circles on preheated baking sheet and bake for approximately 12 minutes, until they are puffed up and begin to turn color. Refrain from opening the oven during the first 4 minutes of cooking. Remove with a metal spatula or pizza peel and place in a bread basket or on a serving platter. Repeat with remaining dough circles until all are cooked.

Place extra pita breads in plastic bags, seal tightly, and freeze until needed. Thaw at room temperature and reheat under the broiler.

Egyptian Fava Falafel

[T'amaya]

4 SERVINGS (3 FALAFEL PER PERSON)

INGREDIENTS

1 cup peeled dried fava beans (broad beans),* soaked overnight in water and then drained

1/4 cup fresh dill leaves

1/4 cup fresh cilantro leaves

1/4 cup fresh parsley leaves

1 small yellow onion, diced

8 cloves garlic, chopped

1 teaspoon ground cumin

1 teaspoon ground coriander

Pinch of cayenne pepper

Salt

Freshly ground black pepper

1 teaspoon baking powder

Expeller pressed corn oil, for frying

1/4 cup white sesame seeds

VARIATION

4 White Pita Breads (page 70)

2 roma tomatoes, thinly sliced

1 cucumber, thinly sliced

1/4 pound feta cheese, crumbled

Egyptian T'amaya *is made of skinned, dried fava (broad) beans instead of chickpeas. This recipe was developed by the Egyptian Christians who had difficulty adhering to the dietary restrictions of their newly adopted religion. To make refraining from meat during the Lenten season more bearable, they came up with the recipe for* T'amaya.

In Egypt, T'amaya *are eaten for breakfast, as a snack, or as a light meal. Families have* T'amaya *night the way some Americans have pizza night. At my sister-in-law Soad's house, it has become a ritual, and the whole family gets involved in the process. Since Soad is a mathematician by trade, and her children also study scientific careers, her kitchen operates with the precision of a German automobile manufacturer. Her daughter Asma (who finishes medical school soon) is in charge of thinly cutting cucumbers and tomatoes. Our nephews Ahmed and Usama are put to work cutting the bread and stuffing the sandwiches. I cut carrots and peppers into neat strips. Then we pile the sandwiches and crudités onto separate platters and serve them. This recipe can be frozen in plastic freezer bags, thawed, and reheated before serving. For making falafel sandwiches see the variation at the end of the recipe.*

Preparation:

Place beans, dill, cilantro, parsley, onion, and garlic into a food processor and mix until a smooth paste forms. Mix in ½ cup water (or enough to make mixture wet and loose—it should resemble the thickness of a thin paste). Add cumin, coriander, cayenne, and some salt and pepper to taste. Stir in baking powder and mix to incorporate. Spoon mixture into a bowl and let stand at room temperature for 1 hour.

Pour 3 inches of corn oil into a large frying pan over medium heat. When oil is hot enough to fry, a piece of bread dropped in it will turn golden and float to the top

continued on next page

Egyptian Fava Falafel

continued from previous page

immediately. Using two teaspoons, gather a heaping teaspoonful of the paste in one spoon and carefully push it off with the other spoon, forming a round patty in the oil. Repeat the process until the pan is full, leaving a ½-inch space between each falafel. While falafel are cooking, sprinkle a few sesame seeds on the uncooked sides. Fry until falafel are dark golden brown, approximately 5 minutes; turn over, and fry the other sides until they are the same color. Line a platter with paper towels. Using a slotted spoon, lift falafel out of oil and drain on paper towels. Repeat with remaining dough. Serve warm with Tahini Sauce (page 160).

* See Where to Buy Guide on pages 203–205 for purchasing information.

Variation:

To make sandwiches with the falafel, cut open a White Pita Bread, place 3 falafel pieces inside and mash down slightly with a fork. Add thinly sliced cucumbers, tomatoes, and/or feta cheese. Serve with crudités and soft drinks—a finishing touch Soad deems essential.

The Hanging Church, Cairo, Egypt

Chickpea, Tomato, and Tahini Salad

[Salata Hommus bil Tomatum wa Tahina]

6 SERVINGS

INGREDIENTS

2 cups canned chickpeas, rinsed and drained

1 cup cherry or grape tomatoes

1/4 cup fresh parsley, finely chopped

Juice of 1 lemon

2 tablespoons tahini*

1/4 teaspoon salt

Freshly ground black pepper to taste

Tender chickpeas, crunchy parsley, and fresh, juicy tomatoes provide a perfect balance of textures in this salad. Because it can be made several hours ahead, it works well for buffet-style dining and picnics. It can also be added to couscous for a light vegetarian meal.

Chickpeas trace their history in the Mediterranean to ancient Egypt where they were actually typical ingredients in Nile festival meals. Tomatoes, however, came from the New World, and didn't become widely available in the Mediterranean until the sixteenth century. Tahini is made from pressing sesame seeds. It is a great source of protein, phosphorous, niacin, and sulfur.

Preparation:

Combine chickpeas, tomatoes, and parsley on a medium serving platter. Pour lemon juice into a small bowl, add tahini, salt, and pepper, and whisk vigorously, adding a few tablespoons of water at a time to create a smooth, creamy dressing. Pour dressing over salad and mix well to combine. Serve at room temperature.

TIP ▶ *To make this salad ahead of time, simply keep the dressing and the salad separate and refrigerate one day ahead. Before serving, pour dressing over salad and mix well.*

*See Where to Buy Guide on pages 203–205 for purchasing information.

Red Lentil Croquettes

[Koftat Ads Ahmar]

Kofta *are traditional ground meat kabobs eaten both at home and in restaurants. In this version red lentils are substituted to make them appropriate for Lent. This is a great recipe to have on hand for your vegetarian family and friends.*

Preparation:

Put the carrots, lentils, onion, garlic, cinnamon, paprika, nutmeg, cumin, lemon juice, peanuts, and 2½ cups water into a large saucepan over high heat. Bring to a boil, and then reduce heat to low. Simmer, covered, for 30 minutes or until all of the liquid has evaporated. Take off heat and set aside until cool enough to handle.

Mix flour and turmeric together on a small plate. Lightly dust hands in flour and form the lentil mixture into 16 (3-inch) ovals. Gently roll the lentil croquettes into the flour mixture to coat.

Heat the oil in a large frying pan over medium-high heat. When oil is hot, carefully lower some of the croquettes into the hot oil being careful not to crowd the pan. Fry for approximately 10 minutes per side or until dark golden. Remove croquettes from oil with a slotted spoon and place onto a platter lined with paper towels. Sprinkle with salt to taste. Repeat with remaining croquettes. Serve warm.

8 SERVINGS

INGREDIENTS

2 carrots, peeled and finely chopped

1¼ cups split red lentils

1 yellow onion, finely chopped

2 cloves garlic, minced

½ teaspoon ground cinnamon

½ teaspoon paprika

¼ teaspoon ground nutmeg

1 teaspoon ground cumin

Juice of 1 lemon

2 tablespoons chopped unsalted peanuts

½ cup all-purpose flour

1 teaspoon ground turmeric

1 cup expeller pressed corn oil

Salt

Caraway Tea

[Carawaya]

SERVES 4

INGREDIENTS

4 teaspoons roasted caraway seeds

Sugar to taste

Caraway is believed to be the world's oldest spice since evidence of it dates back to the Stone Age. Caraway seeds were also found in ancient Egyptian tombs. They are known for their power as digestive aids and for their peppery, nutty, licorice flavor. Both rye and Irish soda breads usually contain caraway, as does sauerkraut sometimes. In Egypt today, caraway is most often used to make a tisane that is drunk after meals. Many people also give it to babies to prevent colic. Caraway seeds should always be added towards the end of cooking a dish so that their flavor doesn't become bitter.

Preparation:

In a medium saucepan, bring 4 cups water and caraway seeds to a boil over high heat. Boil for 2 minutes and then strain into 4 teacups. Sweeten with sugar if desired.

Easter

Preceded by the Lenten fasting period, Easter is the most important holiday on the Egyptian Coptic calendar. During various times in Egyptian history, Muslims shared in the Christian festivities. Under Fatimid rule in the tenth century, for example, Easter was celebrated along the Nile by everyone, regardless of religion, in order to foster harmonious relations between the communities. It is said that even the Muslim Caliph could attend the celebrations. According to Jailan Abbas, author of *Festivals of Egypt*, "in 1528 the Sultan ordered the palace to distribute sweets, fruits, and 20,000 eggs" to the Christians for Easter.

Today Easter morning is spent going to mass. Afterwards, families go home to enjoy dinners that often include the following especially-anticipated treats.

Easter Menu

▶ Jew's Mallow Soup

▶ Roasted Marinated Chicken

▶ Roasted Leg of Lamb with Potatoes

▶ Stuffed Vine Leaves

▶ Savory Phyllo Pastries with Meat

▶ Artichokes with Dill Sauce

▶ Date Dome Cookies

▶ Mint Tea

Jew's Mallow Soup
[Shorbat Maloukhiya]

4 SERVINGS

INGREDIENTS

4 cups chicken stock

1 (14 ounce) package frozen *maloukhiya* (Jew's Mallow)

Salt

Freshly ground black pepper

1 tablespoon clarified butter (*ghee*)

6 cloves garlic, minced

1 teaspoon ground coriander

Maloukhiya is a green leafy herb native to Egypt and is one of the traditional bitter herbs used on Egyptian Jewish Seder plates. In English, Maloukhiya is known as Jew's Mallow or Jew's Courgette. Legend has it that when Muizz li Din Allah (the leader of the Fatimid dynasty) first arrived in Egypt from Tunisia, he was very sick. The Egyptians prepared Maloukhiya for him and he was cured. Since that time, one of Egypt's most ordinary plants gained royal status. In 1021 AD, the caliph Al Hakim decided to ban Maloukhiya from the lower classes so that there would never be a shortage.

To this day, Maloukhiya enjoys widespread popularity in Egypt. Although it can be used for any occasion, my friend Gerges Samael Azez tells me that Maloukhiya is a popular Easter herb. It is usually made into a soup and served with rabbit or chicken and rice. The Nubians sometimes stuff bread with it.

Preparation:

Bring chicken stock to a boil in a medium saucepan. Add frozen *maloukhiya* and some salt and pepper to taste. Bring back to a boil, reduce heat to low, and simmer for 5 minutes.

In a small saucepan over medium heat, melt clarified butter. Add garlic and coriander and cook, uncovered, until garlic begins to turn color. Stir garlic mixture into the soup, taste, and adjust salt and pepper if necessary. Serve hot.

Roasted
Marinated Chicken
[Firakh Mashwi Fee al Forn]

The Middle Ages were very opulent times in Egypt, and particularly Cairo due to its bustling trade revenue. Hospitals treated needy patients free of charge, and refused to release them until they could eat an entire roasted chicken. This is a large quantity for modern standards, let alone during the Middle Ages. In comparison, during the late sixteenth century, King Henry IV of France told the citizens of his country that his goal was to enable each French family to afford a single chicken for their Sunday supper. Rabbi Meshulam of Volterra, Italy, was quoted in E.N. Adler's Jewish Travelers as saying: "We arrived in Cairo on Sunday, June 17, 1481…. if I were to write about its wealth and its people, all of this book would not be sufficient. I swear that if I were to put Rome, Venice, Milan, Padua, Florence, and four more cities together, they would not equal in wealth and population half that of Cairo."

To make a quick one-dish dinner with this recipe, add chopped potatoes, zucchini, tomatoes, and carrots to the pan halfway through cooking.

6 SERVINGS

INGREDIENTS

¼ cup extra-virgin olive oil

Juice of 1 lemon

Juice of 1 lime

1 yellow onion, quartered

4 tablespoons chopped fresh mint

1 tablespoon chopped fresh parsley

1 tablespoon chopped fresh oregano

1 tablespoon poultry seasoning

Salt

Freshly ground black pepper

1 whole chicken (3 to 4 pounds), cleaned and giblets removed

Preparation:

Mix together olive oil, lemon juice, lime juice, onion, mint, parsley, oregano, poultry seasoning, and some salt and pepper to taste in a large bowl. Place chicken in bowl and turn to coat. Place a piece of the onion inside the cavity. Cover bowl and marinate the chicken in the refrigerator for 12 to 24 hours.

Preheat oven to 425 degrees F. Roast the chicken, covered, for 1½ hours or until top is golden brown and thigh meat juices run clear when pierced with a fork. Remove from oven. Let rest for 10 minutes. Serve warm.

Roasted Leg of Lamb with Potatoes

[Fakhda Mashwiya bil Batatas]

10 SERVINGS

INGREDIENTS

1 (5-pound) leg of lamb

1 head of garlic, peeled and slivered

Salt to taste

3 tablespoons dried mint

Freshly ground black pepper to taste

2 cups chicken stock or water

8 medium Yukon Gold potatoes, peeled and quartered

Juice of 1 lemon

2 large yellow onions, sliced into rings

3 tablespoons expeller pressed corn oil

2 large tomatoes, chopped or ½ cup chopped canned tomatoes

2 cinnamon sticks

Succulent, juicy lamb is always served well-done in Egypt. This is an excellent celebratory dish that your guests will appreciate. Although it takes a long time to bake, it is simple to prepare. Once you put the leg of lamb in the oven, begin making the rest of the meal. Before you know it, you'll have a feast!

Preparation:

Preheat oven to 350 degrees F.

With a pairing knife, make 1-inch slits in various places on leg of lamb. Insert garlic slivers into the slits in the lamb. Rub some salt, the mint, and some pepper into the leg of the lamb. Place lamb in a large roasting pan. Pour 1 cup of the chicken stock or water into the pan. Bake for 1 hour, uncovered, basting every 20 minutes.

Add potatoes to the pan. Pour lemon juice over the potatoes and lamb and season with salt and pepper. Place onion rings over the lamb. Drizzle corn oil over the onions and potatoes. Scatter the tomatoes around the sides of the pan. Add cinnamon sticks and remaining 1 cup of stock to the pan. Return to the oven and bake, uncovered, an additional 2 hours, basting every 20 minutes, until lamb is falling off the bone and potatoes are tender.

Remove from the oven and cover pan with lid or aluminum foil. Allow lamb meat to stand at room temperature for 10 minutes before carving. Spoon tomatoes and potatoes into a serving bowl. Remove and discard cinnamon sticks. Place lamb on a serving platter and carve. Serve warm.

Stuffed Vine Leaves

[Wara' El Aghnib]

Plump stuffed vine leaves are usually served as side dishes in Egyptian homes and restaurants, as an accompaniment to the main courses. Since they are filled with rice, separate rice dishes are usually not included in the same meal. Outside of Egypt, fresh vine leaves can sometimes be found at Middle Eastern and Greek grocers in the spring season.

While recipes for Stuffed Vine Leaves vary, the following recipe is from my sister-in-law Soad and is my favorite version. In addition to tasting flavorful and slightly piquant, the vine leaves evoke warm, happy memories of Soad and Egypt itself. Stuffed Vine Leaves can be rolled a day in advance and cooked the day of serving.

6 SERVINGS

INGREDIENTS

- 1/2 pound fresh vine leaves or 1 (8 ounce) jar preserved vine leaves, drained
- 1 cup Egyptian or other short-grain rice
- 1/3 cup fresh dill, finely chopped
- 1/3 cup fresh parsley, finely chopped
- 1/3 cup fresh mint leaves, finely chopped
- 1 cup canned chopped tomatoes, drained
- 1 medium yellow onion, grated
- 1/4 cup expeller pressed corn oil
- 1 teaspoon salt
- 1/2 teaspoon freshly ground black pepper
- Dash of chili powder
- 1 teaspoon ground cumin
- Juice of 1 lemon

Preparation:

Place vine leaves in a large bowl. Cover with boiling water and let stand for 10 minutes. Drain vine leaves. Place leaves on a work surface vein side up. Cut the excess piece of stem from the bottom of each leaf.

In a medium bowl, mix rice, herbs, 3/4 cup of the tomatoes, onion, corn oil, salt, pepper, chili powder, and cumin. Place 1 tablespoon of filling into the middle of a leaf. Shape the filling to resemble the width of a pencil across the width of the leaf. Loosely roll the leaf up, starting from the bottom. Tuck in the sides of the leaf as you go, making an envelope. Refrain from rolling the leaf too tightly or it will tear as the rice cooks and expands inside. Continue with remaining leaves.

Place stuffed vine leaves seam side down, next to each other in a heavy saucepan. The stuffed leaves should be touching one another and fit into the pan without any spaces. Repeat a second layer on top, if necessary. Place a plate upside down on top of the stuffed leaves in the saucepan to keep them from rising. Pour boiling water over the leaves until they are almost but not completely covered.

Add the remaining 1/4 cup tomatoes, some salt and pepper, and the lemon juice to the pan. Cover the saucepan and simmer on low heat until rice is fully cooked and leaves are tender, approximately 1 to 1 1/2 hours.

To test the doneness of the stuffed vine leaves, break one in half and taste it. Serve warm or at room temperature.

Savory Phyllo Pastries with Meat

[Goulash bi Lahma]

**12 SERVINGS
(24 PIECES)**

INGREDIENTS

1 tablespoon unsalted butter

1 small yellow onion, diced

1 pound ground beef

1/4 teaspoon ground nutmeg

1/2 teaspoon ground cumin

1/4 teaspoon ground cinnamon

1/4 teaspoon paprika

Salt to taste

Freshly ground black pepper to taste

1 package phyllo dough, thawed at room temperature for 2 hours

1 cup clarified butter (*ghee*)

Goulash is the Egyptian word for phyllo. Any dish, sweet or savory, that uses phyllo dough is referred to as a different form of goulash. Layering phyllo dough with meat or cheese creates the most common savory goulash dishes, which are often included in holiday buffets and are popular potluck dishes.

Preparation:

Heat butter in a large frying pan over medium heat. Add onion and sauté until translucent, about 5 to 7 minutes. Add beef, stir in nutmeg, cumin, cinnamon, and paprika, and brown thoroughly. Season meat with salt and pepper to taste. Remove from heat and set aside to cool. (This can be done a day in advance.)

Preheat oven to 350 degrees F. Open the box of phyllo dough. With a sharp knife, trim phyllo sheets to fit into a 13x9x2-inch baking pan.

Place 1 phyllo sheet over the bottom of the baking dish and brush with clarified butter. Continue stacking phyllo dough, buttering each sheet, until you have used 1/2 of the sheets. Put browned meat mixture on top of the phyllo and spread into an even layer leaving a 1/2-inch border around the edges.

Cover with another phyllo sheet, brush with butter, and continue stacking and buttering until all phyllo sheets are used up. With a sharp, serrated knife, cut the phyllo into 24 squares (4 across and 6 lengthwise). Place in oven and bake for approximately 45 minutes or until golden.

Artichokes with Dill Sauce

[Kharshuf bi Shabbat]

The ancient tradition of eating artichokes is prevalent all around the Mediterranean today. In addition to their tender texture and elegant, mellow flavor, baby artichokes contain beneficial antioxidants. Dill is rich in mineral salts and a tasty addition to many Egyptian dishes. Although this recipe calls for fresh artichokes, canned or frozen artichoke hearts may be substituted.

Preparation:

Clean the artichokes by soaking them in water, and changing the water until it remains clear after soaking. Pull off the outside leaves of the artichokes. Use kitchen scissors to clip the tops off of the remaining artichoke leaves off so that the top of the artichoke is a uniform height. Remove the thorny choke from the center. At this stage, the artichoke should resemble a flower.

Place artichokes in a large saucepan, add some salt, cover with water, and bring to a boil over medium-high heat. Once artichokes start to boil, reduce heat to medium and continue boiling artichokes until they are tender.

Drain the artichokes and set on a small serving platter. Place lemon juice, olive oil, Dijon mustard, and dill into a blender. Blend together to form a vinaigrette and season with salt and pepper to taste. Pour dressing over artichokes. Serve warm or at room temperature.

4 SERVINGS

INGREDIENTS

12 baby artichokes

Salt to taste

Juice of 2 lemons

3 tablespoons olive oil

1 tablespoon Dijon mustard

1/4 cup fresh dill, finely chopped

Freshly ground black pepper to taste

Date Dome Cookies

[Ma'moul]

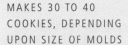

MAKES 30 TO 40 COOKIES, DEPENDING UPON SIZE OF MOLDS

INGREDIENTS

DATE FILLING:

1/2 pound dried dates, pitted

2 tablespoons butter

1 teaspoon orange blossom water*

COOKIE DOUGH:

1 cup unsalted butter, at room temperature

1 1/2 cups sugar

2 teaspoons fresh orange or lemon juice

1 teaspoon orange blossom water

1 large egg

1/2 teaspoon ground cherry kernels (*mahlab*)* (optional)

3 cups unbleached, all-purpose flour

1 cup fine grade semolina*

1/2 teaspoon salt

Confectioners' sugar for sprinkling

These scrumptious cookies are indigenous to Saudi Arabia and probably arrived in Egypt in the seventh century with the Arabians. They are to the Middle East what chocolate chip cookies are to Americans. They can be purchased everywhere, from bakeries to grocery stores that sell pre-boxed varieties. Their fillings range from dates to apples to pistachios to walnuts. By far, the date ones are the most coveted. Many people like to eat Ma'moul *for breakfast.*

Ma'moul are made with special wooden (and nowadays plastic) molds called qaleb. The molds are engraved with various designs that decorate the cookies in intricate patterns. Both the date filling and the cookie dough can be made a day in advance. Refer to the Where to Buy Guide on page 203–205 for purchasing information for the molds, or shape the cookies into balls by hand. For best results, use double air-cell or stone cookie sheets to prevent the cookies from burning on the bottom.

Preparation:

Preheat oven to 350 degrees F. Position racks in the middle of the oven. Line two double air-cell or stone cookie sheets with silicone liners or parchment paper.

Prepare date filling: Combine dates, butter, and orange blossom water in a food processor. Pulse on and off until filling has a paste-like consistency. Set aside.

Prepare dough: Combine butter and sugar in a large bowl and cream until light yellow in color, approximately 3 to 5 minutes. Add orange or lemon juice and orange blossom water; mix well and then add egg and mix well again. Add the cherry kernels, if using, and stir to incorporate.

Mix flour, semolina, and salt in a separate large bowl. Slowly add flour mixture to the butter mixture. Mix until a smooth dough forms and then shape it into a ball.

continued on next page

Date Dome Cookies

continued from previous page

continued from previous page

To assemble the *ma'moul*: Determine which size of mold you are using. For a large mold, break dough off into 2-inch pieces. For a small mold, break dough off into 1½-inch pieces. Roll the dough into balls between the palms of your hands. Flatten each ball and place 1 teaspoon date mixture into the center of each circle. Stretch the dough to cover filling and roll into balls. Place one of the dough balls in a cookie mold. Push it into the mold until it is level with the mold and fills the entire space. Hold the stick of the mold and tap its neck with the cookie facing away from you onto a hard surface to un-mold the cookie dough.

Place cookie design side up onto the cookie sheet. Repeat with the remaining dough. Cookies may be placed ½ inch apart from one another since they do not spread.

Bake approximately 20 minutes and do not let the tops of cookies turn brown. Remove from the oven and top with sifted confectioners' sugar. Allow cookies to cool on cookie sheets on wire racks.

TIP ▶ *These cookies can be frozen up to a month in advance in an airtight container between sheets of wax paper.*

*Refer to Where to Buy Guide on pages 203–205 for more information.

Mint Tea

[Shai bil Na'na]

4 SERVINGS

INGREDIENTS

4 teaspoons dried mint

4 cups water

Sugar to taste

This is a calming tisane that promotes digestion and clears the nasal passages and throat.

Preparation:

Place mint in a teapot or medium saucepan. Cover with water and bring to a medium boil over high heat. Once it boils, remove from heat and steep for 5 minutes. Strain and pour into tea cups. Add sugar to taste. Serve warm.

Housny Restaurant, Ramadan Dining, Alexandria, Egypt

Ramadan Pre-Dawn Breakfast

Sohoor

Islam came to Egypt in 640 AD with the Arabian armies led by Amr ibn al As, ten years after the death of the Prophet Mohammed. Islam is a monotheistic religion like Judaism and Christianity. The Qu'ran is the main holy book from which Islam was derived. It was revealed in the seventh century AD to the Prophet Mohammed by the Angel Gabriel in Mecca, Saudi Arabia. The five pillars of the Islamic religion are:

1. *Shahada,* meaning the declaration that there is only one God, and that the Prophet Mohammed (peace be upon him) is his last and final messenger.
2. *Salat,* which means prayer, and refers to the five obligatory prayers that Muslims are required to pray at specific times each day.
3. *Zakat,* meaning charity, mandates that all Muslims who are financially able must donate a portion of their earnings to charity.
4. *Sawm,* or fasting, meaning that all adult Muslims who are physically able must abstain from food and drink (as well as other regulations) during the holy month of Ramadan.
5. *Hajj,* the annual pilgrimage to Mecca that must be completed once in a lifetime by Muslims who are physically and financially able to do so.

During the holy month of Ramadan, Muslims abstain from food and drink from sun up to sundown to fulfill religious obligations and learn self-restraint, patience, and piety. People who are ill or traveling, children, and non-Muslims are not required to fast. The month of Ramadan is considered to be holy by Muslims because it is the lunar month in which the Torah, Bible, and Qu'ran were revealed. Since the Islamic calendar is lunar, the date of Ramadan changes each year.

Before dawn in Egypt and many other countries with large Muslim populations, men called Messaharati walk through the streets beating a drum and chanting "Wake up believers … prayer is better than sleep." If the Messaharati knows the names of the people living in the buildings, they will mention them by name. It is customary for families to pay a tip for this service in addition to the blessing they will receive from God.

Then pots and pans start clanking, and lights from homes start to illuminate the streets. A light hum of talking takes place as families enjoy their morning meals together. A few minutes before dawn, everyone stops eating. The dawn calls to prayer begin sounding from the minarets of nearby mosques, and everyone prepares to pray. Afterwards many people read the Qu'ran and make additional supplications. During vacations or days off of work and school, many people go to sleep after the morning prayer and wake up in the afternoon. Others go to school and work and rush home before the sunset prayer to enjoy meals with their families. Many businesses close after the mid-afternoon prayer until after the sunset prayer so that people are able to go home.

Traditionally, the breakfast menu items are quick to prepare because they have to be done so early in the morning. Otherwise, they are started the night before and reheated the next day. Antipasto-type platters full of various kinds of purchased cheeses, pastrami, olives, and pickled vegetables are typically served as well. Try serving this menu as a late breakfast or brunch to houseguests anytime.

Ramadan Pre-Dawn Breakfast Menu

▶ Fava Bean Puree

▶ Creamy Wheat Berry Cereal

▶ Eggs with Tomatoes and Feta Cheese

▶ Yogurt with Honey

▶ Egyptian Pound Cake

Ramadan Memories

September 24, 2006, Shiben el Khom, El Menofia, Egypt

Yesterday the town was restless as people prepared for the month of fasting. Everyone hustled back and forth to buy dried fruits, mixed nuts, bread for the morning meal, and most importantly, Ramadan lanterns for the children. Cars honked as they went up and down our street. Honking is a sound that becomes a backdrop to daily life in Egypt. Her cities, after all, are full of people, movement, and light. Cars here use their horns as signals—for they share the road with horse- and donkey-drawn carts, as well as pedestrians, motorcycles, bicycles, scooters, and children playing soccer.

This morning I am struck by the image of people walking by at this early hour. They seem to glide by … their feet as light as air, dressed in long white robes. Some of them hold prayer beads. Set amidst the backdrop of the rising sun, in between tall gray buildings whose roofs are occupied by pigeons, their faces are obscured … it is as if they are angels surrounded by halos of light.

The morning solitude is where peace, hope, and prosperity reside. The cool air is a welcome change from the heat of the day. More and more people begin passing by and the town becomes alive with smooth, respectful movements, and powerful intent. Across the street, colored lights—partially hidden by clothes hanging to dry—flicker on the balcony. Another neighbor has displayed red, white, and green lights above their garage. It is now 4:55 AM and the first horn of the day has sounded. A motorcycle glides down the street, a stray cat meows, starting a chorus of what seems to be every cat in the world. People begin returning home from the morning prayer. The month of Ramadan has begun.

Fava Bean Puree

[Fuul Medammes]

4 SERVINGS (½ CUP EACH)

INGREDIENTS

2 teaspoons extra-virgin olive oil

1 (15-ounce) can cooked fava beans (*fuul medammes*) with juice*

1 teaspoon ground cumin

⅛ teaspoon salt

Freshly ground black pepper

Juice of 1 lemon

Pita bread, for serving

Fava beans (also known as broad beans) are believed to be the world's oldest agricultural crop. One of the pharaohs's favorites, this traditional Egyptian dish is still a popular breakfast and snack food. Recently, Egyptian doctors released research proving that a breakfast of fava bean puree, eggs, and pita bread provides all of the nutrients needed during a day's worth of activity. Most people start their days during Ramadan with Fuul Medammes. In general, Egyptians tend to eat protein-packed breakfasts. Starting the day with thirty grams of protein is actually recommended by neuro therapists for optimal brain function.

Preparation:

Heat 1 teaspoon olive oil in a medium frying pan over medium-low heat. Add beans and juice from can, cumin, salt, and some pepper and stir well to combine. Cook for 5 minutes or until most of the liquid is absorbed. Reduce heat to low and mash the beans slightly with a fork or potato masher and stir in lemon juice.

Spoon the fava mixture onto a serving plate. Make a hole in the center and drizzle remaining 1 teaspoon olive oil into it. Serve with pita bread.

TIP ▸ *This dish can also be eaten as a vegetarian lunch or dinner.*

*Cooked fava beans may be purchased in the international aisle at most grocery stores, or check the Where to Buy Guide on pages 203–205 for mail order sources.

Creamy Wheat Berry Cereal

[Bileela]

This could very well be the world's oldest cereal recipe. Bileela is a comforting whole wheat berry cereal that is enjoyed all over Egypt. It is even sold in plastic bags at street-side stalls at breakfast time for people who don't have time to boil it at home. To quicken the preparation, I suggest covering the bileela with boiling water in a thermos overnight. When you wake up, the cereal will be ready, and you don't have to wait an hour for it to cook.

INGREDIENTS

1 cup whole wheat berries, rinsed*

1/3 cup sugar or honey, or to taste

1/2 cup warm milk

Handful of raisins, if desired

Preparation:

The night before, place whole wheat berries in a large thermos and cover with boiling water. The next morning, the wheat will be puffed and tender. Stir sugar or honey into wheat, if desired, and distribute into 4 cereal bowls. Top with warm milk and raisins, if using.

*Wheat berries can be purchased at organic, Middle Eastern, and health food stores.

Eggs with Tomatoes and Feta Cheese

[Beid bil Gebna wa Tomatum]

4 SERVINGS

INGREDIENTS

1 teaspoon expeller pressed corn or olive oil

4 (¼-inch thick) slices feta cheese

4 eggs

1 ripe tomato, diced

Salt to taste

Freshly ground black pepper to taste

Egyptians enjoy eggs prepared this way with pita bread. Eggs cooked sunny-side up are referred to as "my eyes." Look for the smoothest feta you can find for this recipe.

Preparation:

Heat olive oil in a large frying pan over medium heat. Place feta slices a few inches apart in the pan and let cook for 2 minutes.

Crack an egg over each feta slice and season with salt and pepper to taste. Sprinkle tomato pieces over each egg and cook for about 10 minutes, until egg is set and cheese is soft. Serve warm.

Red date tree

Yogurt with Honey

[Zabadi bil 'Asal]

The Egyptian love of honey can be traced back to ancient times when it was used as a cure for just about every ailment in the world. The Bible also mentioned the healing power of honey. When the majority of Egyptians converted to Islam in the seventh century, they found that even the Qu'ran declared the virtues of honey. Today, many Egyptians bring pure comb honey as gifts to sick people and take a teaspoon of it a day as a tonic. The term 'Asal (honey) is used as an expression of approval in the Egyptian dialect. It is common to refer to people, places, and things as "honey" if they are viewed as exceedingly special.

Egyptians often eat plain, full-fat honey with yogurt for breakfast like Greeks do. Look for good-quality Middle Eastern or Greek yogurt for this dish.

4 SERVINGS

INGREDIENTS

4 cups good quality full-fat plain Greek yogurt

4 teaspoons good quality honey

Preparation:

Divide yogurt into four ramekins. Top each with 1 teaspoon of honey and serve.

Egyptian Pound Cake

[Torta]

10 SERVINGS

INGREDIENTS

1 cup unsalted butter, at room temperature

1 cup sugar

Grated peel of 1 orange

1 teaspoon vanilla extract

4 large eggs, beaten until foamy

½ cup plain full-fat Greek yogurt

1¾ cups unbleached, all-purpose flour

2 teaspoons baking powder

Each time I return to Egypt, pound cake has become more and more popular. I see it everywhere from breakfast buffets to receptions to coffee shops. The first time I had it was at a resort in the breathtaking El Fayoum Oasis. The resort's restaurant served two kinds of breakfasts, Masri (Egyptian) or Continental. The Egyptian consisted of fava bean puree and eggs, while the Continental consisted of this cake and yogurt. Our family got both so that we could sample everything. Serve this cake for breakfast with spreadable cheese, jams, and coffee. Or try it for dessert topped with Creamy Orange Pudding (page 58) and whipped cream. This cake can be wrapped in plastic wrap and aluminum foil and frozen for up to 1 month.

Preparation:

Preheat oven to 350 degrees F. Position rack in the center of the oven. Butter and flour a 10-inch loaf pan.

Combine butter, sugar, orange peel, and vanilla in a large bowl and beat until everything is incorporated and light. Add the eggs to the butter mixture in 4 parts, beating well after each addition. Stir in the yogurt.

Sift the flour and baking powder into the mixture. Stir well to incorporate and pour the batter into the prepared pan. Bake for 40 to 45 minutes, or until a toothpick inserted in the center comes out clean. Remove cake from the oven and allow to cool completely.

Turn the cake out of the pan. If cake does not come out easily, carefully run a butter knife around all of the edges and lift gently to help it come out. Slice into 1-inch-thick slices and serve.

Ramadan After-Sunset Dinner

Iftaar

As the sun begins to set, cannons are fired throughout Egypt to announce the end of the day's fast. Then the minarets start calling Muslims to the sunset prayer. The decorative street lights and lanterns are illuminated in urban and rural areas alike. People stand at traffic lights carrying little bags of dates and sometimes whole boxed meals to toss into the cars of the unfortunate people who are not at home enjoying meals with their families.

At restaurants, the tables, which have been reserved in advance, are already set with small plates of appetizers, dates, and apricot juice so the patrons can sit down and start their meal before ordering.

Socializing and festivities during Ramadan evenings last until dawn. After the breakfast meal, people go out into the streets to walk, window shop, attend supplemental prayers called *Tawareah* at mosques, and socialize. In Cairo, the area around the Hussein and Al Azhar mosques becomes a beacon of human activity. The bazaar in the Attaba neighborhood is packed with wall-to-wall bargain hunters looking for deals for presents that are to be exchanged on the Eid al Fitr, the three-day holiday marking the end of Ramadan. All along the Nile, boats light up as many people reserve places on cruises to break their fasts in style.

In Alexandria, the European-style cafés that line the Mediterranean shore are decked out in white lights. The old Arab quarter and majestic mosques echo an atmosphere reminiscent of Sufi mystics and prestigious sultans. Restaurants in popular quarters add to the communal atmosphere of the month by extending their restaurants outside with sidewalk service found only during Ramadan.

My friends in Luxor tell me that the streets have actually been blocked off to hold Ramadan dinners. Whoever would normally have been traveling stops at the road block and participates in the festivities. In the past, both Christians and Muslims have participated.

Ramadan is the time when I am most nostalgic for Egypt. For that one short month highlights the generosity, kindness, wonderful food, folklore, and family atmosphere that makes Egyptian culture unique. While Ramadan *iftaar* menus could be made up of any of the recipes in this book, for this menu I chose those that are religiously and culturally significant. Keep in mind that since Ramadan lasts for a month, each night's menu and dinner table is transformed into a feast. As many Egyptian Americans say, "It's like thirty Thanksgiving nights."

This menu includes the preliminary fast-breaking items, the main meal, desserts, and what I like to call "round two." Round two are the things that you munch on until the wee hours while visiting with friends and relatives. In this menu, they would include the Lupine Beans, Fresh Fruit Plate, and Mixed Nut Plate. They are usually brought out a few hours after the meal, never at the dinner table, and served in separate courses. If your guests stay until it is almost dawn, it is customary to offer them a place to sleep and invite them to have the morning pre-dawn breakfast with you.

Ramadan After-Sunset Dinner Menu

▶ Macerated Dates with Apricots and Raisins

▶ Homemade Apricot Juice

▶ Eggplant Puree

▶ Vermicelli, Meat, and Tomato Soup

▶ Macaroni with Meat and Béchamel Sauce

▶ Veal, Rice, and Toasted Bread Casserole

▶ Fried Honey Fingers with Sweet Syrup

▶ Sweet Nut-Filled Pancakes

▶ Lupine Beans

▶ Assorted Fresh Fruit Plate

▶ Mixed Nut Plate

Ramadan Table Spread

Macerated Dates with Apricots and Raisins

[Khoshaf]

Macerated dates are enjoyed in many Muslim countries during the month of Ramadan because the Prophet Mohammed used to break his fast with dates. Traditionally, Muslims are to break their fast with dates, pray the sunset prayer, and then enjoy the iftaar *meal.*

The word "dates" appears 248 times in the 146 hadith *(recorded sayings and actions of the Prophet Mohammed [peace be upon him]) according to the Bukhari translation. In seventh-century Arabia they were used for everything from settling debts to charity to entertaining. While the original* Khoshaf *contained only water and dates, modern cooks combine various kinds of dried fruits, sugar, nuts, and coconut in their drinks. Since the dates get soaked in water for a long period of time, it is best to use the hardest dates you can find for this recipe. Soft ones will disintegrate. Serve* Khoshaf *in small ramekins set on dinner plates.*

4 SERVINGS

INGREDIENTS

1 pound firm dried dates, pitted

1/2 pound raisins

1/2 pound dried apricots, chopped into small pieces

1/4 cup sugar

1 teaspoon orange blossom water*

1 teaspoon rose water*

Preparation:

Place dates, raisins, and apricots in a large bowl. Pour 4 cups of boiling water on top of them. Stir in sugar, orange blossom water, and rose water. Let stand until water reaches room temperature and fruit becomes tender. Serve in small ramekins or mugs with a spoon.

*See Where To Buy Guide on pages 203–205 for purchasing information.

Dried fruits for making Khoshaf

Homemade Apricot Juice

[Assir Amr Din]

6 SERVINGS

INGREDIENTS

1 pound dried apricots,
   chopped into small pieces

1 cup sugar

In Egypt, dried fruits are traditionally reserved for Ramadan when large lines form outside of stores specializing in dried fruits and nuts.

Apricot juice is significant because the ancient Arabians discovered that combining apricot flesh and water prevented dehydration. Since it is forbidden to drink during daylight hours of Ramadan, apricot juice became the traditional drink of the break-fast meals.

During Ramadan, Egyptian restaurant tables, which have been reserved in advance, are set with small plates of appetizers, dates, and apricot juice. Restaurant patrons can sit down and start their meal before ordering. Since charity is an important pillar of Islam, many famous Egyptians sponsor large, free communal meals throughout the cities and villages.

During Ramadan, large colored cloths are draped over store fronts, in windows, and used as decorative tents. Special lanterns called fanoos are specific to Ramadan and used as typical decorations in homes and businesses. Strands of small lantern-shaped lights are also used to adorn streets and alleys. Some people also use miniature tabletop mosques and fill them with Nubian-style figurines of people praying, reading the Qu'ran, preparing food, and performing other tasks of daily life.

Preparation:

Place the apricots in a large, heat-proof bowl and cover them with 6 cups boiling water. Allow to soak until the apricot pieces dissolve (this can take anywhere from a few hours to overnight, depending on the apricots).

Stir the sugar into the apricots until it dissolves. Puree the mixture in a blender. Refrigerate until cold.

Eggplant Puree

[Baba Ghanoug]

This popular appetizer is just one of many that are included in traditional restaurant dinners. I tend to like the more rustic versions in which the eggplant is mashed by hand and pieces of the eggplant can be distinguished from the puree itself. If you prefer a smooth, creamy puree, simply put the mixture into a food processor and pulse on and off a few times to create the desired consistency.

4 SERVINGS

INGREDIENTS

2 eggplants (each 8 to 9 inches long)
2 tablespoons tahini*
Salt to taste
Juice of 1 lemon
Extra-virgin olive oil, as needed
Dash of sumac* for garnish

Preparation:

Preheat broiler. Prick eggplants with a fork and place on a baking sheet. Broil 15 to 20 minutes, turning once, until eggplants are blistered and collapse. Allow to cool. Peel and remove flesh and place in a colander to drain. Press down with a fork until all liquid is removed. Place the eggplant in a medium bowl and mash down with a fork to cut it into bite-size pieces, or pulse the eggplant a few times in a food processor—be careful not to process the eggplant too much as it should not be completely smooth.

With a fork, stir tahini, salt, and lemon juice into the eggplant. Add olive oil, tablespoon by tablespoon, until the texture resembles crunchy peanut butter. The amount of olive oil needed will depend on the water content and size of the eggplants used.

Place the eggplant puree in a mound on a serving plate. Make a small well in the center and fill with olive oil. Sprinkle with sumac. Serve at room temperature along with pita bread or crudités.

* See Where to Buy Guide on pages 203–205 for purchasing information.

Vermicelli, Meat, and Tomato Soup

[Shorbat bil Sharleya, Lahma, wa Tomatum]

8 SERVINGS

INGREDIENTS

2 medium tomatoes

1 tablespoon unsalted butter

1 medium yellow onion, diced

1 medium carrot, diced

1 celery stalk, diced

1 pound ground beef

$1/2$ teaspoon ground allspice

$1/2$ teaspoon ground cumin

$1/2$ teaspoon ground nutmeg

Salt to taste

Freshly ground black pepper to taste

4 cups beef or chicken stock

1 cup vermicelli*

Juice of 1 lime

Soups are always served as a first course after people have broken their fast with dates. This is a light and satisfying soup that I was served by Chef Nasser Saiyd from Cairo.

When I returned to the United States from Egypt, I prepared the soup to bring to a potluck at a friend's house. One of the guest's four-year-old daughter (who had never sampled Egyptian cuisine before) ate four bowlfuls of the soup! Her mother was astounded, noting "She doesn't even like soup!" I urge you to serve this soup at your next family gathering. Maybe it will inspire a soup lover in your family as well.

Preparation:

Fill a large saucepan three-quarters full of water and bring to a boil. Add tomatoes and boil 1 to 2 minutes or until skin begins to crack. Drain tomatoes and submerge in a bowl of ice-cold water. When tomatoes are cool enough to handle, peel skins off, cut in half, remove seeds, and dice.

Melt butter in a large stockpot over medium heat. Add onion, carrot, and celery. Sauté for 5 to 7 minutes or until onions are translucent. Add beef and brown, stirring occasionally and breaking the meat into tiny bits. Stir in allspice, cumin, nutmeg, and some salt and freshly ground pepper to taste. Add tomatoes, stock, and 4 cups water. Increase heat to high and bring to a boil, skimming off scum as it appears at the top of the soup. Reduce heat to low, cover, and simmer for 20 minutes.

Remove lid, stir, and add vermicelli. Simmer, uncovered, until vermicelli is tender. Taste and adjust salt and pepper, if necessary. Squeeze lime juice into soup and stir. Serve hot.

*See Where to Buy Guide on pages 203–205 for purchasing information

Macaroni with Meat and Béchamel Sauce

[Macarona Bechamel]

Various forms of pasta existed in the ancient Mediterranean area. Béchamel sauce gained popularity in Egypt during Napoleon's three-year campaign there. In Egypt, béchamel sauce is made with stock, eggs, and milk, instead of all milk, like the original French recipe. It is used as a topping for vegetables, beef slices, and this macaroni dish. My friend Hanaa El Abd often replaces the meat in the recipe with sliced broiled eggplant, which is equally delicious.

Preparation:

To make the béchamel sauce: Melt butter in a medium saucepan over medium heat. Add flour and whisk well to incorporate. Slowly whisk in the milk and stock 1/2 cup at a time, whisking after each addition. Increase heat to medium-high, boil gently for two minutes, reduce heat to low and simmer while stirring slowly with a wooden spoon until sauce is reduced to half its original volume. Remove from heat and let cool slightly. Taste and add salt and pepper to taste as necessary. Whisk egg in a small bowl and add 2 tablespoons of béchamel sauce, one at a time and whisk well after each addition. Slowly add the egg mixture into the béchamel sauce, whisking well. Set sauce aside until needed.

To make the meat filling: Heat butter in a large skillet over medium heat. Add beef, onion, and beef seasoning and cook until beef is brown, approximately 5 minutes. Add tomato puree, salt, and freshly ground pepper to taste. Reduce heat to low and cook, uncovered, until tomato puree has been absorbed by the meat mixture. Remove pan from heat, taste and adjust salt and pepper, if necessary.

8 SERVINGS

INGREDIENTS

BÉCHAMEL SAUCE:

4 tablespoons butter

4 tablespoons all-purpose flour

2 cups warm whole milk

2 cups warm chicken or vegetable stock

Salt

Freshly ground black pepper

1 egg

MEAT FILLING:

2 tablespoons unsalted butter

2 pounds ground beef

1 onion, grated

1 teaspoon beef seasoning or 1/2 teaspoon ground coriander and 1/2 teaspoon ground cumin

1/4 cup tomato puree

Salt

Freshly ground black pepper

1 pound rigatoni or penne

1/2 cup grated pecorino Romano cheese (or Egyptian *gebna rumi*), for topping

To assemble and bake the macaroni: Preheat oven to 350 degrees F. Boil pasta according to package directions. Stop cooking 1 to 2 minutes early (pasta will continue to cook in the oven) and drain Spread approximately ¼ cup of béchamel sauce over the bottom of a 9x13x2-inch pan. Reserve 1 cup of béchamel sauce for top of casserole. Mix remaining béchamel sauce with pasta. Taste and adjust salt if necessary.

Spoon half of pasta mixture into the baking dish and smooth out top. Spread meat filling evenly over pasta. Spread remaining pasta mixture over the meat filling. Smooth the top, and pour reserved béchamel sauce evenly over the top of the pasta. Sprinkle grated pecorino Romano cheese evenly over the entire dish. Bake casserole for approximately 45 minutes or until the top is golden brown.

TIP ▶ *The béchamel sauce and meat filling may be made a day in advance, stored in the refrigerator, and then assembled with freshly boiled pasta and baked on the day of serving.*

Veal, Rice, and Toasted Bread Casserole

[Fattah bil Bitello]

Nile Style

PART 2 | Significant Ceremonies

Egyptian Fattah *differs from other* Fattah *recipes in the Middle East because it contains rice as a base instead of yogurt and is usually topped with a garlicky tomato sauce. This version does not contain tomato sauce, which is a typical modern addition, because in the Middle Ages when it became popular, tomatoes were not present in the Mediterranean and Middle Eastern region. Beef or lamb cubes could be substituted for the veal in this recipe. This book also contains a recipe for Lamb Fattah (page 120).*

Preparation:

Place veal cubes, onion, salt, pepper, cinnamon, nutmeg, and paprika in a large saucepan. Cover with water and bring to a boil over high heat. Lower heat to medium-low, cover and simmer until veal is tender. Taste and adjust salt if necessary.

Preheat broiler. Place pita bread pieces on a baking sheet and brush lightly with clarified butter on both sides. Place under broiler, turning once, until toasted on both sides. Set aside.

In a small saucepan, heat vinegar over medium heat. Add garlic and coriander and cook until liquid is half of it's original quantity.

Stir bread pieces into Egyptian rice and spoon mixture onto the bottom of a serving platter, leaving a 2-inch border around the sides of the dish. Arrange the veal pieces around the rice border. Drizzle vinegar-garlic sauce over the rice and veal broth over the veal pieces. Scatter parsley on top of dish. Serve warm.

6 SERVINGS

INGREDIENTS

2 pounds boneless veal shoulder cubes

1 large onion

1 teaspoon salt

1/2 teaspoon freshly ground black pepper

1/2 teaspoon ground cinnamon

1/2 teaspoon ground nutmeg

1/2 teaspoon paprika

2 pita breads, cut into 1-inch squares

1/4 cup clarified butter (*ghee*)

1/4 cup distilled white vinegar

13 cloves garlic, peeled and minced

1 teaspoon dried coriander

2 cups prepared Egyptian Rice (page 22)

4 tablespoons finely chopped fresh parsley

Hot sauce, for serving

Sweet Fritters with Lemon Syrup

[Balahe Sham]

MAKES 40

INGREDIENTS

LEMON SYRUP:

2 cups sugar

3 strips lemon peel

Juice of 1/2 lemon

SWEET FRITTERS:

1 cup expeller pressed corn oil, plus extra for frying

2 1/4 cups unbleached, all-purpose flour

1 tablespoon sugar

1/2 teaspoon salt

2 egg yolks

1 teaspoon vanilla extract

These delicious treats are classic Egyptian pastries. Their name means "date of the Sham region," which refers to the Levantine region of the Middle East. Egypt and this region share many recipes because of their shared history. In Iran, the same sweet goes by the name of zalbia. *During Ramadan, the* Balahe Sham *are offered plain, topped with sweet syrup or chocolate, or split open and filled with* ishta *cream and topped with ground pistachios.*

This recipe was taught to me by Pastry Chef Hashem Kassem Mohamed who goes by the name of Ahmed Hashem at the Tut Hotel in Luxor, Egypt, where I was completing an assignment as a Culinary Consultant. Ahmed and I worked side by side for weeks making breads and pastries. I was very impressed by his willingness to learn, his ingenuity, and his wide range of knowledge. In many bakeries in Egypt, the chefs specialize in either Eastern or Western desserts, local breads, or international breads. Ahmed, however, could produce exquisite Egyptian pastries one minute and Kaiser rolls or intricately decorated French gateaus the next. While I was teaching him my favorite Italian and American recipes, I mentioned the trouble I was having with Balahe Sham. *The night before I left, he taught me this recipe and gave me a plate full as a parting gift. These pastries are best eaten the day they are made and while still hot to prevent them from getting soggy. You will need a pastry bag fitted with a large star-shaped tip.*

Preparation:

Make the syrup by combining sugar, lemon peel, lemon juice, and 3/4 cup of water in a medium saucepan. Stirring slowly, bring to a boil over medium heat. Once mixture comes to a boil and sugar is dissolved, stop stirring and reduce heat to low. Simmer for 10 minutes and then remove from heat and set aside to cool. Discard lemon peel and set aside. (This can be done up to 1 month in advance; cover and store in the refrigerator.)

Bring 2 cups water and oil to a boil over high heat. Reduce heat to low and carefully stir in flour, sugar, and salt. Continue stirring until ingredients are incorporated and begin to form a dough that pulls away from the sides of the pan. Set aside to cool.

continued on next page

Sweet Fritters
with Lemon Syrup

continued from previous page

When dough is room temperature, stir in egg yolks, one at a time, and vanilla.

Spoon batter into a pastry bag fitted with a large star attachment. Push dough down towards the bottom and twist the top of the bag so that it stays compact.

Pour syrup into a large shallow bowl and set near frying area. Place a slotted wire spoon, a spatula, another large bowl with a colander over it, and a knife near frying area along with filled pastry bag. Heat 2 inches of corn oil in a large wide skillet over medium-high heat.

Holding pastry bag completely perpendicular above hot oil with one hand, squeeze a 3-inch log out of bag and quickly run a knife or spatula across the tip of the bag to release it into the hot oil. Working quickly, continue to add pastry logs until you have about 10 equal-size logs in the oil at once. With the slotted wire spoon, carefully turn logs to ensure even browning and cook until they are dark golden. (This should take 2 to 4 minutes, if it takes longer, increase the heat slightly; if they fry too quickly, decrease the heat slightly.) Using the slotted spoon, lift logs out of the oil and gently shake off excess oil. Drop them in the syrup and with another spoon and turn them to coat evenly. Place them into the colander to drain. Repeat the process, working in batches, until all of the dough is used. Serve warm.

Amy Riolo with Chef Ahmed Hashem

Nile Style

PART 2 | Significant Ceremonies

Sweet Nut-Filled Pancakes

[Atayef]

SERVES 4

INGREDIENTS

PANCAKE BATTER:

1 1/2 teaspoons active dry yeast

1 1/2 teaspoons sugar

2 cups unbleached, all-purpose flour

1/8 teaspoon salt

SYRUP:

1 cup sugar

Juice of 1/2 lemon

3 strips lemon peel

1/2 teaspoon orange blossom water*

1/2 teaspoon rose water*

FILLING:

1/4 cup blanched almonds, ground

1/4 cup walnuts, ground

Canola oil, for frying

Atayef are synonymous with Ramadan in Egypt. I remember one year at 4:10 AM on the first day of Ramadan, the first call to prayer sounded. Various mosques around town continued their chorus of prayer calls until 4:40 AM whence silence once again befell a country that seemed to never sleep. Five minutes later, two foldable tables were set up on the sidewalk of the empty street in front of our apartment. Using lanterns as their guides, two men and a woman began preparing batter that would be transformed into Atayef *once the day started. The* Atayef *makers decorated their downstairs apartment with red, white, and green lights in a U-shaped formation to call attention to their sweets. Some pastry shops use red, green, and yellow food coloring to dye the pancake batter.*

Preparation:

To make batter: Mix yeast with sugar and 1/4 cup of warm water. Stir until dissolved. Sift flour and salt into a large mixing bowl. Make a well in the center. Pour in yeast mixture and 1 1/4 cups warm water. Whisk mixture until a smooth batter is formed. Cover bowl with plastic wrap and kitchen towels and place in a warm, draft-free area. Allow to rise for 1 hour. Batter is ready when it is bubbly.

In the meantime, prepare the syrup: Combine 3/4 cup of water with sugar, lemon juice, and lemon peel in a medium saucepan. Stir and cook over medium-high heat, stirring often until sugar is dissolved. Bring mixture to a boil, stop stirring, and lower heat to medium-low. Simmer for 10 minutes. Remove from heat and set aside to cool. When syrup has cooled, remove and discard lemon peel. Stir in orange blossom water and rose water.

When batter is ready, heat 2 tablespoons of canola oil in a large frying pan. Using a batter dispenser or a tablespoon, carefully pour 1 tablespoon of batter into the oil and spread to form a 4-inch round pancake. Continue with some of remaining batter, do not crowd pan. When tops of pancakes are full of holes, remove them with a spatula and place on a paper towel-lined tray, cooked side down. When all of batter has been used, begin to fill the pancakes.

continued on next page

Sweet Nut-Filled Pancakes

continued from previous page

Mix ground almonds and walnuts together. Holding a pancake in the palm of your left hand, fill it with 1 teaspoon of the nut mixture on the uncooked side of the pancake. Fold pancake in half and gently press the very tip of the edges to seal in the form of a half moon. (Be careful not to make a thick ridge around the edge like ravioli or it will cause the *atayef* to fry unevenly.) Place filled pancakes on a plate and continue filling and sealing the remaining pancakes.

Heat 2 inches of oil in a large frying pan. When oil is hot, fry the filled pancakes for 2 minutes per side or until golden. Remove pancakes and place on a platter lined with paper towels. While still warm, place the pancakes on a serving platter and pour syrup over the top. Allow to cool enough to handle and serve warm.

TIP ▶ *The batter, filling, and syrup may all be made the day before serving and stored separately in the refrigerator. On the day of serving the pancakes will just need to be cooked, filled, fried, and topped.*

*See Where To Buy Guide on pages 203–205 for purchasing information.

Making Atayef *in Alexandria, Egypt*

Lupine Beans

[Termis]

**MAKES APPROXIMATELY
4 CUPS**

INGREDIENTS

1 (16-ounce) jar Ready-to-Eat
Lupine Beans

Lupine beans have been popular in Egypt since antiquity. In ancient times, they were not only eaten, but used in creams and facial scrubs to improve the skin's appearance and reduce wrinkles. According to Pliny, eating them "freshens the complexion." They were also boiled with rain water to make a mixture that cured gangrene and ulcers.

Throughout the Mediterranean region, lupine beans are eaten during holidays. In southern Italy, for example, they are an ever-present staple at Christmas dinners. During Ramadan in Egypt, people often spend the hours between the last evening prayer and the dawn prayer visiting with family members. Termis are the perfect snack for socializing. Nut shops and roasters all over Egypt sell ready-to-eat lupine beans. Outside of Egypt, glass jars of lupine beans can be purchased from Italian and Middle Eastern import stores. Look for jars marked "Ready to Eat." Many of the older varieties were packed with salt, and it took days to rinse them of the residue. Nowadays, with the Ready-to-Eat varieties, one quick soaking is enough.

Preparation:

Soak lupine beans in cold water for a day and then drain.

To eat lupine beans, hold them in your hand and squeeze the bean through its shell. Eat the bean and discard the shell.

Assorted
Fresh Fruit Plate

[Tabaa Fakha Tazig]

Typical Ramadan dinners end with a plate of fresh fruit. At intimate family dinners this may mean a plate of a single type of seasonal fruit, carved by a male member of the family and distributed to each person present. In restaurants, the fruit plates can be very elaborate—an opportunity for chefs to demonstrate their carving skills. Egypt's plethora of sweet fruits is transformed into edible works of art. When creating your own fruit plates, use local availability, personal preferences, and your own imagination to dazzle your guests.

4 SERVINGS

INGREDIENTS

4 tangerines, peeled

6 large strawberries

2 Gala apples, cored and sliced into ¼-inch wedges

2 golden apples, cored and sliced into ¼-inch wedges

Preparation:

Place a doily on a round serving plate. Arrange the whole tangerines in the form of a cross in the center of the plate. Place a strawberry on top of the center of each tangerine and one on the side of the two tangerines that are on the right and left side. Arrange the gala apple slices on the left side of the plate between the strawberry and tangerine on the top and bottom. Arrange the golden apple slices on the right side of the plate between the strawberry and the tangerine on top and bottom.

Mixed Nut Plate

[Tabaa M'kassarat]

Community vendors sell many versions of almonds, pistachios, walnuts, peanuts, pine nuts, chickpeas, pumpkin seeds, and hazelnuts during the Ramadan season. They are usually sold in small paper bags, and many people walk around the urban areas, or along the Nile or Mediterranean, munching on them. It is also common to serve them to guests after dinner. Use your own taste preferences to determine the kind of nuts you serve.

MAKES 1¼ POUNDS NUTS

INGREDIENTS

¼ pound pistachios

¼ pound walnuts

¼ pound roasted salted almonds

¼ pound salted peanuts

¼ pound salted pumpkin seeds

Preparation:

Place pistachios, walnuts, almonds, peanuts, and pumpkin seeds in individual mounds on a serving platter.

Eid al Fitr Celebration (Marking the End of Ramadan)

The Eid al Fitr is celebrated by Muslims worldwide with a three-day holiday directly following the month of Ramadan. On the first day of the holiday, everyone attends congregational prayer held at mosques and arenas. The rest of the holiday is spent visiting family and friends, eating celebratory meals, and exchanging gifts.

Usually the tone of this holiday is about comfort and ease. Since during the month of Ramadan people wake up before dawn to eat and then fast all day, the evening meals tend to be heavy. Eid al Fitr marks a return to normalcy when people can dictate when and where they would like to eat. In our family, this means Traditional Eid Cookies for breakfast with coffee or tea and milk and a large, yet light, meal in the middle of the day (a time when we would have been fasting during Ramadan). Most people truly look forward to lighter meals made of fish and a variety of salads for this meal because they need a break from the large *iftaar* during Ramadan.

Eid al Fitr Menu

▶ Egyptian Rice with Mixed Vegetables

▶ Pickled Herring (purchased)

▶ Grilled Fresh Sardines

▶ Arugula Salad

▶ Traditional Eid Cookies

▶ Honey-Filled Eid Cookies

Khan el Khalili Spice Shop, Cairo, Egypt

Egyptian Rice with Mixed Vegetables

[Roz bil Khodar]

Nowadays Egyptian rice is a common export to the Arab world. Its short grain and high starch content differentiate it from the long grain and Basmati rice that are eaten in many other Middle Eastern countries. See the Where to Buy Guide on pages 203–205 for purchasing information. This is a quick and homey recipe to have on hand.

Preparation:

Place bell peppers and carrots in a medium saucepan filled three-quarters of the way with water and bring to a boil. Reduce heat and simmer, uncovered, for 10 minutes. Drain and set aside.

Heat olive oil in a medium saucepan over medium heat. Add onion slices and sauté until light golden. Remove from pan and add to vegetables.

Add the rice to the oil that the onion sautéed in. Cook over medium-low heat for 3 to 5 minutes or until translucent. Add the vegetables, tomatoes, and stock. Season with salt and pepper and stir to incorporate. Bring to a boil over high heat. Reduce heat to low and simmer, covered, for 20 to 25 minutes, or until all water is absorbed. Serve warm.

6 SERVINGS

INGREDIENTS

2 green bell peppers, diced

2 carrots, diced

2 tablespoons olive oil

1 yellow onion, thinly sliced

2 cups Egyptian or other short-grain rice

3/4 cup chopped tomatoes

3 cups chicken or vegetable stock

1/2 teaspoon salt

1/4 teaspoon freshly ground black pepper

Grilled Fresh Sardines

[Sardine Ma'li]

6 SERVINGS

INGREDIENTS

1 tablespoon extra-virgin olive oil

3 pounds fresh sardines (approximately 6-inches long), cleaned and gutted

1 bunch fresh rosemary

Salt

Freshly ground black pepper

2 lemons, cut into quarters

In Egypt, marinated fresh sardines are a popular delicacy. People make them at home, or buy them from stores that marinate them in house. When fresh sardines become available in the United States in the fall, I like to grill them, allowing their fresh flavor to shine through. I stuff them with rosemary, which is said to stimulate brain function and was found in the tombs of ancient Egypt dating back to the First Dynasty. Rosemary oil is used to relieve rheumatism, cure headaches and infections, and stimulate circulation and digestion. In Egypt, we light incense while we prepare sardines to keep the scent of the fish from lingering.

Preparation:

Heat grill or grill pan over medium-high heat. If using a grill pan, brush with olive oil. Stuff each sardine with a sprig of fresh rosemary and season with salt and pepper to taste. Place on grill and cook for 3 to 5 minutes per side until lightly golden and cooked through. Place on a platter and garnish with remaining rosemary sprigs and lemon quarters.

Arugula Salad

[Salata bil Gargeer]

While arugula is considered a gourmet food item in the United States, it is abundant in Egypt and thought of as a peasant food. It has been eaten since antiquity, and its oil is also extracted as a traditional medicine used for treating skin conditions. Arugula is a typical accompaniment to fish in Egypt and throughout the Arab world. It is served on heaping platters next to fish dishes, and sometimes dressed with the broth from cooked fish. Arugula is never served cooked in Egypt.

6 SERVINGS

INGREDIENTS

3 bunches fresh arugula

Juice of 3 lemons

1/4 cup extra-virgin olive oil

Salt

Freshly ground black pepper

Preparation:

Wash arugula well by placing in a large bowl of water and letting it soak for a few minutes. Drain arugula, rinse bowl with water, and soak again. Continue draining and soaking until water remains clear. This could take more than 10 separate soakings because arugula tends to collect sand and dirt.

Dry the arugula thoroughly and pile it onto a dinner plate. In a medium bowl, whisk lemon juice and olive oil to obtain a light dressing. Season dressing with salt and pepper to taste and pour over the arugula.

Traditional Eid Cookies

[Kahk a L'Eid]

**MAKES APPROXIMATELY
2 DOZEN**

INGREDIENTS

5 cups unbleached, all-purpose
   flour

1 tablespoon sesame seeds

1 cup clarified butter (*ghee*)

1 cup milk

¹/₄ teaspoon salt

¹/₂ tablespoon active dry yeast

1¹/₂ tablespoons baking
   powder

¹/₂ teaspoon rose water*

¹/₂ teaspoon almond extract

¹/₂ teaspoon ground cinnamon

¹/₂ teaspoon ground cloves

¹/₂ teaspoon ground ginger

¹/₂ cup confectioners' sugar, for
   decoration

The Abbasids of Baghdad ruled Egypt from 750 AD to 905 AD. Their Muslim caliphate was founded by descendents of the Prophet Mohammed's uncle, Al Abbas. During the Abbasid caliphate, a noteworthy amount of education and scientific knowledge was spread throughout Islamic society.

The Abbasids also placed great importance on cooking, and the philosopher Al-Kindi began to write about it as an art form. The Abbasid cooking tradition, which was based largely on Persian cuisine, was adapted to native Egyptian ingredients during their rule in Egypt. When the Islamic alchemists perfected distillation, rose water became an indispensable ingredient in Middle Eastern cuisine, as well as a widely popular perfume and home fragrance. Rose water is one of the ingredients in these delicious cookies.

After a month of rising and eating beans, eggs, and bread before dawn, the Traditional Eid Cookies make the perfect celebratory breakfast. This is a recipe that I adapted from my sister-in-law Soad's version. They can be made in advance and frozen. To serve them, thaw for a few hours at room temperature and dust with another coating of powdered sugar. To enable the cookies to "grab" onto more powdered sugar, their tops are decorated using a ma'alıt, which looks like a cross between tweezers and a staple remover, to make dents on the top. If you don't have one, you can use a fork to make deep grooves in the tops of the cookies.

Preparation:

Preheat oven to 350 degrees F. Line 2 baking sheets with parchment paper or silicone liners. Pour flour in a large bowl and make a well in the center. Sprinkle sesame seeds in the well. Heat the clarified butter in a small saucepan over medium heat until it begins to boil. Remove from heat, and using a wooden spoon carefully incorporate into the flour. Stir until ingredients are mixed well and flour mixture turns cool.

In a separate bowl, mix milk, salt, yeast, baking powder, rose water, almond extract, cinnamon, cloves, and ginger. Add milk mixture to dough ¹/₄ cup at a time, mixing

continued on next page

Traditional Eid Cookies

continued from previous page

well to incorporate after each addition. When all of milk mixture is incorporated, form dough into a ball and turn out onto a lightly floured surface and knead for 5 to 10 minutes.

Break off small pieces of dough and roll to form 2-inch balls. Place balls 1-inch apart on the baking sheets. Flatten the tops slightly and use a *ma'alit* or fork to make 3 or 4 lines of dents down the tops of the cookies. Bake both cookie sheets side by side for 14 to 18 minutes, or until light golden. Take out of oven and carefully transfer cookies to wire racks to cool. Continue with remaining dough. Sprinkle cookies with confectioners' sugar.

*See Where To Buy Guide on pages 203–205 for purchasing information.

Eid cookies at Vinous Patisserie in Alexandria, Egypt

Honey-Filled Eid Cookies

[Kahk bil Agameya]

MAKES APPROXIMATELY 4 DOZEN

INGREDIENTS

FILLING:

4 tablespoons clarified butter (*ghee*)

4 tablespoons unbleached, all-purpose flour

1 cup orange blossom honey

4 tablespoons chopped walnuts or dates, if desired

DOUGH:

1 teaspoon sugar

2 teaspoons active dry yeast

7 cups unbleached, all-purpose flour, sifted with 1 teaspoon salt

1 teaspoon ground cinnamon

1 teaspoon ground cloves

1 teaspoon ground ginger

2 cups clarified butter (*ghee*)

1 cup confectioners' sugar, for topping

These rich, buttery cookies have been a part of the Eid al Fitr celebration in Egypt since the tenth century when Fatimid Sultans ordered that the cookies be prepared in the palace kitchens, stuffed with gold coins, and distributed to the poor for the holiday. Before the Eid al Fitr, financially-able Muslims must pay a charity, called zakat al fitr, *to the mosques in order for their fasting to be accepted by God. Many people give additional food and charity during the month, and these cookies were born out of that tradition. Today, fillings for these cookies range from dates and walnuts, to the honey mixture used in this recipe. The honey mixture is the most symbolic because it looks like liquid gold.*

Preparation:

To make the filling: Melt clarified butter in a large saucepan over medium heat. Add the flour and stir with a wooden spoon until the mixture changes color. Remove from heat and stir in the honey, mixing well to incorporate. Return the pan to the heat and continue stirring until the mixture is thickened, about 10 to 20 minutes. Remove from heat, stir in nuts or dates, if desired, and allow to cool completely. When mixture is cool, break off very small pieces of the filling and roll into pea-sized balls. Place on a sheet of wax paper or plastic wrap until ready to fill the cookies.

To make the dough: In a small bowl, dissolve the sugar in ¼ cup of warm water. Add the yeast and stir. Let mixture sit for 10 minutes. Mix the flour with salt, cinnamon, cloves, and ginger in a large mixing bowl and make a well in the center. Bring the clarified butter to a boil in a medium saucepan over medium heat. Pour into the center well of the flour mixture and stir to incorporate ingredients, stirring until mixture has cooled. Once dough is completely cool, stir in the yeast mixture.

Line 2 cookie sheets with parchment paper or silicone liners. Dust a clean work surface with extra flour. Turn the dough out onto the work surface and knead for 10

continued on next page

Honey-Filled
Eid Cookies

continued from previous page

minutes, until the dough is soft and smooth. Break off 1-inch pieces of the dough and form into egg shapes. Make a hole in the center of each and insert a ball of the filling. Cover the hole and shape the cookies into balls. Place cookies 1 inch apart on the prepared cookie sheets. Make 3 or 4 rows of lines across the tops of the cookies with a fork or a *ma'alit*. Cover cookies with a kitchen towel and allow to rest for 1 hour.

Preheat the oven to 375 degrees F. Bake cookies for 20 minutes or until set. Remove from oven. Sift confectioners' sugar on the top and allow to cool on the pans.

Eid al Adhu ("The Feast of the Sacrifice")

The largest holiday on the Muslim calendar is the Eid al Adhu, also known as the Eid Kabeer or the Big Eid in Egypt. This holiday is proceeded by the Hajj, the fifth pillar of Islam that requires that Muslims who are physically, emotionally, and economically able make a ritual pilgrimage to Mecca once in their lifetime. The Hajj occurs during the twelfth month of the lunar Islamic calendar, and the Eid al Adhu comes directly after it from the tenth to fourteenth days of the month.

According to the Qu'ran, the Prophet Abraham received a message from God through a dream. In the dream, Abraham was ordered to sacrifice his son Ismael. (The biblical version of the story depicts Isaac as the son who is to be sacrificed.) Ismael, who was still a child, told weeping Abraham not to be afraid, and that he should follow God's command before his own sentiments. Just as Abraham began to draw his sword to his beloved son, the angel Gabriel appeared before him and told him that his dream was only a test to measure Abraham's devotion. He continued that God would never require a believer to do something so difficult. The angel Gabriel told Abraham to sacrifice a sheep instead.

To this day, Muslims around the world sacrifice sheep and other animals to commemorate God's mercy. According to Islamic law, one-third of the meat must be distributed to the needy, one-third must be shared with the family, and the other third may be kept by the person who purchased the animal. This tradition is called the *adheya*. It is customary for the people who receive the meat as a gift to thank the person who gave it to them and say special prayers in their honor. Taking this custom a step further, many Egyptians sacrifice sheep and distribute the meat to the needy to give thanks for blessings such as wealth and children throughout the year. The Eid al Adhu menu is made up of various courses highlighting the meat obtained from the sacrifices. It is considered a waste to throw the meat away.

Eid al Adhu Menu

▶ Phyllo Triangles Filled with Lamb
▶ Lamb Broth and Orzo Soup
▶ Lamb, Rice, and Fried Bread Casserole
▶ Stewed Green Beans with Tomatoes and Thyme
▶ Cucumber and Yogurt Salad
▶ Banana, Honeydew, and Cantaloupe Cocktail
▶ Peanut, Coconut, and Raisin Baklava

Phyllo Triangles Filled with Lamb

[Sambusak bil Lahma Dani]

Salah ad Din al Ayyub (Saladin), a Kurdish soldier from Lebanon, came to power in Egypt in 1169 AD. Saladin surrounded Cairo with a wall and erected the Citadel, one of Egypt's most beautiful monuments to date, to protect it from the crusaders. His dynasty, the Ayyubids, were based in Damascus, Syria, and financially supported by Baghdad, Iraq. The Ayyubid empire's union helped to unify the cuisine that is referred to as Middle Eastern today by combining the cooking styles of Lebanon and Syria with those of the Abbasid courts in Iraq and the Fatimid palaces in Egypt. For this reason, many classic Middle Eastern dishes, like these phyllo triangles, are enjoyed throughout the region.

8 SERVINGS
15 PHYLLO TRIANGLES

INGREDIENTS

$1/2$ pound ground lamb, rinsed and drained well

1 small yellow onion, grated

$1/2$ teaspoon ground cumin

$1/2$ teaspoon ground cinnamon

$1/2$ teaspoon ground nutmeg

$1/2$ teaspoon paprika

Salt to taste

Freshly ground black pepper to taste

9 phyllo pastry sheets (18x14-inch), thawed according to package directions

$1/3$ cup clarified butter (*ghee*)

Preparation:

Make lamb filling: Heat a large frying pan over medium heat. Add ground lamb, onion, cumin, cinnamon, nutmeg, and paprika. Cook the mixture, stirring occasionally, until meat is browned. Season with salt and pepper to taste, stirring well to incorporate. Allow mixture to cool to room temperature. (The filling can be made a day in advance and refrigerated.)

Preheat oven to 350 degrees F. Line 2 baking sheets with parchment paper or silicone liners.

Open the phyllo sheets and spread them out on a work surface long side facing you. Layer three sheets on top of each other, brushing the top one with clarified butter to cover. Cut 5 equal strips (from top to bottom) going down the length of the rectangle. Place one teaspoon of lamb mixture at the top of each strip. Fold the phyllo over the filling on the diagonal. Continue to fold the phyllo in a flag-folding fashion into a triangle. Continue with remaining phyllo and filling.

Place triangles on prepared baking sheets. Brush clarified butter over the tops of each triangle. Bake for 20 to 25 minutes or until golden. Serve warm or at room temperature.

Lamb Broth and Orzo Soup

[Shorba bi Lissan al Asfoor]

MAKES APPROXIMATELY 6 QUARTS

INGREDIENTS

2 black peppercorns

1 cinnamon stick

2 pieces lamb meat with bone attached

1 onion, coarsely chopped

1 carrot, coarsely chopped

1 stick celery, coarsely chopped

2 tablespoons salt or to taste

2 cups orzo

Juice of 1 lemon

Handful of fresh parsley, finely chopped

A slightly more narrow version of orzo is called Lissan al Asfoor *or "birds' tongues" in Egypt. In the olden days, many women made the* Lissan al Asfoor *from scratch. Outside of Egypt, orzo makes a good substitute. What is essential to the success of this simple soup, however, is homemade lamb stock. It can be made ahead and frozen, then at the time of serving, it is reheated and the orzo is added.*

Preparation:

To make the lamb stock: Fill an 8 quart stockpot three-quarters of the way full with water. Add peppercorns, cinnamon stick, lamb meat, onion, carrot, and celery to the pot. Add salt, stir, and bring to a boil over high heat. Skim scum off the top with a slotted spoon as it forms. Once water is boiling, reduce heat to low, cover, and simmer for 2 to 3 hours. Strain stock into another stockpot and discard spices and vegetables. Peel the meat off the bone and shred into tiny pieces. Add to the stock. (At this point, stock may be refrigerated for up to a week or frozen for up to a month.)

Preheat oven to 350 degrees F. Place orzo on a baking sheet and toast in the oven, stirring 2 or 3 times until orzo is golden brown. Remove from oven and set aside.

Bring stock back to a boil over high heat. Taste and add more salt if needed. Pour in the toasted orzo, bring to a boil, and then reduce heat to low. Cook soup for approximately 10 minutes, stirring occasionally, until orzo is tender but not overly soft. Remove from heat, stir in lemon juice, taste and adjust salt and pepper, if necessary. Transfer to a soup tureen or individual soup bowls, top with parsley, and serve hot.

TIP ▶ *Since this recipe makes a large quantity of soup, freeze the rest in a combination of single and family serving-size freezer containers to use at another time.*

Lamb, Rice, and Fried Bread Casserole

[Fattah bil Lahma Dani]

This dish is said to have been Napoleon's favorite while he was in Egypt from 1798 to 1801. Napoleon invaded Egypt to gain control of trade routes to India, and during his occupation, thousands of Egyptian and French soldiers lost their lives. When he returned from Egypt after the unsuccessful military campaign, Napoleon mentioned that even though he was unsuccessful in colonizing Egypt and many people lost their lives, the campaign was still worthwhile because of "the knowledge that was gained" from his time spent in Egypt. Napoleon is credited with having created the precursor to the work of the modern Egyptologists by hiring hundreds of people to study and record the history, culture, and sociology of Egypt. Napoleon published their research in twenty-four volumes called Descriptions de l'Egypte, which can still be viewed today in a condensed version. Portions of the original are on display at museums and galleries around the world. He also initiated a new system of weighing and measuring in Egypt as well as a French style of government.

This is my favorite version of Fattah, which was prepared for us by Chef Nasser Saiyd from Cairo while we were on a Nile cruise from Luxor to Aswan. The taste combines the perfect balance of rich, buttery meat and rice with a perfectly piquant tomato sauce. I also learned this method of serving Fattah, which is the most elegant I've seen, from Chef Nasser. Although this dish is easy to make, it contains quite a few steps. Be sure to read the recipe carefully before beginning it, and have all of the ingredients ready to make preparation easier. The stock and tomato sauce could be made a day in advance and reheated before assembling. Contact your local supermarket or butcher to obtain the correct piece of meat beforehand.

4 SERVINGS

INGREDIENTS

LAMB STOCK AND MEAT:

2 teaspoons clarified butter (*ghee*)

2 pounds lamb leg sirloin, cut into 3-inch pieces with bone in

2 medium yellow onions, quartered

1/4 teaspoon ground nutmeg

1/2 teaspoon ground cinnamon

1/4 teaspoon paprika

1 teaspoon salt

1/4 teaspoon freshly ground black pepper

4 cups lamb (page 119), chicken, or beef broth

TOMATO SAUCE:

1 tablespoon expeller pressed corn oil

1/2 head of garlic, peeled, minced

1 1/4 cups chopped tomatoes

1 teaspoon ground coriander

Salt to taste

Freshly ground black pepper to taste

Pinch of chili powder, if desired

Handful of freshly chopped parsley or cilantro

1 tablespoon distilled white vinegar

Preparation:

Prepare stock and meat: Preheat oven to 375 degrees F. Heat clarified butter over medium heat in a large ovenproof frying pan. Add lamb and brown on all sides. Add onions to the pan along with nutmeg, cinnamon, paprika, salt, and pepper. Pour broth over meat. Place in oven and cook until tender, about 1 1/2 to 2 hours.

RICE:

2 teaspoons expeller pressed corn oil

1 cup Egyptian or other short-grain rice

1 teaspoon salt

1³/₄ cups fresh lamb stock (from cooking meat)

BREAD:

¹/₂ cup expeller pressed corn oil, plus extra for greasing ramekins

1 pita, spread open and cut into 2-inch pieces

1 teaspoon dried coriander

1 tablespoon chopped fresh parsley or cilantro, for garnish

Prepare tomato sauce: After meat has cooked about 45 minutes, begin preparing the tomato sauce by warming the corn oil over medium heat in a medium saucepan. Add the garlic and cook, stirring slowly, until it begins to color. Add the tomatoes to the pan, mix well, and stir in coriander, some salt and pepper, and chili powder. Continue to cook over medium-high heat until the mixture begins to boil. Stir in the parsley or cilantro and reduce heat to medium-low and cover the pan. Simmer sauce, stirring every 15 minutes or so, until the mixture becomes thick. Sauce is ready when it has reduced to less than half of its original volume, about 30 minutes. Stir in vinegar and cook for 5 more minutes. Remove from heat and leave covered until ready to serve.

Prepare the rice: Heat oil in a medium saucepan with a tight-fitting lid. Add rice and salt and stir to coat rice. Add 2 cups of the warm lamb stock (from preparing the lamb meat). Bring to a boil over medium-high heat. Stir, reduce heat to low, cover, and simmer for 15 to 20 minutes, until stock is absorbed and rice is done. Taste and adjust salt if necessary. Remove from heat and keep covered until ready to serve.

Prepare the bread: Heat corn oil in a large frying pan over medium-high heat. When oil is hot add pita pieces and sprinkle with coriander and fry until golden on both sides. Remove with a slotted spoon and drain on a plate lined with paper towels. When bread has cooled slightly, gently mix it in with the rice.

To serve the *Fattah*: Oil 3- to 4-inch ramekins and divide rice mixture between them, pressing down and smoothing the tops. Turn the ramekins over onto individual serving plates, using a knife to release the rice if necessary. Top each rice dome with some tomato sauce (usually just the top of the rice dome is covered) and sprinkle with a teaspoon of reserved parsley or cilantro. Arrange lamb pieces around rice and add a few more dabs of sauce on empty portions of the plates, if desired. Serve warm.

Stewed Green Beans with Tomatoes and Thyme

[Lubiya Matboukh bil Tomatum]

Throughout the Middle East, a variety of wild thyme known as zataar *is used both fresh and dried. There are also various spice mixes called* zataar *that usually contain* zataar *itself, along with sumac, sesame seeds, and salt. This recipe calls for plain* zataar, *not the mix. Fresh thyme works well as a substitute for the* zataar *in this recipe. Green beans are a good source of vitamins A, C, and folate.*

Preparation:

Heat olive oil in a medium saucepan over medium heat. Add onion and sauté until translucent, about 3 to 5 minutes. Stir in garlic and cook for 1 minute. Stir in tomatoes, thyme, and some salt and freshly ground pepper to taste.

Bring to a boil over high heat, add green beans, stir, and reduce heat to low. Simmer for 10 to 15 minutes, or until green beans are tender. Taste and adjust salt and pepper if necessary. To serve, spoon onto a serving platter and top with fresh parsley.

*See Where To Buy Guide on pages 203–205 for purchasing information.

4 SERVINGS

INGREDIENTS

1 tablespoon olive oil

1 small yellow onion, diced

1 clove garlic, chopped

1³/4 cups chopped tomatoes

1 teaspoon fresh thyme, finely chopped, or ¹/2 teaspoon dried *zataar**

Salt to taste

Freshly ground black pepper to taste

1 pound fresh green beans, ends trimmed

1 tablespoon finely chopped fresh parsley

Cucumber and Yogurt Salad

[Salata Khoyar bil Laban]

6 SERVINGS

INGREDIENTS

- 3 cups plain full-fat yogurt, drained in a cheesecloth-lined colander for a minimum of 6 hours
- 6 small cucumbers, diced and drained
- 1 tablespoon fresh dill, finely chopped, or ½ teaspoon dried dill
- 1 small yellow onion, grated and drained well
- Salt to taste

This is one of the dishes that Egyptian and Turkish kitchens have in common. In 1250 AD, a Turkish military power known as the Mamlukes took control of Egypt. During their two centuries of power, Egypt was embellished with some of the most impressive Islamic architecture in the world, which the Mamlukes financed through trade. The Mamlukes built the Qaitbay and Sultan Hassan mosques in Cairo. The kitchens of the entire Mediterranean region became infused with Turkish flavors. During the reign of Sultan al Nasir Muhammad, the kitchens of the Cairo citadel produced more than twenty-five thousand tons of food per day. A typical banquet included thousands of animals and tons of sugar for desserts and sorbets.

Preparation:

Place yogurt in a medium bowl. Add cucumbers, dill, and onion and stir. Season with salt to taste. Serve immediately to prevent salad from becoming runny.

Cairo Citadel

Banana, Honeydew, and Cantaloupe Cocktail

[Cocktail bil Mowz wa Shammam]

This is a delicious combination of thirst-quenching fruits. I recommend making it only when these items are in season. Since the Eid al Adhu comes at different times each year, it will not always be appropriate for the celebration. During other seasons, choose another cocktail that features other seasonal fruits, or serve Egyptian Lemonade (page 17) or Hibiscus Punch (page 21) instead.

Preparation:

Place banana, ice, and 1 tablespoon honey in blender. Blend on highest speed until smooth and frothy. Pour equal amounts into 4 clear glasses.

Rinse out the blender and put cantaloupe and 1 tablespoon honey inside. Whip until frothy and pour over the back of a spoon on top of the banana juice in the glasses (this prevents cantaloupe and banana from mixing).

Rinse blender and fill with honeydew and remaining 1 tablespoon honey. Whip until frothy and pour over the back of a spoon on top of the cantaloupe juice. Serve immediately.

4 SERVINGS

INGREDIENTS

1 banana, cut into rounds

1 cup ice

3 tablespoons honey

1 cup bite size pieces cantaloupe, chilled

2 cups bite size pieces honeydew, chilled

Nile Style

PART 2 | Significant Ceremonies

Peanut, Coconut, and Raisin Baklava

[Goulash bi Fuul Sudani, wa Zabeeb]

MAKES 30 SERVINGS

INGREDIENTS

SYRUP:

1 1/2 cups sugar

2 large strips orange peel

Juice of 1 small orange

FILLING:

1 cup roasted, unsalted peanuts, coarsely chopped

1/4 cup golden raisins

1/4 cup black raisins

1/2 cup dried coconut #1

BAKLAVA:

1 (1 pound) package phyllo dough, thawed according to package instructions

1 cup clarified butter (*ghee*)

My husband's cousin's mother-in-law Saadeya Osman U'aah prepared this delicious baklava for me when she came to visit us at our home in Egypt during Ramadan one year. It was the first time I had ever tasted peanuts in baklava, and it was extraordinary. Southern Egypt, like the southern United States, is famous for its peanuts. Markets in Aswan offer many freshly roasted varieties for sale. In Egypt, a teaspoon of the peanut, coconut, and raisin combination is often used to top sweet drinks and puddings. For best results, use unsalted peanuts and dried coconut to make this recipe.

Preparation:

Preheat oven to 350 degrees F. Butter a 9x13-inch or 12-inch-round baking pan.

Make the syrup: Combine sugar, 1 cup water, orange peel and juice in a medium saucepan. Bring to a boil over medium heat, stirring until sugar dissolves. Discontinue stirring, reduce heat to low, and simmer for 10 minutes (see Tip). Set aside to cool. Remove and discard orange peel.

Make the filling: Combine peanuts, golden raisins, black raisins, and dried coconut together in a medium bowl and stir well.

To assemble the baklava: Remove phyllo dough from package. Trim the sheets with a sharp knife to fit the pan you are using.

Cover bottom of baking pan with 1 sheet of phyllo dough. Brush clarified butter over the top. Place another sheet on top and brush with more clarified butter. Continue stacking and brushing with butter until half of the phyllo dough is used.

Spread filling evenly across the top of the phyllo. Top with another sheet of phyllo and brush with butter. Continue layering remaining phyllo dough and brushing with clarified butter. Brush top layer with clarified butter. With a long, sharp knife, cut phyllo three-quarters of the way through into 30 squares (5 across and 6 lengthwise).

continued on next page

Peanut, Coconut, and Raisin Baklava

continued from previous page

Bake for 40 to 50 minutes or until golden, rotating pan halfway through to ensure even browning. Remove pan from oven and pour syrup over the top. Allow to sit until syrup is absorbed and baklava has cooled to room temperature. Using a knife and a small metal spatula, carefully cut around the baklava squares and lift up from the bottom to serve.

TIP ▶ *You can tell when the syrup is ready by looking at the orange peel strips. When the strips appear to look like candied orange peel, the syrup is at the right consistency.*

Baklava at Metropolitan Restaurant in Luxor, Egypt

Ashoora

The tenth day of *Muharam*, the first month of the Islamic calendar, is known as *Ashoora* (sometimes spelled *Ashura*). *Ashoora* is a special day for Egyptian Jews, Christians, and Muslims (although it is remembered by each group on different dates). Muslims are encouraged to fast on *Ashoora* because the holiday commemorates God saving the Prophet Moses and the Jewish people from the tyranny of the pharaoh. The Prophet Mohammed recommended that Muslims fast the day before or the day after *Ashoora* as well. After the fast, families congregate for a communal meal.

Ashoora Menu

▶ Chicken, Pea, and Potato Soup
▶ Stuffed Baby Eggplants and Zucchini
▶ Lamb and Potato Stew
▶ Savory Cheese Phyllo Pastry
▶ Ashoora Wheat Pudding
▶ Ginger Tea

Sinai

Chicken, Pea, and Potato Soup

[Shorbat bil Firakh, Bisella, wa Batatis]

This is a substantial soup that makes a nice meal with bread and salad. Alternately, it can be served in small amounts as a first course. This soup can be frozen and reheated when needed.

Preparation:

Heat corn oil in a medium stockpot over medium heat. Add onion and sauté for 5 minutes or until translucent. Add chicken pieces and brown on all sides. Add peas, potatoes, and chicken stock and stir. Add turmeric, paprika, ginger, coriander, salt, and freshly ground pepper.

Increase heat to high and bring to a boil. Skim the white scum off the top as it appears. Reduce heat to low, cover, and simmer for 20 to 30 minutes or until chicken is cooked through and vegetables are tender.

Taste the soup and adjust salt and pepper, if necessary. Transfer to tureen or individual soup bowls and sprinkle cilantro on top. Serve with lime quarters.

4 SERVINGS

INGREDIENTS

- 1 tablespoon expeller pressed corn oil
- 1 medium yellow onion, diced
- 2 pounds boneless chicken breast, cut into 1-inch cubes
- 1 cup frozen petite peas, thawed and drained
- 2 Yukon Gold potatoes, peeled and cubed
- 5 cups chicken stock
- 1/8 teaspoon ground turmeric
- 1/2 teaspoon paprika
- 1 teaspoon ground ginger
- 1 teaspoon ground coriander
- 1 teaspoon salt
- 1/2 teaspoon freshly ground black pepper
- 2 tablespoons finely chopped fresh cilantro
- 1 lime, quartered

Stuffed Baby Eggplants and Zucchini

[Mahshi Bittingan wa Koosa]

SERVES 4

INGREDIENTS

10 (3 to 4 inches long x 1¹/₂ inches wide) baby eggplants

10 (3 to 4 inches long x 1¹/₂ inches wide) baby zucchini

2 cups Egyptian or other short-grain rice, rinsed

2 cups chopped tomatoes, drained with juice reserved

²/₃ cup fresh parsley, finely chopped

²/₃ cup fresh cilantro, finely chopped

²/₃ cup fresh mint, finely chopped

1 small yellow onion, grated

1 teaspoon ground cumin

Pinch of dried crushed red pepper flakes

1 teaspoon salt

¹/₄ teaspoon freshly ground black pepper

2 tablespoons expeller pressed corn oil

1 quart water or vegetable stock (or enough to fill stock pot three-quarters full)

I stock up on baby eggplants while they are in season in the Washington, D.C. area in July and August so that I can make this dish. In Egypt, the eggplant season is much longer than it is on the East coast of the United States, and this dish can be enjoyed for a greater period of time. Many people like to serve both eggplant and zucchini together, but you can also do one at a time.

To cut down on preparation time, you can core the eggplants and zucchini and make the filling a day before stuffing and cooking them. At Egyptian open-air produce markets, many of the women selling their produce will also core them for you for an added price. A long vegetable corer is essential for making this dish. The coring process, although intimidating at first, is very easy once you get the hang of it. I recommend buying extra vegetables the first time, and making this dish when you have time to practice. (Check your local kitchen supply store or Middle Eastern market for a corer, or see Where to Buy Guide on pages 203–205 for more information.)

Preparation:

To core eggplants and zucchini: Line a work surface with newspapers and place vegetables and corer on them. Cut off the stems of the eggplants and zucchini. Use the tip of the corer to punch holes in a circle formation around the top of the vegetable. Place tip of corer on top of circle formation, and holding vegetable straight up and down push all the way down to the bottom of the vegetable in one slow movement, paying special attention not to puncture the vegetable or break through the bottom. Pull the corer out and repeat the process all the way around the circle. Holding the vegetable in your left hand, insert the corer back into the vegetable, and use the flat side as you turn the corer in a clockwise fashion slowly to cut away the flesh of the vegetable. Once you have loosened the flesh on the inside of the vegetable, carefully pull the corer out with the inside attached to it. Continue this process until most of the inside has been removed. Then, use the scraper side to carefully scrape the edges of the inside

continued on next page

of the vegetable by pushing it down and dragging it along the inside of the vegetable, removing all white flesh, until you are left with only the shell of the vegetable. Repeat with remaining eggplants and zucchini.

Prepare the filling: Mix the rice, tomatoes, parsley, cilantro, mint, onion, cumin, crushed pepper flakes, salt, and pepper together in a large bowl. Heat corn oil in a large skillet over medium heat. Add rice mixture. Cook, uncovered, stirring occasionally, for 5 minutes, until the mixture becomes more solidified and rice turns translucent. Remove from heat and let sit until cool enough to handle.

Find a saucepan with a lid that will accommodate all of the eggplant and zucchini standing up and snuggled next to one another.

Stuff vegetables: Place one vegetable in your hand and fill with a tablespoon of filling mixture by placing the filling in your free hand and with your fingers carefully pushing it down to the bottom of the cavity, until vegetable is three-quarters full. Be careful not to over pack the vegetable or it will burst while cooking—the filling needs to have room to expand while it cooks. Using a paper towel or your hands, wipe the excess rice off the sides of the vegetable. Continue stuffing all vegetables.

Place vegetables snugly and standing with filling end up in the large saucepan. Place an inverted plate over the vegetables inside the saucepan. Pour water or stock into the saucepan, covering the vegetables three-quarters of the way up. Add salt, pepper, and reserved tomato juice to the saucepan. Cover saucepan with a lid and bring to a boil over high heat. Once the liquid starts to boil, immediately reduce heat to low, and cook for 45 minutes to 1 hour, until vegetables are tender and rice is cooked. (The cooking liquid will probably not be completely evaporated at this time.) Taste and adjust salt and pepper, if necessary. Serve warm or at room temperature.

Soad's Stuffed Baby Eggplant

Lamb and Potato Stew

[Tagin Lahma Dani bil Batatis]

6 SERVINGS

INGREDIENTS

- 1 tablespoon clarified butter (*ghee*)
- 1 onion, coarsely chopped
- 2 pounds boneless lamb shoulder cubes (2-inch pieces)
- 1 teaspoon ground cumin
- 1/2 teaspoon paprika
- 1/2 teaspoon ground cinnamon
- 1/2 teaspoon ground nutmeg
- 1 cup chicken stock
- 1 cup chopped tomatoes
- 2 cups peeled and diced Yukon Gold potatoes
- Salt to taste

This comforting stew is served in Egyptian homes and restaurants. Beef could be substituted for the lamb. This stew can be made in advance and frozen for up to a month.

Preparation:

Preheat oven to 375 degrees F. Heat clarified butter in a large, ovenproof skillet over medium heat. Add onion and sauté until translucent. Add lamb and brown on all sides. Season with cumin, paprika, cinnamon, and nutmeg and stir. Add chicken stock, increase heat to high, and bring to a boil. Cover skillet and transfer to oven to bake for 1½ hours, until meat is tender.

Add tomatoes and potatoes, stir, cover, and let simmer for 30 more minutes, until potatoes are tender. Taste and add salt and adjust seasonings if necessary. Serve warm.

Savory Cheese Phyllo Pastry

[Goulash bil Gebna]

Egypt produces many delicious varieties of locally produced artesan cheeses, most commonly made from cow and sheep milk. Three of the most common are gebna rumi, *a hard, slightly aged sheep's or cow's milk cheese similar to asiago;* gebna ararish, *a skimmed cow's milk cheese similar to ricotta; and* gebna bayda, *a creamy cheese similar to feta. Outside of Egypt, some of these cheeses can be found in Middle Eastern and Egyptian grocers. This recipe has been modified to include cheeses widely available in the U.S. without sacrificing the flavor of the dish.*

12 SERVINGS

INGREDIENTS

1 cup clarified butter (*ghee*)

1 package phyllo dough (18x14-inch), thawed

½ pound asiago or gruyere cheese, grated

½ pound full-fat cottage cheese

½ pound whole milk ricotta

Preparation:

Preheat oven to 350 degrees F. Grease a 13x9-inch pan with 1 teaspoon of clarified butter. Open the phyllo package and carefully open the phyllo sheets. Remove 4 sheets of phyllo and reserve for later use by covering with a slightly damp kitchen towel.

Layer 1 sheet of remaining phyllo dough on the bottom of the pan. Gently brush with clarified butter to cover. Push the sides up along the edge of the pan and brush with clarified butter. Layer another sheet on top and brush with butter, pushing the sides up against the sides of the pan. Continue buttering and layering until all phyllo sheets are used except for the 4 reserved sheets.

Make the filling by combining the asiago or gruyere cheese, cottage cheese, and whole milk ricotta. Spread over phyllo sheets and fold the sides of phyllo down over the cheese like a frame. Next cover the top of the dish with one of the reserved phyllo sheets, butter the top, and fold sides over the edges of the pastry inside the pan. Continue buttering and layering the remaining three phyllo sheets.

Bake, uncovered, for 30 minutes; rotate pan and bake 30 minutes longer. Remove from oven and let stand at room temperature for 10 minutes. To serve, cut 6 equal vertical strips along the length of the pan, then cut 4 horizontal strips across the width of the pan to make 24 squares. Serve warm or at room temperature.

Ashoora Wheat Pudding

[Ashoora]

4 SERVINGS

INGREDIENTS

1 cup whole wheat berries, rinsed*

1/2 cup sugar or honey, or to taste

1 cup warm milk

1 tablespoon cornstarch

Handful of raisins

1 teaspoon unsalted roasted peanuts, chopped

1 teaspoon slivered almonds

1 teaspoon chopped walnuts

1 teaspoon unsweetened dried coconut

The ingredients in this pudding are basically the same as those in Creamy Wheat Berry Cereal (page 90). The difference is that this pudding is cooked twice, sweetened more, and garnished with mixed nuts. Its name, Ashoora, is the same as the holiday it is served on. Keep in mind that the wheat berries needs to be soaked for at least 8 hours before serving.

Preparation:

Eight hours or the night before serving, place whole wheat berries in a large thermos, cover with boiling water, and close thermos. The next morning, the wheat will be puffed and tender.

In a medium bowl, mix together sugar or honey, milk, and cornstarch. Place milk mixture in a medium saucepan over medium heat. Increase heat to high and boil, stirring, for 2 minutes. Reduce heat to low, and cook, stirring constantly, until pudding has thickened. Taste and adjust sugar, if necessary. Stir in raisins and divide among 4 dessert bowls.

Mix peanuts, almonds, walnuts, and coconut together and sprinkle on top of pudding. Serve warm.

*Wheat berries can be purchased at organic, Middle Eastern, and healthfood stores.

Ginger Tea

[Ginzabil]

Ginger arrived in Egypt via India during the spice trades. In India, Ayurvedic doctors regard it as a traditional therapy known to activate the body's fire element, which in turn burns up toxins. It is used to relieve muscle inflammation, motion sickness, morning sickness, and indigestion. Its zingy, warm flavor is added to soups, cookies, stews, and beverages. It is even mentioned in the Qu'ran as being one of the ingredients that will be enjoyed in heaven: "And in it, their drink is mixed with ginger." (Qu'ran 76:17)

8 SERVINGS

INGREDIENTS

4 teaspoons ground ginger or chopped fresh ginger root

4 cups boiling water

Honey or sugar to taste, if desired

Preparation:

Place ginger in a teapot or medium saucepan and pour in boiling water. Steep the ginger tea, covered, for 10 minutes. Remove lid, strain tea into tea cups, and sweeten with honey or sugar, if desired.

The Prophet Mohammed's Birthday
Moulid an Nabi

During their reign in Egypt, the Fatimids reinstated many of the ancient festivals that were forgotten, introduced the Egyptian *moulid* festivals, and even encouraged cross-religious celebrations. The *moulid* festivals, which still take place in Egypt today, are religious festivals that are celebrated to honor special religious figures. "*Moulid*" means birth, so the *moulids* are held on the birthday of the person who is being honored. There are Jewish, Christian, and Muslim *moulids* held in Egypt today. The Jewish *moulid* is held in the village of Damanhour and commemorates the life of Rabbi Yaakov Abu Hasira, a Moroccan Jew who immigrated to Egypt and was known for his piety. Christian *moulids* are held throughout Egypt in honor of the Virgin Mary and various saints.

The largest *moulid* for the Prophet Mohammed is held around the Hussein Square in Islamic Cairo. It is celebrated with Sufis (a mystical sect), who chant to honor the Prophet Mohammed from dusk until dawn. Brightly colored tents with Islamic design motifs are set up around the mosque. Inside them, men, women, and children recite verses of the Qu'ran and praise God (this act is called a *zikr* in Arabic). Tables are set up around the perimeter of the tents for people to sit and listen to the chanting. Adjacent falafel shops, restaurants, cafés, and pastry shops extend their services to the people present.

Culinarily speaking, the most typical and anticipated *moulid* foods are the sweets. The entire month of the *moulid*, pastry shops, makeshift tents, and street-side stalls all display their traditional offerings made with various types of nuts and chickpeas that are set in sugar, caramel, or nougat and molded into a variety of shapes. It is common to give gifts of an assortment of these sweets.

There are also special sugar treats given to the children. In the olden days, sugar was boiled and poured into wooden molds to make dolls for the girls and toy soldiers on horses for the boys. Nowadays plastic dolls dressed up like brides, *aroosa* in Arabic, are more common. They are sold in pastry shops where whole windows are used to display the pretty dolls in their brightly colored outfits. During the *moulid* celebrations, the tables set up around the tents where the chanting takes place are topped with glasses full of fresh mint to be added to tea. As you sit, sipping your tea, or enjoying a snack, leaders of different Sufi sects walk by wearing green, white, yellow, and red turbans on their heads that denote the group to which they belong. The Sufi leaders come to Cairo from all over Egypt for this event. Along their way, they often stop in towns and villages where they walk through the downtowns and chant praises. Many people offer them payment for their services. Vendors present at the *moulids* sell children's toys, incense, popcorn, and lupine beans.

Moulid Menu

▶ Calf's Liver, Pepper, and Onion Sandwiches

▶ Lamb Pita Sandwiches

▶ Sesame Candy

▶ Turkish Delight

▶ Rose-Infused Punch

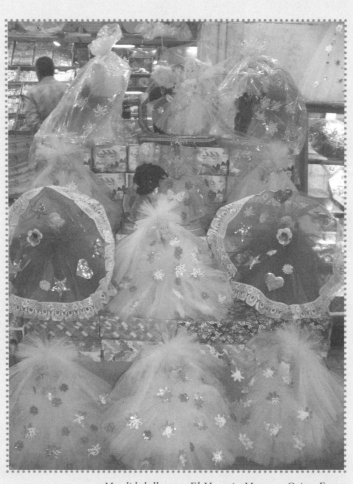

Moulid dolls near El Hussein Mosque, Cairo, Egypt

Calf's Liver, Pepper, and Onion Sandwiches

[Sandaweech Kibda bil Filfil]

4 SERVINGS

INGREDIENTS

1 onion, coarsely chopped

Juice of 1 lime

1/4 cup expeller pressed corn oil

4 cloves garlic, peeled

Dash of dried crushed red pepper flakes

1 teaspoon ground cumin

Salt

Freshly ground black pepper

2 pounds calf's liver, cut into thin strips

1 green bell pepper, cut into long, thin strips

1 red bell pepper, cut into long, thin strips

4 long, thin, soft sub rolls

These sandwiches are typical North African street fare. In Egypt, liver is always thinly sliced and fried, grilled, or braised. In this recipe, marinating the meat enhances its flavor and makes it more tender.

Preparation:

Combine onion, lime juice, corn oil, garlic cloves, red pepper flakes, cumin, and a little salt and pepper in a large bowl. Add calf's liver and toss to coat. Cover the bowl and allow the liver to marinate 1 hour at room temperature or overnight in the refrigerator.

Preheat a large frying pan over medium-high heat. Pour liver and marinade in the skillet and brown liver on both sides, turning only once. Add peppers to the skillet and continue to cook the liver for 3 to 4 minutes more per side, or until cooked through.

Warm the rolls and slice them in half. Using a slotted spoon, remove the liver and peppers from the liquid and fill the rolls. Serve immediately.

Lamb Pita Sandwiches

[Shwarma bil Lahma Dani]

This is the lamb version of the pita sandwiches. Since the rotisserie at most shwarma *shops slowly roasts meats, often inexpensive cuts are used in restaurant varieties. For home cooking, it is best to use a more expensive cut of meat to compensate for the quick cooking time. Keep in mind that the lamb needs to be marinated for 24 hours.*

Preparation:

Place lamb slices, onion, garlic, cumin, cinnamon, paprika, nutmeg, lemon peel, lemon juice, vinegar, and corn oil into a large, shallow dish. Turn well to coat. Cover and refrigerate for 24 hours.

After lamb has finished marinating, preheat oven to 425 degrees F. Remove cover from lamb and drain well. Spread lamb meat onto a baking sheet with sides. Top with tomato slices and dab clarified butter around meat. Bake for 30 minutes, turning once, until lamb is cooked through and tender.

Place pitas on a baking sheet and heat in the oven for 1 to 2 minutes. Place lamb and tomato slices in a pile on top of the pitas. Serve warm. To eat, fold pitas in half (as you would a soft taco).

4 SERVINGS

INGREDIENTS

2 pounds lamb filet, sliced into thin 1/2-inch strips

1 onion, chopped

5 cloves garlic, chopped

1 teaspoon ground cumin

1/2 teaspoon ground cinnamon

1/2 teaspoon paprika

1/4 teaspoon nutmeg

Juice and grated peel of 1 lemon

1/4 cup white vinegar

1/4 cup expeller pressed corn oil

2 large tomatoes, sliced

2 tablespoons clarified butter (ghee)

4 regular-size pitas

Sesame Candy

[Simsimeya]

MAKES 20 (2-INCH) PIECES

INGREDIENTS

1 cup sesame seeds
2/3 cup honey

One of the best places to buy moulid sweets in Cairo is the El Abd pastry shop downtown. Weeks before the moulid, people form long lines outside of the store to buy their delicious confections. Using only a few traditional ingredients such as honey, sugar, and egg whites, both nuts and legumes are transformed into elegant delicacies. They are then wrapped in plastic, piled into large, decorative boxes, and tied with ribbons. It is traditional to bring these sweets to friends and relatives.

Preparation:

In a large saucepan bring sesame seeds and honey to a boil over medium-high heat. Stirring slowly, allow the mixture to boil for 4 to 6 minutes or until mixture turns amber colored and thickens. Test it by spooning a tiny piece out of the pot and dropping it into a glass of ice cold water; if it forms a ball, its ready to be poured out.

Cover a heatproof work space with a piece of wax paper. Pour honey mixture onto the wax paper and smooth it out. Allow to cool for a few minutes and then cut into 2-inch pieces. To make circles or other shapes, lay cookie cutters on wax paper and spoon the sesame mixture into the center of the cookie cutters. Allow to cool completely and then remove the cookie cutters and peel the candy off of the wax paper.

*Old-fashioned
Moulid candy mold*

Turkish Delight

[Malban]

The Arabic name for Turkish Delight, Malban, *refers to liquid cooking starch. Turkish Delight is a popular kind of candy made throughout the Middle East. It has been made for centuries with the same traditional method of adding a mixture of cornstarch and water to a thickened sweet syrup and flavoring it with rose water.*

The Egyptians used starch to glue pieces of papyrus strips together for writing tablets in 4000 BC. The Greeks began using it in cooking and the Turks came up with this recipe, which was originally written using old Turkish means of weighing and measuring that are no longer in use.

In Cairo, old-time confectioners make Malban *fresh daily. Surprisingly, it is quite simple and inexpensive to make at home. Keep in mind, however, that it needs about 1½ hours simmering time on the stove, and it needs to set overnight before cutting and serving. Some people sprinkle ground walnuts or pistachios on top of Turkish Delights.*

16 SERVINGS

INGREDIENTS

1 tablespoon lemon juice

4 cups sugar

1 cup cornstarch

1 teaspoon cream of tartar

2 tablespoons rose water*

¼ teaspoon red food coloring (optional)

1 cup confectioners' sugar

¼ cup finely ground dried, unsweetened coconut #1**

Preparation:

Grease the sides and bottom of a 9-inch round or square baking pan. Line sides and bottom with wax paper and grease the wax paper with vegetable oil.

Combine lemon juice, sugar, and 1½ cups water in a medium saucepan over medium heat. Stir the mixture until sugar dissolves and it comes to a boil. Once mixture boils, reduce heat to low and simmer for approximately 45 minutes or until it registers 240 degrees F on a candy thermometer. Remove from heat.

Combine cornstarch, cream of tartar, and 3 cups water in a large saucepan over medium heat. Stir briskly to remove lumps and cook stirring constantly until mixture resembles a clear, thick paste.

Carefully, wearing oven mitts, stir the sugar syrup into the cornstarch mixture over low heat. Cook, stirring constantly, for 5 minutes. Simmer mixture on the lowest temperature possible for 1 hour, or until mixture turns slightly golden and has decreased in volume by about a half.

Add the rose water and red food coloring, if desired, and stir well to combine. Pour into prepared baking dish and spread the mixture evenly, smoothing the top. Cover and allow to stand a minimum of 12 hours.

Sift confectioners' sugar and coconut together. Turn Turkish delight out onto another plate or work surface. Remove wax paper. Oil a sharp knife and cut the candy into even 1-inch pieces. Coat the candy pieces with coconut mixture. Serve at room temperature or store in an airtight container between sheets of wax paper or parchment paper.

*See Where to Buy Guide on pages 203–205 for purchasing information.

**Dried, unsweetened, coconut #1 can be purchased at Middle Eastern and Egyptian markets. If you cannot find it, mix cornstarch with the powdered sugar instead. This will prevent the Turkish Delight from sticking together.

Pastry Shop Mohandiseen, Cairo, Egypt

Rose-Infused Punch

[Assir Ward]

This is a delicious and refreshing rose-infused drink. During last year's moulid, *one family made large amounts of it and offered it to passersby for free. The first time I tasted it, the sweet floral taste tingled on my tongue while my ears were flooded with the hypnotic sounds of the* zikr *(traditional chanting method), and my eyes were filled with the vivid colors of the happy event. I was told to drink the Rose-Infused Punch all at once, not in small sips. Serve in small, clear punch or cocktail glasses.*

4 SERVINGS

INGREDIENTS

2 cups water, chilled

1 cup sugar

4 tablespoons lemon juice

10 drops red food coloring

½ cup rose water*

Preparation:

Combine water, sugar, lemon juice, food coloring, and rose water in a pitcher. Stir well to incorporate all ingredients. Taste and adjust sugar, if necessary. Serve chilled.

*See Where to Buy Guide on pages 203–205 for purchasing information.

Al Hussein Mosque

Part 3
Modern Celebrations

I n addition to its ancient festivals and religious ceremonies, Egyptians also celebrate many modern holidays. No matter what month you travel to Egypt, some kind of festivity will be taking place. It is always interesting to see the ancient Egyptian love of celebrations being translated into modern lifestyles. As with the ancient festivals, music, food, flowers, and family take center stage with each holiday.

In modern Egypt new dining styles blend modern restaurant concepts and international hospitality standards with time-honored traditions. This section contains recipes that are prepared and served frequently in Egypt today, and are a testimony to Egypt's multicultural and multi-religious past. Use the recipes in this section to celebrate festivities of your own.

Modern Celebrations include:

▶ Supper by the Sea

▶ Welcome Home Dinner

▶ Mother's Day

▶ Birth Celebration

▶ Valentine's Day Dinner

▶ New Year's Eve

▶ Nile-Style Street Food

Supper by the Sea

Seaside dining is one of the pleasures of visiting Egypt's northern Mediterranean shore. In Alexandria, hundreds of varieties of seafood are served within hours of being caught. While strolling along Alexandria's seaside *corniche*, you can often see fishermen coming to shore with the day's catch as well as fishing boats unloading large quantities of squid, red mullet, prawns, and more. Modern-day food in Alexandria combines fresh seafood and produce, strong Greek roots, and European influences with Egyptian hospitality.

According to Herodotus, King Amasis of Egypt (569–525BC) loved the Greeks. Many modern Egyptian scholars attribute King Amasis with the beginning of the Greek period in Egypt. He demonstrated his affections to the Greeks by building them a city called Naucratis in Egypt. Greeks were welcomed into Egypt and the priests of ancient Memphis appointed Alexander the Great to the throne. In 332 BC, Alexander founded a city on Egypt's northern Mediterranean shore, which he never actually stepped foot in, and named it Alexandria. This new port opened up trade and communication between not only Egypt and Greece but the entire Mediterranean as well. The lighthouse of Alexandria beamed through the night sky and beckoned visitors who came to Egypt from afar seeking knowledge. It was considered to be one of the wonders of the ancient world.

Shortly after Alexander founded Alexandria, he was killed. A member of his army, Ptolemy I, became the ruler of Egypt and began a new dynasty that ruled Egypt for three centuries. Although the Ptolemaic rulers were of Greek origin, they assimilated into Egyptian culture, and the Greek style of daily living became heavily influenced by Egypt. Music, dancing, art, legal systems, and business trends were all affected by Egyptian philosophies. The Greeks had scribes write down records of all of the achievements of the ancient Egyptians. By the time Cleopatra and her brother ruled, many of these advancements had been taken back to Greece and were eventually introduced to the western world as European discoveries.

Archaeologist Zahi Hawass found a statue of a goddess named Aphrodite-Isis at Kom Abu Billo, which demonstrates that the ancient Greeks and Egyptians even combined their religious beliefs. For this reason, both of these countries most celebrated dishes have common roots. During modern times (eighteenth to twenty-first centuries), Egypt has also been home to English, French, Greek, and Italian immigrants who came to Egypt in search of economic opportunities. Many of these immigrants settled in Alexandria. French and Italian pastry shops, cafés, and Greek grocers and cheesemakers greatly impacted the cuisine of Alexandria.

In Alexandria, many restaurants located along the shore, in the residential neighborhoods, and in shopping malls in the newly developed outskirts of the city offer freshly caught fish cooked to order. When you enter a seafood restaurant, you are escorted to an area (usually to the side of the entrance) that displays all of the fresh seafood. You can tell the waiter how many people are in your party, which kind of

Fishing boats on the Mediterranean

seafood you would like, and how you would like it cooked. The seafood is usually grilled and dressed simply with garlic and oil, or baked or roasted with a spicy tomato or creamy tahini sauce, or deep fried and dusted with a touch of spice. Then you are escorted to a table where you are immediately served a multitude of *salatat*, Egyptian appetizers collectively referred to as *mezze* in the rest of the Arabic-speaking world. Depending upon the size of your party and the quality of the restaurant, you could be offered as little as 2 or 3 or as many as 15 appetizers/salads. They range from Tahini Sauce (page 160) and Eggplant Puree (page 98) to Chickpea and Tahini Puree (page 165) and Fava Bean Puree (page 89). The price of each appetizer will be charged to your bill. The waiter will then take your drink order and ask you what accompaniments you would like for your fish (rice, potatoes, soup, pasta, etc.). Then freshly baked bread is brought to the table to eat with the salads. If there's still room, many of the restaurants offer excellent desserts afterwards. The following menu is a small sampling of what a true Alexandria seafood restaurant offers.

Supper by the Sea Menu

▶ Egyptian Garlic Aioli

▶ Pea and Potato Salad

▶ Grilled Prawns

▶ Spice-Dusted Shrimp with Rice

▶ Calamari with Tahini

▶ Fish Kabobs

▶ Cherry Kernel Cookies

▶ Blackberry Juice

Egyptian Garlic Aioli

[Salata bil Toum]

This dish is very popular in Alexandria. Originally, a mortar and pestle was used to crush the garlic before the other ingredients were added. This is very similar to the Greek Skordalia and Italian garlic sauce. It is worth searching for good-quality Yukon Gold potatoes and garlic, since they are the backbone of the dish. Egyptian potatoes are excellent—golden and buttery on their own without condiment, and are often exported for sale in Europe. In Egypt, this aioli is served as a dip with hot, fresh pita bread and other appetizers and salads. It can also be slathered on burgers, vegetables, fish, and chicken as a condiment.

6 SERVINGS

INGREDIENTS

3/4 pound Yukon Gold potatoes, peeled and quartered

6 cloves garlic, minced

1/4 cup good quality extra-virgin olive oil, unfiltered if possible

Juice of 1 lemon

Sea salt to taste

Freshly ground black pepper to taste

Preparation:

Place potatoes in a medium saucepan and cover with water. Bring to a boil over high heat, reduce heat to medium and cook for 10 to 15 minutes or until fork tender. Drain the potatoes and mash lightly. Place potatoes and garlic in a food processor and process while slowly pouring the olive oil and lemon juice in through the spout. Taste and season with salt and freshly ground pepper as needed.

Alexandria, Egypt

Pea and Potato Salad

[Salata Batatis wa Bisella]

4 SERVINGS

INGREDIENTS

1 pound Yukon Gold potatoes, peeled and cut into bite-size chunks

1 pound frozen green peas, thawed

1/4 cup mayonnaise

1 teaspoon Dijon mustard

1 tablespoon finely chopped fresh mint

1 tablespoon finely chopped fresh parsley

1 tablespoon finely chopped fresh cilantro

Sea salt to taste

Freshly ground black pepper to taste

This delicious appetizer was served to us at the El Housny restaurant in Alexandria during the month of Ramadan. It can be made a day ahead of time, and stored, covered, in the refrigerator.

Preparation:

Place potatoes in a large saucepan and cover with water. Bring to a boil over high heat. Reduce heat to medium and cook 15 to 20 minutes, until fork tender. Drain potatoes and immerse in cold water.

When potatoes are room temperature, drain and place in a serving bowl. Stir in the peas, mayonnaise, mustard, mint, parsley, and cilantro. Season with sea salt and freshly ground pepper to taste. Serve immediately or refrigerate.

Reopened in 2002, the Bibliotecha Alexandrina is built on the grounds of Alexandria's famous ancient library. It contains six specialized libraries, three museums, nine art galleries, a planetarium, a children's science "Exploratorium," conference centers, and seven research institutes.

Grilled Prawns

[Gambari Mashwi]

The Kadoura restaurant in the Mohandiseen neighborhood of Cairo is also famous for its fresh, fantastic seafood. One of their specialties is grilled prawns dressed with a tomato and coriander sauce and served on a bed of chopped cilantro or arugula. If fresh prawns are not available, you can substitute shrimp.

Preparation:

Place prawns or shrimp, tomatoes, coriander, ½ cup cilantro, chili powder, and a sprinkling of salt and freshly ground pepper in a large bowl. Cover and marinate at room temperature for 1 hour.

Preheat grill pan or broiler. Evenly divide prawns or shrimp onto 4 metal skewers and brush with leftover marinade. Grill or broil for approximately 6 minutes, turning frequently, until shrimp turn pink in color and are tender. Taste and adjust salt and pepper if necessary.

Place remaining 1 cup of cilantro on a serving platter and place skewers of shrimp on top to serve.

4 SERVINGS

INGREDIENTS

2 pounds prawns or colossal shrimp, peeled and deveined

1 cup chopped tomatoes

1 teaspoon ground coriander

1½ cups fresh cilantro, finely chopped

Pinch chili powder

Salt

Freshly ground black pepper

Grilled Prawns

Spice-Dusted Shrimp with Rice

[Gambari Makri bi Roz]

4 SERVINGS

INGREDIENTS

- 1/2 cup unbleached, all-purpose flour
- 1/2 teaspoon ground cumin
- 1/2 teaspoon salt
- 1/4 teaspoon freshly ground black pepper
- 2 pounds jumbo shrimp, rinsed, shelled, and deveined*
- 3 tablespoons butter or olive oil
- 2 medium yellow onions, finely chopped
- 1 head of garlic, peeled and finely chopped
- 3/4 cup vegetable or fish stock
- Juice of 1 lemon
- 4 cups prepared Egyptian Rice (page 22)
- 5 tablespoons finely chopped fresh parsley

Ancient Roman emperors would often send envoys to traverse the Mediterranean to fish for shrimp and prawns off the coasts of Libya and Egypt. This delicious dish takes only twenty minutes to prepare. It is quick and easy enough to make on the most hectic of days, yet special enough to serve to guests. You may substitute scallops or fish cubes for the shrimp if fresh shrimp are not available.

Preparation:

Pour the flour into a shallow dish or plastic storage bag. Add cumin, salt, and freshly ground pepper. Toss shrimp in flour, coating all sides.

Heat the butter or olive oil in a wide frying pan over medium heat. Add onions and garlic and sauté until translucent, about 4 to 5 minutes. Carefully add shrimp and cook on top of the onions until they begin to turn light pink in color, 3 to 4 minutes. Turn shrimp over and cook on the other side for another 2 or 3 minutes.

When shrimp have all turned pink, add the stock to the pan. Lower heat to low and cook, uncovered, for about 2 minutes or until broth is reduced to half its original volume. Remove from heat and stir in lemon juice.

Place rice on a serving platter. Top with shrimp and sauce. Sprinkle with fresh parsley and serve warm.

* To devein shrimp: With a pairing knife, make an incision along the top of the curved part of the shrimp and remove the black vein inside of the shrimp. Most supermarkets sell shrimp deveined, which cuts down on preparation time significantly.

Calamari with Tahini

[Calamara bil Tahina]

Fresh calamari from the Mediterranean Sea is a specialty of cooks along Egypt's northern coast. This is a wonderful appetizer, or light lunch or dinner with a salad. Be sure to buy calamari that is already cleaned. The bodies look like white tubes that are sealed at one end. The heads and tentacles are not used in this recipe.

4 SERVINGS

INGREDIENTS

- 1/4 cup unbleached, all-purpose flour
- 1 teaspoon salt
- 1/4 teaspoon freshly ground black pepper
- 1 teaspoon ground cumin
- 2 cups canola oil
- 2 pounds squid bodies, cut into rings
- Cayenne pepper, for sprinkling
- Tahini Sauce (page 160)

Preparation:

Pour flour into a large, shallow bowl. Stir in salt, freshly ground pepper, and cumin.

Heat the canola oil over medium-high heat in a large, heavy saucepan. Coat squid rings with flour mixture, shake off excess, and place on a platter. When oil reaches 300 degrees F, add the squid rings. Do not crowd pan—you will have to fry in batches. Fry calamari 3 to 5 minutes per side, until golden. Remove from oil and place on a dish lined with paper towels. Continue frying the remaining calamari.

Sprinkle calamari very lightly with cayenne pepper and salt. Taste calamari and adjust salt, if necessary. Serve hot with Tahini Sauce.

Fish Kabobs

[Kabob Samac]

4 SERVINGS

INGREDIENTS

Juice of 2 limes

1 teaspoon ground cumin

1 teaspoon salt

1/2 teaspoon freshly ground black pepper

1/4 cup extra-virgin olive oil

2 onions, quartered

2 pounds skinless, boneless tuna or swordfish fillets, cut into 2-inch chunks

Chef Saber at the Housny restaurant in Alexandria is a kabob master. He and his colleagues cook hundreds of perfectly grilled sword-length skewers of fish, meat, and chicken each hour. A trick to producing juicy kabobs is to turn the skewers frequently. If I couldn't see the grill while watching Chef Saber and his coworkers, I would think they were playing a very intense game of foosball—that is how quickly and energetically kabobs should be turned!

Preparation.

Combine lime juice, cumin, salt, freshly ground pepper, and olive oil in a large bowl. Whisk to combine and then add onions and fish chunks, turning to coat. Cover bowl and let stand at room temperature for 30 minutes or in the refrigerator overnight.

Preheat the grill or grill pan over medium-high heat (or preheat the broiler).

Skewer fish cubes evenly onto metal skewers (if using wooden skewers, soak them first to prevent splintering). Take care not to push the fish pieces too closely together. They should be touching, yet loose.

Place skewers on grill, grill pan, or on a baking sheet under the broiler and grill for approximately 10 to 15 minutes, turning often, until fish is cooked through. Serve hot.

Cherry Kernel Cookies

[Mahlabayat]

Alexandria's famous bakeries, like Patisserie Vinous, often showcase these cookies stacked high on enormous trays. Mahlab, which is made from crushed cherry kernels, is the star of these ring-shaped cookies. It is a widely used ingredient in the Middle East. These cookies can be stored in the freezer for up to one month. They are wonderful additions to celebratory cookie trays, and are delicious with coffee or tea for breakfast.

Preparation:

Preheat oven to 350 degrees F. Place the butter, corn oil, sugar, and 1/2 cup water in a large mixing bowl. Cream together until everything is evenly incorporated. Add the baking powder, flour, ground cherry kernels, salt, and anise extract. Stir well to form a dough.

Break off pieces of the dough and form into 1-inch balls. Place the balls 2 inches apart on ungreased cookie sheets. Press the balls flat and make a hole in the center by using the base of the handle of a wooden spoon. Bake 15 to 20 minutes, until lightly golden. Remove from oven and cool on cookie sheets.

*See Where to Buy Guide on pages 203–205 for purchasing information.

MAKES ABOUT 4 DOZEN

INGREDIENTS

- 1/3 cup unsalted butter, melted
- 1/3 cup expeller pressed corn oil
- 1/2 cup sugar
- 1 1/2 teaspoons baking powder
- 4 cups unbleached, all-purpose flour
- 3 teaspoons ground cherry kernels (*mahlab*)*
- 1/2 teaspoon salt
- 1 teaspoon anise extract

Cherry Kernel Cookies

Blackberry Juice

[Assir Toot]

4 SERVINGS

INGREDIENTS

1 pint blackberries
4 cups ice cold water
1/2 cup sugar, or to taste

Blackberry juice is very popular in Egypt—during blackberry season it is found at breakfast buffets, juice bars, and on restaurant menus. Try this delicious drink next time fresh blackberries are available in your area.

Preparation:

Put blackberries, water, and sugar in a blender and whip on high speed until frothy. Strain through a fine sieve into a pitcher. Serve chilled or over ice.

Welcome Home Dinner

 A large percentage of Egyptian citizens live and work abroad. When they return to Egypt for vacations and holidays, their relatives often treat them to amazing meals with as many traditional dishes as possible. Luckily, I've learned to cook these dishes, so I don't have to wait until I go back to Egypt to sample them. When I return to Egypt, however, I realize that there is one aspect of the atmosphere I can never duplicate—the sounds.

On a typical morning in any residential area in Egypt, you can hear the sound of the gas tank seller as he clanks a metal spoon on gas tanks attached to the back of his bicycle as he drives up and down the streets. The bells of the horses pulling carriages full of *aish baladi*, Egyptian whole-wheat pita bread, make a continuous jingle sound. Car drivers in Egypt choose to use their horns in place of turn singles, so incessant honking is part of the atmosphere as well. Roosters crowing, donkeys braying, calls to prayer, pigeons cooing, children playing, and music blaring from cars, the street, and houses are all a part of daily life in Egypt, reminding you that ancient and modern are present, and that Egypt is a land like no other.

This menu is only a portion of what my husband's cousin's wife Rasha prepared for our Welcome Home Dinner on a recent trip to Egypt.

Welcome Home Dinner Menu

▶ Rice, Tomato, and Spinach Soup

▶ Stuffed Cabbage

▶ Pea, Carrot, and Tomato Stew

▶ Beef Croquettes

▶ Tahini Sauce

▶ Mixed Country Salad

▶ Crème Caramel

▶ Anise Tea

Rice, Tomato, and Spinach Soup

[Shorbat Roz, Tomatum, wa Sabanik]

8 SERVINGS

INGREDIENTS

1 tablespoon unsalted butter

1 small yellow onion, diced

1 (1 pound) bag frozen spinach, thawed and drained well

3/4 cup Egyptian or other short-grain rice

3 large ripe tomatoes (approximately 1 1/2 pounds) peeled,* seeded, and diced, or 1 1/2 pounds canned diced tomatoes

4 cups chicken stock

1 teaspoon ground coriander

Salt to taste

Freshly ground black pepper to taste

This light, flavorful soup, which makes a lovely first course, is one that Chef Nasser Saiyd prepared for us in Egypt. If you cannot find Egyptian rice, substitute any short-grain rice.

Preparation:

Heat butter in a large saucepan over medium heat. Add onion and sauté until translucent, 5 to 7 minutes. Add spinach, rice, tomatoes, stock, coriander, and a sprinkling of salt and pepper. Increase heat to high and bring to a boil. Reduce heat to low and simmer, uncovered, 20 to 30 minutes, until rice is tender. Taste and adjust salt, if necessary. Serve hot.

* To peel tomatoes: Fill a large saucepan three-quarters full of water and bring to a boil on high heat. Add tomatoes and cook for 1 to 2 minutes or until skin splits. Remove from heat, drain, and immerse tomatoes in cold water. When tomatoes are cool enough to touch, peel the skin off with your hands. Remove seeds with your hands as you are cutting tomatoes.

Stuffed Cabbage

[Mahshi Cromb]

Cabbage was enjoyed by ancient Egyptians, Greeks, and Romans. The ancient Romans believed it had many healthful properties, including the ability to prevent intoxication. There is a well-known saying in Egypt that "If you give an Egyptian a vegetable, they'll stuff it." Seasonal availability determines which stuffed vegetables are on the menu at which time of year. Cabbage season, for example, is in the spring, and at that time Stuffed Cabbage is served warm as an accompaniment to roasted meats and poultry. If you prefer a vegetarian filling, use the one for Stuffed Baby Eggplant and Zucchini (page 129).

6 SERVINGS

INGREDIENTS

1 medium cabbage (about 2 pounds)

6 teaspoons salt

SAUCE:

3 cups chicken stock

Juice of 1 lemon

2 teaspoons dried mint

1 cinnamon stick

1 head garlic, separated and peeled

FILLING:

2 pounds ground beef

1 cup Egyptian or other short-grain rice

1 1/2 teaspoons salt

1 teaspoon ground cinnamon

1 teaspoon ground cumin

1/4 teaspoon paprika

1/4 teaspoon ground nutmeg

1 onion, grated

Freshly ground black pepper to taste

Preparation:

With a sharp knife, cut the core out of the cabbage. In a large 6- to 8-quart stockpot, bring 4 cups water and 6 teaspoons salt to a boil over high heat. Carefully drop in the cabbage and push it down with a spoon. Boil the cabbage until the leaves begin to separate, 3 to 5 minutes. Using tongs, carefully remove the leaves and drain them.

Trim 1-inch off the bottom of the cabbage leaves so that their bottoms are even. Carefully remove the thick portions of the ribs without cutting through the leaves. Place the leaves on a work surface until ready to use.

Prepare the sauce: Combine chicken stock, lemon juice, mint, cinnamon stick, and garlic cloves in a medium saucepan. Bring the mixture to a boil over medium-high heat. Reduce the heat to low and simmer, uncovered, while stuffing cabbage leaves.

Prepare the filling: Mix the ground beef, rice, salt, cinnamon, cumin, paprika, nutmeg, onion, and some pepper together in a large bowl.

Place 1 tablespoon of filling in the center of a cabbage leaf. Fold the sides over the filling and roll up the leaf. Continue with the remaining cabbage leaves. Line a 3- to 4-quart pot with any broken cabbage leaves. Place the stuffed cabbage leaves, seam-side down, snugly in the bottom of the pot so that they are all tucked in together with no gaps. If necessary, make a second or third layer.

Place a small plate upside down over the cabbage rolls to keep them submerged. Pour sauce over cabbage rolls to cover. Bring the mixture to a boil over medium-high heat. Reduce heat to low, cover, and simmer approximately 1 hour or until cabbage is tender and filling is cooked through. Wearing oven mitts, carefully remove the plate. Transfer cabbage rolls to a serving platter. Strain the sauce over the cabbage rolls and serve warm.

Soad's Stuffed Cabbage

Pea, Carrot, and Tomato Stew

[Bisella wa Gazar Matboukh]

This is a quick and easy side dish to have on hand. It is the perfect accompaniment for Beef Croquettes (page 159).

Preparation:

Melt the clarified butter in a medium saucepan over medium heat. Add the onion and sauté until translucent. Add peas and carrots and stir to combine. Add stock, tomatoes, wild thyme, and salt and pepper to taste.

Bring to a boil over high heat. Reduce heat to low, stir, cover, and let simmer for 20 minutes or until vegetables are tender. Taste and adjust seasonings if necessary. Serve hot.

*See Where to Buy Guide on pages 203–205 for purchasing information.

6 SERVINGS

INGREDIENTS

- 2 teaspoons clarified butter (*ghee*) or expeller pressed corn oil
- 1 medium yellow onion, finely chopped
- 3 cups frozen peas and carrots, thawed and drained
- 2 cups vegetable, chicken, or meat stock
- 1/2 cup chopped tomatoes
- 1 teaspoon wild thyme, *zataar,** or oregano
- Salt to taste
- Freshly ground black pepper to taste

Beef Croquettes

[Kofta]

4 SERVINGS

12 KOFTA

INGREDIENTS

2 pounds lean ground beef

1 medium yellow onion, diced

6 cloves garlic, chopped

2 teaspoons ground cumin

1 teaspoon salt

1/2 teaspoon freshly ground
black pepper

Kofta are easy, economical kabobs that can be enjoyed for lunch or dinner. Ground chicken, turkey, beef, or lamb could also be used. Kofta *can be grilled, baked, or broiled. Keep in mind that if you use wooden kabob skewers you will need to soak them in water before using them so that they do not burn under the hot flame. Flat metal skewers are the easiest to use because they require no soaking and ensure that the* kofta *will not spin around as you turn them.*

Preparation:

Place beef, onion, garlic, cumin, salt, and pepper in a food processor. Process until mixture turns into a thick paste. Turn the mixture out onto a work surface. Form 12 thin finger-shaped sausages (about 2 1/2 inches long) and then flatten slightly to resemble disks.

Keep a bowl of water next to you to wet your hands as you shape the *kofta* onto the skewers. The moisture helps the *kofta* adhere to the skewers. Pierce skewer through the middle of the kofta, threading three kofta onto each skewer. Shape the kofta around the skewer so that it doesn't brake or fall off during cooking. Do not crowd or push kofta too close together.

Preheat grill, grill pan, or broiler. If using broiler, place the skewers on a baking sheet, otherwise, place directly onto grill or grill pan. Grill *kofta* for approximately 10 minutes per side. If *kofta* are cooked before the rest of the meal, wrap them in aluminum foil until needed.

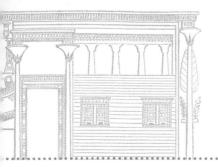

Tahini Sauce

[Tahina]

An eighty-year-old widowed taxi driver in Luxor once told my husband and me that he hoped to meet a nice woman and get remarried. Even though he was old, he said, he was still very strong because he ate tahini every day. Now every time we mention tahini, we cannot help thinking of that taxi driver and wondering if he ever did find his new bride.

In Egyptian restaurants large vats of Tahini Sauce are prepared and served on sandwich-size plates to dip bread and kabobs into as an appetizer. It is also added to mashed chickpeas to make Hommus bil Tahina (page 165) and to Baba Ghanoug (page 98), as well as many other salads.

Tahini can be purchase in Middle Eastern, Indian, organic, and health food stores, or in the international aisle of most supermarkets.

6 SERVINGS

INGREDIENTS

3/4 cup tahini*

Juice of 1/2 a lemon

Salt to taste

Freshly ground black pepper to taste

Pinch of chili powder or to taste

Dash of paprika

Preparation:

Place tahini in a medium bowl. Add lemon juice and stir to form a thick paste. Add some water, a tablespoon at a time (approximately 1/2 cup total), until tahini becomes light and creamy. Add salt, pepper, and chili powder to taste.

Transfer to a small serving plate or bowl and using the back of a spoon, smooth out the surface and make circle designs on the top. Sprinkle top with paprika. Serve cold or at room temperature as an appetizer or as an accompaniment to *kofta*.

* See Where to Buy Guide on pages 203–205 for purchasing information.

Mixed Country Salad

[Salata Baladi]

6 SERVINGS

INGREDIENTS

3 radishes, finely diced

1 cucumber, finely diced

1 carrot, shredded

1 bunch flat-leaf parsley, finely chopped

1 green pepper, finely diced

1 large tomato, finely diced

1/4 cup olive oil or expeller pressed corn oil

Grated peel and juice of 3 lemons

Dash of ground cumin

Dash of chili powder

Salt to taste

Freshly ground black pepper to taste

1/2 teaspoon sugar, if needed

This is the most commonly served salad in Egypt. The types of vegetables used in making it vary depending on the time of year and availability. Be sure to dice the vegetables finely in order to achieve the proper texture.

Preparation:

Place radishes, cucumber, carrot, parsley, green pepper, and tomato in a large bowl.

In a separate medium bowl, whisk olive oil, lemon peel, lemon juice, cumin, chili powder, and salt and pepper to taste. Taste dressing again and add sugar, if needed. Pour dressing over vegetables and toss to combine.

Crème Caramel

Egyptians love to serve Crème Caramel for dessert. Although I've eaten it many times, I was really surprised to see the version that my husband's cousin's wife Mona Shanab prepared for me. I went to their home to visit them while I was in Chicago for an International Association of Culinary Professionals conference. Mona prepared a huge feast, even though I was their only guest. For dessert she prepared Basboosa (page 49), a cake, and this recipe for Crème Caramel. Her recipe is now my favorite because it is easy to make and tastes as light as air. She made it in a beautiful crescent-shaped pan, so that when she turned it out it looked stunning.

10 SERVINGS

INGREDIENTS

1½ cups sugar
4 cups whole milk
8 large eggs
1 teaspoon vanilla extract

GARNISHES

Whipped cream, if desired
Maraschino cherries, if desired

Preparation:

Make the caramel by placing 1 cup sugar in a small heavy saucepan with ¼ cup of water to moisten. Bring to a boil over high heat, swirling the saucepan to dissolve the sugar. Then boil without stirring until the syrup turns a dark caramel color, approximately 7 to 10 minutes. Immediately pour the caramel into a 4-cup soufflé dish or a 10-inch oval baking dish. Holding the dish with oven gloves, quickly swirl the dish to coat the base and sides (the caramel will harden quickly as it cools). Place the dish in a roasting pan.

Preheat oven to 325 degrees F. Make the crème by putting the remaining ½ cup of sugar, milk, eggs, and vanilla into a blender and whipping for 3 minutes. Pour mixture into the soufflé or baking dish on top of the caramel. Pour enough boiling water into the roasting pan to come halfway up the sides of the soufflé or baking dish. Bake the custard, uncovered, for 40 to 45 minutes, until it is set and a knife inserted in the middle comes out clean. Remove the soufflé pan from the roasting pan and let the custard cool for 30 minutes, then refrigerate overnight.

To turn out, carefully run a sharp knife around the edge of the dish to loosen the custard. Cover the dish with a serving plate with a short lip around the edges and, holding them tightly together, invert the dish and plate. Gently lift one edge of the dish, letting the caramel run over the sides, and then slowly remove the dish. Garnish with whipped cream and maraschino cherries, if desired.

Anise Tea

[Yansoon]

4 SERVINGS

INGREDIENTS

4 teaspoons dried anise
Sugar or honey to taste

Anise is known to be both a breath freshener and digestive aid, which makes it a very popular after-dinner drink in Egypt. Middle Eastern stores often sell anise in tea bags, even though making it from scratch is not difficult and is less expensive.

Preparation:

In a tea kettle or saucepan bring 4 teaspoons dried anise and 4 cups water to a boil over high heat. Remove from heat and steep, covered, for 10 minutes. Strain into 4 tea cups and sweeten with sugar or honey, if desired.

Mother's Day

Mother's Day is celebrated on March 21st in Egypt. Large colorful banners are set up in urban areas wishing mothers a happy day. Many Egyptian pop singers sing songs dedicated to their mothers, and television channels air programs and movies with motherhood themes. Florists sell large bouquets of gladiolas, country roses, and birds of paradise for the occasion. Pastry shops sell decorative tortes with Mother's Day motifs. Most people celebrate the holiday with a homemade meal in honor of their mother. For this menu, I've chosen traditional items that mothers typically prepare for their children. For this holiday, however, their children should make this meal for their mothers.

Mother's Day Menu

▶ Chickpea and Tahini Puree

▶ Egyptian Rice with Vermicelli

▶ Beef and Okra Stew

▶ Cracked Wheat, Tomato, and Cucumber Salad

▶ Creamy Milk Pudding

▶ Coconut Butter Cookies with Sweet Syrup

▶ Strawberry Banana Cocktail

Chickpea and Tahini Puree

[Hommus bil Tahina]

4 SERVINGS

INGREDIENTS

- 1 cup cooked or canned chick-peas, peeled
- 1 garlic clove, minced
- 1/3 cup tahini*
- 1/8 cup extra virgin olive oil, plus two teaspoons for garnish
- Salt to taste
- Dash of cayenne pepper or to taste
- Dash of paprika, for garnish
- Pita Bread for serving (page 70), or use store bought

The word hommus *means "chickpeas" in Arabic. The full name for this dish is* Hommus bil Tahina *or "chick-peas with sesame paste" in English. To peel chickpeas, hold them in between your thumb and index finger over a bowl and squeeze. The chickpea will come through and you will be left with the skin in your hand. I like to peel them while I'm watching television or talking on the phone, and leave them ready in the refrigerator, so that later on I can make this dish.*

Preparation:

Place chickpeas in a food processor, reserving a few for garnish. Add the garlic, tahini, olive oil, some salt, and cayenne pepper to the food processor. Puree until smooth.

Add some water, tablespoon by tablespoon, puree-ing until you get an extra-creamy consistency (you should need less than 1/4 cup in total) and scraping down the sides of the food processor for about 1 to 2 additional minutes. Taste and adjust seasonings if necessary.

If not serving immediately, store the puree in a covered container in the refrigerator. Otherwise, spoon onto a small round dish. Using the back of a spoon, make dents in the top and fill the dents with remaining olive oil. Sprinkle with paprika and arrange remaining chickpeas on the top. Serve with warm pita bread.

*See Where to Buy Guide on pages 203–205 for purchasing information.

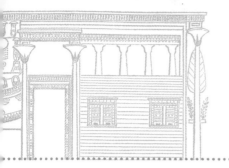

Egyptian Rice with Vermicelli

[Roz bil Shareya]

In this rice recipe, vermicelli is browned before the rice is cooked, so the finished dish combines golden vermicelli strands with white rice grains. Indian manufacturers, however, sell pre-toasted vermicelli that eliminates the need to brown the vermicelli before cooking the rice. If you live near an Indian grocer, look for brown roasted vermicelli (called sev*), and substitute it for the regular version in this recipe.*

4 SERVINGS

INGREDIENTS

1 teaspoon clarified butter (*ghee*)

½ cup vermicelli

1 cup Egyptian or other short-grain rice

2 cups vegetable or chicken stock

¼ teaspoon salt, or to taste

Preparation:

Melt clarified butter over medium heat in a medium saucepan. Add the vermicelli. Stir once and continue to cook for 2 to 3 minutes until vermicelli is golden. (Skip this step if you use pre-roasted vermicelli.)

Add the rice to the vermicelli and stir to combine. Cook for 2 to 3 minutes until rice starts to turn translucent. Add the stock and salt and stir to mix well. Bring to a boil, lower heat to low, and cover the pot with a tight-fitting lid. Simmer 15 to 20 minutes or until all of the liquid is absorbed. Remove from heat and allow rice to stand covered at least 5 minutes before serving. Serve warm.

Beef and Okra Stew

[Lahma bil Bamya]

6 SERVINGS

INGREDIENTS

- 1 teaspoon clarified butter (*ghee*) or expeller pressed corn oil
- 1 large yellow onion, chopped
- 2 pounds boneless beef shoulder, cut into 1- to 2-inch cubes
- 1/4 teaspoon ground cumin
- 1/4 teaspoon ground cinnamon
- 1/4 teaspoon ground nutmeg
- 1/4 teaspoon paprika
- 2 cups chicken or beef stock
- Salt
- Freshly ground black pepper
- 1 cup tomato puree
- 1 pound fresh okra or baby okra, stems removed and cut into 1/4-inch rounds, or frozen chopped or baby okra, thawed
- Juice of 1 lemon or lime

This classic Egyptian stew can be eaten for lunch or dinner. The Spanish Umayyad Prince Abd al Rahman brought okra to Europe from Egypt in the ninth century. When choosing okra, choose firm, bright green ones. A soft texture and discoloration are signs that they are beyond their peak. Baby okra can be left whole and used in this recipe. If you're not a fan of okra, you could substitute green beans instead. Lamb can also be used in place of the beef. This is a great stew to make in advance, because it tastes just as good on the second day.

This dish convinced Branden and Matthew, my then teenage cousins who were accustomed to eating chicken nuggets, burgers, and pizza, to seek out homemade foods instead. While they were resistant at first, once they tried it, they couldn't get enough. Eating Egyptian Beef and Okra Stew became a tradition that they wanted to honor every time they came to our home.

Preparation:

Heat clarified butter or corn oil in a large saucepan over medium heat. Add onion and cook and stir until it turns translucent. Add beef cubes and brown on all sides. Add cumin, cinnamon, nutmeg, paprika, stock, and a sprinkling of salt and pepper. Increase heat to high and bring to a boil. Reduce heat to low, cover, and simmer for 1 hour, stirring occasionally.

Add tomato puree and okra, stir, and cover. Cook for another 30 minutes, until okra is tender. Taste and adjust salt and pepper, if necessary. Stir in lemon or lime juice. Serve warm.

Cracked Wheat, Tomato, and Cucumber Salad

[Tabbouli]

Tabbouli *originated in Lebanon where it is known as* Tabouleh. *It is a nutritious lunch or picnic item that is often included in everyday family meals. The cracked wheat provides fiber and the herbs are packed with vitamins and minerals. Cucumbers possess a property that levels the body temperature in warmer climates. They are also rich in potassium and are said to prevent eczema, fevers, psoriasis, and fluid retention.*

To make Tabbouli *more than 1 day in advance, simply omit the citrus juices while preparing the salad, refrigerate it, and add the lemon and lime juice before serving. To eat, place some of the salad inside of a romaine leaf and roll it up.*

Preparation:

Pour bulgur into a large bowl. Cover it with enough water to cover plus 2 inches. Let stand for 1 hour.

Drain the bulgur and mix it with the olive oil, lemon juice, lime juice, and salt and pepper to taste. Add cucumbers, tomatoes, onion, parsley, and mint and stir. Taste and adjust seasonings if necessary. Refrigerate an hour or up to 12 hours. Serve with large whole romaine leaves.

8 SERVINGS

INGREDIENTS

1 cup bulgur wheat #1*

1/4 cup extra-virgin olive oil (first cold press if possible)

Juice of 1 lemon

Juice of 1 lime

Salt to taste

Freshly ground black pepper to taste

4 small cucumbers, diced

4 Roma tomatoes, diced

1 small onion, grated

3/4 cup fresh parsley, chopped

1/4 cup fresh mint, chopped

1 head of romaine lettuce leaves, cleaned and dried

*Bulgur is a parboiled and dried wheat that is processed into grains. See Where to Buy Guide on pages 203–205 for purchasing information.

Creamy Milk Pudding

[Mahallabiya]

6 SERVINGS

INGREDIENTS

4 tablespoons rice flour or cornstarch

4 cups cold whole milk

1 cup sugar

1 teaspoon rose water*

1 teaspoon ground almonds

1 teaspoon ground pistachios

1 teaspoon ground walnuts

Mahallabiya *is a light and creamy custard—a quick, easy, and inexpensive dessert to make for any occasion. Traditionally, the milk pudding is thickened by rice flour (ground rice), as corn was not available in Egypt prior to the seventeenth century. Nowadays, many people use cornstarch instead. Pure vanilla or almond extracts could be substituted for the rose water. This is a great dessert to make ahead of time because it needs to be chilled before serving. I like to make double quantities so that I can serve it one time as a pudding and later on in the week use the other half (which has been stored in the refrigerator) to make Cream-Filled Baklava (page 173).*

Preparation:

Dissolve the rice flour or cornstarch in 1/4 cup cold milk. In a medium saucepan, mix the sugar with the 3 3/4 cups remaining milk. Cook over medium heat until liquid reaches the boiling point. Slowly pour the rice flour/cornstarch mixture into the milk mixture and increase the heat to high.

Stirring constantly with a wooden spoon or plastic whisk and being sure to scrape the sides and bottom of the saucepan to prevent the milk from scalding, boil the pudding for two minutes. Reduce the heat to low and continue whisking until the pudding resembles a thick custard, approximately 10 minutes. Remove from heat and stir in the rose water. Ladle 1/2 cup of pudding into each of 8 ramekins. Allow to cool to room temperature and then place ramekins in the refrigerator and chill until firm.

When ready to serve, mix almonds, pistachios, and walnuts together and sprinkle over the tops of the pudding.

*See Where to Buy Guide on pages 203–205 for purchasing information.

Coconut Butter Cookies with Sweet Syrup

[Remoosh El Set]

These cookies are very popular in Luxor, Egypt. In Arabic, their name means "Lady's Eyelashes" due to their teardrop shape. I love their buttery, sweet mellow taste. Be sure to serve them with coffee or tea.

Preparation:

Make the syrup: Combine the sugar, lemon peel, lemon juice, and 3/4 cup water in a medium saucepan. Stirring slowly, bring to a boil over medium heat. Once mixture comes to a boil and sugar is dissolved, stop stirring, reduce heat to low, and simmer for 10 minutes. Remove from heat and allow to cool. Discard lemon peel and set aside. (Syrup can be made up to 1 month in advance, covered, and stored in the refrigerator.)

Preheat the oven to 350 degrees F. Line two baking sheets with parchment paper or silicone liners.

Combine butter and confectioners' sugar in a large bowl and beat well until light in color. Beat in the egg and vanilla, then stir in the ground coconut and flour. Mix well to incorporate.

Break off walnut-size pieces of dough, roll them into balls, and place on prepared baking sheets. Flatten the balls slightly and taper the sides and top to look like a teardrop. Space 12 cookies evenly on each cookie sheet, leaving about an inch between each cookie. Press an almond vertically into the center of each cookie.

Bake cookies for 15 to 20 minutes or until lightly golden. When cookies are done, remove from oven and set on cooling racks. Using a spatula, carefully lift the cookies onto another baking sheet and pour syrup over the top while the cookies are still hot. Serve at room temperature. Refrigerate leftovers, covered, for up to a week.

MAKES 24 COOKIES

INGREDIENTS

SYRUP:
2 cups sugar
3 strips lemon peel
Juice of 1/2 lemon

COOKIES:
1 1/2 sticks unsalted butter, at room temperature
1/2 cup confectioners' sugar
1 egg
1 teaspoon vanilla extract
1/3 cup ground dried coconut #1*
2 1/4 cups unbleached, all-purpose flour
24 whole blanched almonds

*See Where to Buy Guide on pages 203–205 for purchasing information.

Strawberry Banana Cocktail

[Cocktail bil Frawola wa Mowza]

4 SERVINGS

INGREDIENTS

2 cups fresh strawberries, trimmed and sliced, plus 4 whole strawberries

1 banana, sliced

1 cup cold milk

4 tablespoons honey, or to taste

1/2 cup whipped cream, for garnish

4 teaspoons finely chopped roasted unsalted peanuts

February and March are strawberry and banana season in Egypt. Large heaps of fragrant strawberries and hanging banana bunches are displayed at open-air markets and juice bars everywhere. My favorite place to sample fresh bananas, however, is Banana Island, Gezirat al Mowz, in Luxor. From the corniche, you can take a felucca (traditional sailboat) across the Nile to this beautiful banana plantation. You can wander among massive towering banana trees, and then sit and enjoy large trays of freshly picked ones on picnic tables while overlooking the Nile. This sweet drink is like a sundae in a glass.

Preparation:

Put strawberries, banana, milk, and honey in a blender. Whip until all ingredients are combined and drink is frothy. Taste and adjust honey, if necessary. Pour drink into 4 clear glasses. Top each with a dollop of whipped cream. Place a strawberry in the middle and sprinkle peanuts over the top.

Birth Celebration

After babies are born in Egypt, it is common to hold an *Isbooh*, a gathering to welcome the baby into the world. Traditionally, it is at this event that the baby's name is revealed. Family members hold the baby and circle a table or room singing a traditional song. Guests are usually treated to desserts, candies, and sweet drinks to denote the "sweet" occasion. Some families invite religious officials to lead special prayers for the baby's health and welfare. Guests usually bring gifts for the baby and/or money for the parents.

Birth Celebration Menu

▶ Cream-filled Baklava
▶ Anise Biscotti
▶ Egyptian Rice, Apricot, and Pistachio Pudding
▶ Mango Juice

Sweets

Cream-filled Baklava

[Goulash bil Halib]

MAKES 30 TO 40 PIECES

INGREDIENTS

SYRUP:

1½ cups sugar

2 large strips of orange peel

Juice of 1 small orange

BAKLAVA:

1 (1 pound) package phyllo
   dough, thawed according to
   package directions

1 cup clarified butter (*ghee*)

1 recipe Creamy Milk Pudding
   (page 169)

Cream-filled Baklava is a heavenly alternative to more common nut filled baklavas. I like to make this recipe for potluck lunches and dinners, and it has become my father's favorite dessert.

Preparation:

Preheat oven to 350 degrees F. Butter an 11x17-inch or 12-inch round baking pan.

Make the syrup: Combine the sugar, orange peel, orange juice, and 1 cup water in a medium saucepan. Bring to a boil over medium heat, stirring until sugar dissolves. Stop stirring and reduce heat to low. Simmer for 10 minutes or until the syrup thickens. (When the strips appear to look like candied orange peel, the syrup is at the right consistency.) Remove from heat, allow syrup to cool, and then discard orange peel.

To assemble the baklava: Remove phyllo dough from package. Trim the sheets with a sharp knife to fit the pan you are using. Wrap excess dough in plastic wrap in the refrigerator. Cover bottom of baking pan with 1 sheet of phyllo dough. Brush clarified butter evenly over the top. Place another sheet over the top and brush with more clarified butter. Continue stacking and brushing with butter until half of the phyllo dough is used.

Spread Creamy Milk Pudding evenly across the top. Continue layering remaining phyllo dough on top of pudding, brushing with clarified butter. Brush top layer with clarified butter.

With a long, sharp knife, cut phyllo three-quarters of the way down into 10 strips horizontally. Cut diagonal lines across the strips three-quarters of the way down to create diamond shapes. Bake for 40 to 50 minutes or until golden, rotating pan every 20 minutes to ensure even browning. Remove pan from oven and pour syrup over the top while still hot. Allow to sit until syrup is absorbed and baklava has cooled to room temperature.

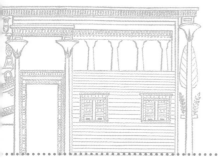

Anise Biscotti

[Biskoweet bil Yansoon]

These crunchy cookies were first introduced in the United States by Italian immigrants. Italians had enjoyed them since ancient times when the Romans would take them on long voyages because they stayed fresh for a long time.

These cookies are also very popular in the northern Mediterranean coastal areas of Egypt between Alexandria and Ismalea where they are intrinsic to the local cuisine. I learned this when my friend Mona Ali, an Ismalea native, baked them for me. When I told her that they were popular Italian cookies, she said that she never knew that Italians made them, and that they were a specialty of her hometown. Since the ancient Romans were attracted to Egypt for its large granaries, and the ancient Egyptians already possessed sugar and sophisticated bakeries, it is likely that the Romans learned the recipe from their stay in Egypt.

These light biscotti make a great breakfast, teatime snack, or dessert. Serve with hot coffee or tea for dunking. Fennel seeds or nigella seeds are sometimes used in place of anise seeds.

MAKES 2 DOZEN

INGREDIENTS

- 4 large eggs, at room temperature
- 1 cup sugar
- 2 cups unbleached, all-purpose flour
- 2 teaspoons anise seeds
- 1 teaspoon vanilla or anise extract

Preparation:

Preheat oven to 375 degrees F. Grease and flour 2 ($8^1/2$ x $4^1/2$ x $2^1/2$-inch) loaf pans.

In a large bowl, whisk eggs by hand or with an electric mixer on high speed until they turn light yellow, about 3 minutes. Slowly add the sugar and continue to beat until incorporated.

With the mixer running on low speed, add the flour, anise seeds, and vanilla. Mix well to incorporate. Pour $1/2$ of the batter into each pan and smooth out the top of the batter. Bake in the middle of the oven for 25 minutes or until dough turns golden. Remove pans from the oven and reduce oven temperature to 325 degrees F.

Let biscotti cool for 10 minutes in the pans. Using oven mitts, turn over loaf pans to unmold cookies. Allow to cool for an additional 10 minutes. Cut each loaf crosswise into 1-inch-wide slices. Lay each slice on its side on a cookie sheet. Bake for 8 to 10 minutes, remove from oven, turn biscotti over, and bake for another 8 to 10 minutes. Cookies should be light brown when finished. Cool thoroughly. Cookies will keep in an airtight container for up to a month.

Egyptian Rice, Apricot, and Pistachio Pudding

[Roz bi Laban bil Amr Din wa Fusdooq]

4 SERVINGS

INGREDIENTS

$^1/_3$ cup Egyptian rice, Arborio rice, or short-grain rice

3$^3/_4$ cups whole milk

1 cinnamon stick

Grated peel of 1 lemon

$^2/_3$ cup sugar

GARNISHES

1 cup dried apricots

$^1/_8$ cup shelled pistachios, ground

$^1/_8$ cup raisin

In Egypt, rice pudding is very popular. It can be made on the stovetop or in the oven. This is a slow-cooking stovetop version that produces a smooth and creamy pudding that has a satisfying textural consistency. My husband and brother-in-law say that it is the "ultimate" rice pudding recipe. Whenever they order rice pudding in restaurants, they reassure me that it is not as good as mine. I hope that everyone who tastes this recipe has the same reaction.

Preparation:

Rinse the rice and drain well. Pour milk into a medium saucepan. Add drained rice, cinnamon stick, lemon peel, and sugar. Stir with a wooden spoon and bring to a boil over medium-high heat. Reduce heat to low, stir, and cover. Simmer pudding for 2 to 2$^1/_2$ hours, until rice is tender and liquid is absorbed.

Remove and discard cinnamon stick. Allow pudding to cool at room temperature and then pour into a serving bowl. Place apricots around the outer edges of the pudding to garnish. Sprinkle pistachios on top of the pudding, in a heart shape, if desired. (I like to place a heart-shaped cookie cutter in the middle and sprinkle the pistachios inside the cutter. Then I remove the cutter and I have a perfect shape.) Arrange the raisins on top of the pudding. Refrigerate leftovers for up to 2 days.

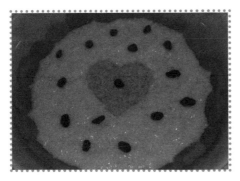

Egyptian Rice, Apricot, and Pistachio Pudding

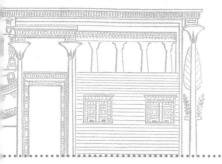

Mango Juice

[Assir Manga]

Mangoes are native to India where they have been consumed for more than 4,000 years. They arrived in the
Middle East via Persian traders. It wasn't until 1825, however, that the Egyptian ruler Mohamed Ali began importing
them into Egypt from India. Today in Egypt, mangoes
(including the popular Sukkary, Alphonse, Beautiful
Cheek, and Lady's Finger varieties) are cultivated in
September and October when their incredibly sweet, rich
flavor is enjoyed fresh and in juices so thick that they need
to be eaten with a spoon. Egyptian companies also bottle
the juices and export them to the United States. The Best and
Mira varieties can be purchased in the Hispanic section of most grocery stores, as well as in many
Middle Eastern, Indian, Latin, Asian, and Caribbean grocers.

    Mangoes are rich in Vitamin A, C, potassium, and antioxidants. When choosing man-
goes in the United States, look for Ataulfo or Champagne mangoes for their sweet flavor.
Smell the mangoes near the stem. If there is no fragrance, there will be no flavor. Most mangoes purchased in supermarkets need to be ripened in paper bags for a few days before being
consumed.

4 SERVINGS

INGREDIENTS

2 fresh ripe mangoes

1 to 2 cups cold water

Sugar or honey to taste, if
   desired

Preparation:

Cut mangoes by slicing off the sides of the fruit starting from 1/2 inch to the side of
the stem. Cut a grid through the flesh of each half to the peel and scoop out the
cubes from their base into a blender. Trim around the pit to remove any extra
mango flesh and discard pit.

Pour 1 cup of cold water into the blender and pulse on and off on high speed for 1
minute until a juice has formed but some large mango chunks remain. Taste the
drink. If it doesn't seem sweet enough, add sugar or honey to taste. If it seems too
thick, add up to another cup of water, a little at a time, pulsing and tasting after each
addition. Serve with a straw and a spoon.

Valentine's Day Dinner

Valentine's Day seems to become more and more popular each year in Egypt, where it is known as "*Eid al Hob*" or "The Feast of Love." The holiday is actually deeply rooted in antiquity, when St. Valentine would secretly marry couples (against the law of the Roman government) in the basement of his church in Terni, Italy. Since St. Valentine risked his life to religiously sanction a couple's love, the holiday marking him became known as a romantic holiday.

Today Valentine's Day is celebrated in Egypt similar to the way it is celebrated in Europe and the United States—with cards, flowers, sweets, and romantic dinners. Love songs bombard the radio and romantic films dominate the television stations throughout the entire month of February. This menu contains items that are served in Egyptian restaurants on that day and have romantic histories and connotations.

Valentine's Day Dinner Menu

▶ Pomegranate, Walnut, and Red Pepper Puree
▶ Couscous with Peas, Carrots, and Eggplant
▶ Chicken and Beef Kabob Bouquets
▶ Fattoush Salad
▶ Double Chocolate Baklava
▶ Coffee with Cardamom

View of the Nile from Metropolitan Restaurant, Luxor, Egypt

Pomegranate, Walnut, and Red Pepper Puree

[Muhammara]

The Arabic name for this dish comes from the word Muhammar, *which means to brown something when cooking it but literally means "to make red" since the word* hamra *means red. While* muhammara *is most often served as a spread with pita triangles, I have also seen it used to stuff phyllo dough triangles for elegant and unexpected appetizers.*

Pomegranates were present in 1550 BC in Egypt and began appearing in Greek mythology three thousand years ago. Throughout history, their juice and seeds were used in natural medicines for curing a wide variety of ailments. Pomegranates made their way to Spain and were introduced to America with Spanish settlers in 1769. They are now grown in California and Arizona. Modern doctors have been researching the fruit and found that it helps reduce the risk of heart disease and colon cancer, and can also lower high blood pressure. It is also thought to inhibit the spread of other cancers.

6 SERVINGS

INGREDIENTS

1 (7-ounce) jar roasted red peppers, drained and rinsed

1/3 cup fresh bread crumbs

1/3 cup walnuts

4 cloves garlic, sliced

Juice of 1 lemon

4 tablespoons pomegranate molasses*

Pinch of cayenne pepper

Salt to taste

1/4 cup extra virgin olive oil

Preparation:

Combine peppers, bread crumbs, walnuts, garlic cloves, lemon juice, pomegranate molasses, cayenne pepper, and a pinch of salt in a food processor. Pulse on and off, gradually pouring the olive oil into the running food processor. Taste the puree and adjust the salt as needed. Serve at room temperature.

* See Where to Buy Guide on pages 203–205 for purchasing information.

Couscous with Peas, Carrots, and Eggplant

[Couscousi ma Khodar]

4 SERVINGS

INGREDIENTS

1 large eggplant (approximately 7 to 8 inches long and 3 inches wide)

Salt

3 medium carrots, peeled and cut into 1½-inch chunks

3 tablespoons extra-virgin olive oil

Freshly ground black pepper

1 cup frozen peas, thawed and drained

1 teaspoon saffron

1 cup couscous

Couscous is a tiny semolina pasta originally made by Berbers in Morocco, Tunisia, and Algeria. The word couscous comes from the Berber word k'seksu, which is similar to the sound that the dry semolina granules make as they are shaken through a sieve. In the Maghreb region (Morocco, Tunisia, and Algeria), couscous is a daily staple. In other areas of the Middle East, couscous is eaten much less frequently, and it is often called maftuul or maghribeya, because the word cous is actually a derogatory term in some Arabic dialects. In modern France, couscous is the most commonly eaten item outside of the home.

Preparation:

Wash eggplant and cut into 1½-inch-wide slices. Place in a large colander and salt generously. Allow to sit for an hour to remove bitter juices. After an hour has passed, rinse and drain the eggplants, and cut into 1½-inch cubes.

Preheat the oven to 450 degrees F. Place eggplant and carrots on a baking sheet. Toss with 2 tablespoons olive oil and season with salt and pepper. Roast until soft and cooked through, about 25 to 30 minutes. Stir in peas and keep warm until serving.

Place 1 cup water, saffron, a pinch of salt, and 1 tablespoon olive oil in a medium saucepan and bring to a boil over high heat. Remove from heat, stir in couscous, and cover. Let stand for 10 minutes. Fluff couscous with a fork, taste, and adjust salt if necessary.

Pour couscous onto a serving platter. Arrange eggplant, carrots, and peas on top. Serve warm.

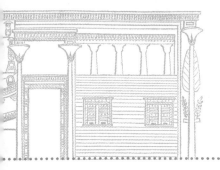

Chicken and Beef Kabob Bouquets

[Kebab Firakh wa Lahma]

NOTE:

Shish Kebab ▶ Beef Cubes with Onions and Peppers

Shish Tawouk ▶ Chicken Cubes with Onions and Peppers

Mixed Grill ▶ Chicken Cubes, Beef Kofta, and Veal Cubes

Kabob and Kofta ▶ Mixed Beef Cube and Ground Beef

Kabobs are popular street and restaurant fare throughout Egypt. The men who make them are known as Kebabgys. When I worked on a consulting project for a restaurant group in Luxor, I spent a lot of time at the Kebabgy restaurant where the master kabob maker transformed grilled meat into edible works of art daily. Grilled whole chickens, pigeons, lamb and veal rib chops, and liver are also popular in Egypt. French fries and Egyptian rice are typical accompaniments to kabob dinners. For formal buffets, kabob skewers are pushed into carved melons or arranged in glass containers to form meat "bouquets."

4 SERVINGS

INGREDIENTS

1/4 cup expeller pressed corn oil

2 cloves garlic, minced

Juice and grated peel of 2 lemons

Pinch of saffron

1 teaspoon salt

1/2 teaspoon freshly ground black pepper

1 pound chicken breast meat, skinned and cubed

1 pound beef cubes for kabobs

1 teaspoon ground cumin

1 melon, for serving

Preparation:

Combine corn oil, garlic, lemon juice and peel, saffron, salt, and pepper in a small bowl. Divide into 2 medium bowls. Add the chicken cubes to one of the bowls, mixing to coat all pieces of chicken well. Add the beef cubes to the other bowl, mixing to coat all pieces of meat well. Cover both bowls and marinate for 1 hour at room temperature or overnight in the refrigerator.

Prepare skewers if needed. (If using wooden skewers, soak them in water for 30 minutes to prevent them from burning. Metal skewers need no preparation.)

Thread the chicken cubes onto 2 of the skewers. Avoid pushing the meat too close together, it should be touching but not crowded in order to ensure even cooking. Thread the beef cubes onto the other 2 skewers in the same way. Sprinkle cumin on the chicken and beef.

Preheat grill or broiler. Place chicken skewers directly on a prepared grill or on a baking sheet under the broiler for 7 to 10 minutes on each side, until chicken is cooked through. Wrap in tin foil and repeat the process with the beef skewers.

To serve, cut the melon in half and place it, cut side down, on a serving platter. Push the pointy end of the kabob skewers down into the melon skin to hold them in place, arranging them close together, as if they were flowers.

Fattoush Salad

[Salata Fattoush]

4 SERVINGS

INGREDIENTS

- 1 cucumber, diced
- 4 tomatoes, finely chopped
- 1 red onion, thinly sliced
- 1 pita bread, cut into 12 pieces
- 1/2 cup extra-virgin olive oil (first cold pressed, if possible)
- 4 teaspoons sumac*
- 2 tablespoons pomegranate molasses*
- Juice of 1 lemon
- Salt to taste
- Freshly ground black pepper to taste

This is a delicious cucumber and tomato salad tossed with crunchy toasted pita bread pieces and dressed with a pomegranate molasses dressing. Pomegranate molasses is also a base for delicious marinades and glazes for meat and poultry. This salad is a great way to use up leftover pita bread. Toss some leftover chicken, lamb, or beef into the salad and you have a complete meal in a bowl.

Preparation:

Preheat broiler. Combine cucumber, tomatoes, and red onion in a large salad bowl.

On a baking sheet, brush pita bread pieces with 2 tablespoons of the olive oil and sprinkle with sumac. Place under broiler and toast for 2 to 4 minutes, until golden on each side. Remove from oven and set aside to cool.

Mix remaining olive oil, pomegranate molasses, lemon juice, and salt and pepper to taste in a medium bowl. Whisk vigorously to form a smooth dressing. Add pita chips to cucumber mixture and toss to combine. Pour dressing over salad and toss again to combine. Serve immediately.

*See Where to Buy Guide on pages 203–205 for purchasing information.

Ultimate Kabob from Kebabgy in Luxor, Egypt

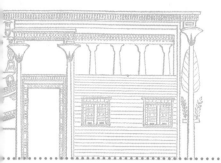

Double Chocolate Baklava

[Ba'lawa bil Chokolata]

What we know as baklava is said to have originated in Persia and was an interpretation of a Chinese dessert made with pastry "leaves." It is believed that Armenian Christians first brought baklava to Istanbul (then Constantinople). The original version of its name, baki-halva, means "Lenten Sweet" because it was made with forty sheets of pastry dough—one for each day of Lent. In Turkey, royal palaces transformed the humble dessert into the rich, syrupy confection that we are familiar with today. Many Arabic-speaking countries, including Egypt, quickly adopted the dessert as their own. As chocolate consumption is consistently on the rise in modern Egypt, my decadent Double Chocolate Baklava recipe goes a step beyond the traditional, creating the ultimate demonstration of gooey gluttony by combining both milk and dark chocolate with buttery phyllo dough.

24 SERVINGS

INGREDIENTS

1 (1 pound) box phyllo dough, thawed according to package directions

1 cup clarified butter (ghee)

1/2 pound milk chocolate (chips or small pieces)

1/2 pound dark chocolate (60% or higher), chopped

2 tablespoons confectioners' sugar

Preparation:

Preheat oven to 350 degrees F. Butter a 13x9-inch baking pan.

Remove phyllo dough from package. Trim it with a sharp knife to fit the pan you are using. Wrap excess dough in plastic wrap in the refrigerator. Cover bottom of baking pan with 1 sheet of phyllo dough. Brush clarified butter evenly over the top. Place another sheet over the top and brush with more clarified butter. Continue stacking and brushing with butter until half of the phyllo dough is used.

Sprinkle milk and dark chocolate evenly across the top. Place another phyllo sheet over the chocolate and brush with some butter. Continue layering remaining phyllo dough and brushing with clarified butter.

With a long, sharp knife, cut phyllo three-quarters of the way through into 24 squares (4 across and 6 lengthwise). Bake for 40 to 50 minutes or until golden, rotating pan every 20 minutes to ensure even browning. Remove pan from oven and cool to room temperature. Sprinkle with confectioners' sugar before serving.

Coffee with Cardamom

[Ahwa bil Habbahan]

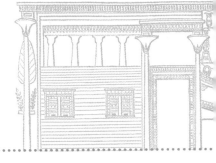

4 SERVINGS

INGREDIENTS

4 espresso-size cups of cold water

1 green cardamom pod, crushed

4 teaspoons Turkish coffee*

Sugar to taste, if desired

Coffee arrived in Egypt via the Sufi clerics who met Yemeni clerics in Mecca, Saudi Arabia, during the annual pilgrimage. Its taste and stimulant properties were appreciated by Imams (Muslim prayer leaders), who would drink coffee to stay awake for long hours of prayer and study. Coffee became known as the "wine of the Arabs" because of its role in Arabian culture, economy, and cuisine.

When the Portuguese took over the spice trade in the sixteenth century, the Egyptian economy, which relied heavily on the spice trade, suffered a serious blow. Luckily, coffee was a commodity in which Egyptians could deal. By the seventeenth century, Cairo alone was home to 650 coffee houses. The coffee houses, complete with backgammon tables and water pipes (sheesha) *used for smoking flavored tobacco, have become integral to Egyptian culture by providing refuge and inspiration for Egyptian writers, artists, and leaders alike.*

In Egyptian homes, coffee with cardamom is enjoyed after meals. A kanaka, *a small, long-handled pot with a spout, is used to prepare the coffee on the stove. Small espresso cups are used to serve the coffee. Ask your guests how much sugar they would like before making the coffee because the sugar is brewed with the coffee, not stirred in later. In Egypt, the term for black coffee is* ahwa saada *(and it is often served at funerals), while* sukar ziada *means with sugar (usually 2 to 3 teaspoons). Cardamom, coincidentally, is considered to be an aphrodisiac in Arabian culture, making it the perfect addition to a Valentine's Day menu.*

Preparation:

Bring water, cardamom, and coffee just to a boil in an Arabic coffee pot.* Remove coffee pot from the heat so that the coffee does not boil over. Remove the foam from the top of the coffee with a teaspoon and place some in the bottom of each espresso cup. Let the coffee stand in the pot for 1 minute and then place back on the flame. Add desired amount of sugar and stir. Bring just to a boil a second time without stirring. Discard cardamom and distribute coffee in coffee cups.

* See Where to Buy Guide on pages 203–205 for purchasing information.

New Year's Eve

The New Year of the Gregorian calendar is celebrated in Egypt as it is in many places around the world. In Cairo, the New Year often starts out with a "bang" with fireworks and concerts at the pyramids. This menu is made up of foods that are available in January and are particularly suited to cooler weather.

New Year's Eve Menu

► Lentil Soup

► Rice with Cinnamon and Saffron

► Chicken Breasts Stuffed with Cheese, Tomato, and Hulled Grains

► Eggplant and Tomato Casserole

► Deep-Fried Cauliflower

► Date K'nafeh

► Powdered Orchid Drink

Mohandiseen Neighborhood in Cairo

Lentil Soup

[Shorbat Ads]

4 SERVINGS

INGREDIENTS

1 teaspoon butter

1 teaspoon olive oil

2 carrots, diced

1 onion, diced

2 celery stalks, diced

1 cup brown lentils, rinsed

1 teaspoon salt

1/2 teaspoon freshly ground black pepper

1 teaspoon ground coriander

4 cups vegetable or chicken stock

Fresh parsley for garnish

During ancient times, Egyptians were the chief exporters of lentils in the world. Since lentils were traded for currency and their shape is reminiscent of small coins, they are often associated with wealth. I like to serve lentils on New Year's to wish my guests, and myself, a prosperous, healthy new year.

Preparation:

Warm butter and olive oil together in a large saucepan over medium heat. When butter begins to foam, add carrots, onion, and celery. Sauté until translucent, about 3 to 5 minutes. Stir in lentils and cook for 1 minute. Season with salt, freshly ground pepper, and coriander. Add stock, stir, and increase the heat to high.

When the stock begins to boil, reduce heat to medium-low and stir. Cover and allow to simmer 45 minutes to 1 hour or until lentils are tender. Taste and adjust salt and pepper if necessary. Garnish with parsley and serve warm.

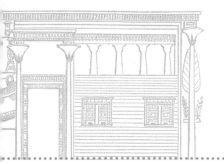

Rice with Cinnamon and Saffron

[Roz bil Irfa wa Saffron]

Rice with Cinnamon and Saffron is a light and tasty alternative to plain and fried rice. Good quality saffron gives the rice a beautiful yellow color and the cinnamon lends it a greater depth of flavor.

Preparation:

In a large saucepan over medium heat, warm clarified butter. Add rice, stir, and cook until it is translucent, about 3 to 5 minutes. Stir in chicken stock, saffron, cinnamon stick, and salt. Increase heat to high and bring to a boil. Reduce heat to low, cover, and simmer until all liquid is absorbed and rice is fluffy, about 15 to 20 minutes.

While the rice is cooking, warm a small skillet over medium heat. Add pine nuts to the skillet and sauté for 2 to 4 minutes, until the nuts release their aroma. Stir and make sure that all of the pine nuts are toasted. If needed, sauté for another 2 to 4 minutes, making sure that pine nuts do not burn. Remove from the heat and set aside.

When rice is finished cooking, let it stand, covered, for 10 minutes. Fluff it with a fork, and spoon into a serving bowl. Garnish with toasted pine nuts and serve hot.

4 SERVINGS

INGREDIENTS

1 tablespoon clarified butter (*ghee*)

2 cups Egyptian or other short-grain rice, rinsed and drained

3½ cups chicken stock

½ teaspoon saffron, crushed

1 cinnamon stick

½ teaspoon salt

2 tablespoons pine nuts

Chicken Breasts Stuffed with Cheese, Tomato, and Hulled Grains

[Sedriyat Firakh Mahshi bil Gebna Rumi ,Tomatum, wa Freekh]

4 SERVINGS

INGREDIENTS

2 tablespoons clarified butter (*ghee*)

1 medium yellow onion, diced

3/4 cup hulled grain, rinsed*

23/4 cups chicken stock

1 tablespoon expeller pressed corn oil

6 cloves garlic, minced

1 cup plus 1 tablespoon diced tomatoes

1 teaspoon ground coriander

Salt to taste

Freshly ground black pepper to taste

1 tablespoon white vinegar

1 ounce shredded sheep's milk cheese (Romano, Kesseri, or Machego)

1/2 cup fresh parsley, chopped

4 boneless chicken breast halves, sliced in half width-wise

1 tablespoon olive oil

Juice of 1 lemon

Hulled grains are a traditional Middle Eastern ingredient that have a smoky taste and slightly chewy consistency. This is a recipe I invented after tasting a bone-in chicken breast stuffed with a similar mixture at Astor Mediterranean, an Egyptian-owned restaurant in Washington, D.C. The ingredients in the stuffing are both nutritious and delicious, and they combine to make a very unique, tasty, and impressive main course.

Preparation:

Melt 1 tablespoon of the clarified butter in a medium saucepan over medium heat. Add the onion and sauté until translucent, about 3 to 5 minutes. Add the hulled grain and stir. Add the chicken stock and increase the heat to high. Bring the mixture to a boil, reduce heat to low, stir, and cover. Cook for approximately 40 minutes to 1 hour, until all of the liquid is absorbed and the grain is tender.

While grain is cooking prepare the tomato sauce: Warm the corn oil over medium heat in a medium saucepan. Add the garlic and cook, stirring slowly, until it begins to color. Add 1 cup of the tomatoes to the pan, mix well, and stir in the coriander and a sprinkling of salt and pepper. Continue to cook over medium-high heat until the mixture begins to boil. Reduce heat to low and allow sauce to simmer, stirring every 5 minutes or so, until the mixture becomes thick. Sauce is ready when it has reduced to less than half of its original volume, about 30 minutes. Stir in vinegar and allow to cook for 5 more minutes. Taste and adjust salt and pepper to taste. Remove from heat and leave covered until ready to serve.

When hulled grain is finished cooking, stir in remaining 1 tablespoon of tomatoes and the cheese and parsley, and then taste and adjust seasonings if necessary.

continued on next page

Chicken Breasts Stuffed with Cheese, Tomato, and Hulled Grains
continued from previous page

Place a large sheet of wax paper on a work surface. Place chicken breasts on wax paper. Cover with another sheet of wax paper. Gently pound chicken breasts to flatten. Remove top sheet of wax paper. Place 1 teaspoon of the hulled grain mixture in the center of each chicken breast. Roll up chicken breasts to cover filling and secure with undyed wooden toothpicks.

Heat remaining 1 tablespoon of clarified butter and olive oil in a large saucepan over medium-high heat. Add chicken breasts and brown on all sides. Squeeze lemon juice over chicken. Add the tomato sauce and reduce temperature to low. Cover and simmer until chicken is cooked through, approximately 20 minutes.

When ready to serve, reheat remaining hulled grain mixture over low heat and spoon onto a serving platter (either in a mound in the middle or covering the bottom like a bed for the chicken). Place chicken pieces around the hulled grain or on top of it, removing the toothpicks from each piece. Top each piece of chicken with some of the tomato sauce. Serve warm.

TIP ▶ *You can make the filling and tomato sauce a day in advance and assemble and cook the chicken breasts the following day.*

*See Where to Buy Guide on pages 203–205 for purchasing information. To rinse hulled grain, place it in a bowl, cover it with water, drain, and continue rinsing it and draining until the water runs clear.

Kebabgy Restaurant, Luxor, Egypt

Eggplant and Tomato Casserole

[M'saa'a]

4 SERVINGS

INGREDIENTS

1 tablespoon expeller pressed corn oil, plus extra for frying

1 small yellow onion, diced

6 large garlic cloves, minced

3 cups strained chopped tomatoes

1 teaspoon ground coriander

1 teaspoon ground cumin

Salt to taste

Freshly ground black pepper to taste

1 large eggplant, sliced into ¼-inch-thick slices

1 cup grated cheddar or mozzarella cheese (optional)

Egyptian Eggplant and Tomato Casserole is the forerunner of Italian eggplant parmesan and Greek moussaka. It can be made with or without ground or minced beef added to the sauce. I first learned to make it when I was working as a consulting chef at the Kebabgy restaurant in Luxor, Egypt. When I witnessed the head chef putting cheddar cheese on top, I could not believe my eyes. Despite the untraditional twist, his M'saa'a was the best I've tasted. Purists, however, may choose to make a cheeseless version. My friend Sabah says that her family serves M'saa'a *at a weekly brunch held after the congregational Muslim prayer on Friday.*

Preparation:

Preheat oven to 350 degrees F. Heat 1 tablespoon corn oil in a large saucepan over medium heat. Add onion and cook, uncovered, until translucent, about 3 to 5 minutes. Add garlic and cook until golden. Add tomatoes, coriander, cumin, and some salt and pepper to taste and stir. Bring mixture to a boil, cover, and reduce heat to medium-low. Simmer for 20 minutes or until thickened.

Meanwhile, prepare the eggplant by heating 1 inch of corn oil in a large wide skillet over medium-high heat. When the oil is hot, add eggplant slices and fry until soft and lightly golden on both sides, approximately 5 minutes. Remove from oil with a slotted spoon and drain on a plate or cookie sheet lined with paper towels.

To assemble the casserole, pour one-third of the tomato sauce on the bottom of a 9- or 10-inch round or oval baking dish. (This can also be made in single-serving-size ramekins or Egyptian tagins.) Top with a layer of eggplant (using half of the eggplant). Pour half of the remaining sauce over the eggplant and continue layering with the rest of eggplant and covering with a final layer of sauce. Sprinkle cheese on top, if using. Bake the eggplant casserole, uncovered, for 20 to 30 minutes, until the top is bubbly and a crust begins to form around the edges.

TIP ▶ *Serve with Egyptian Rice (page 22) for a great vegetarian lunch or dinner.*

Deep-Fried Cauliflower

[Arnabit Ma'li]

These delicious fritters are popular all over the Mediterranean. In Egypt, they are often eaten with breakfast. I have chosen to include them in a dinner menu because that is when people are most apt to prepare them outside of Egypt. This dish is best eaten the day it is prepared. I assure you that you probably will not have to worry about leftovers—like chips and popcorn, deep fried cauliflower is almost addictive.

4 SERVINGS

INGREDIENTS

1 cup water

2 large eggs, lightly beaten

1 cup unbleached, all-purpose flour

1 teaspoon saffron, crushed

1 teaspoon salt

1 head cauliflower, about 1½ pounds, cut or broken into florets

Expeller pressed corn oil, for frying

Preparation:

Place the water and eggs in a medium bowl. Gradually incorporate the flour by stirring with a whisk to combine. Stir in saffron and salt and set aside.

Wash the cauliflower and remove any brown spots; place in a colander and drain well. Bring a large pot of water to a boil. Add salt and the cauliflower florets. Cook, uncovered, for 3 to 5 minutes, until tender. Drain and rinse the cauliflower under cold water to stop the cooking.

Heat 2 inches of corn oil in a medium saucepan over medium-high heat. When the oil is hot, dip the cauliflower florets into the batter, then carefully lower a few at a time into the oil. After 1 or 2 minutes, when they are golden on one side, turn them over and cook for another 1 or 2 minutes on the other side. Remove from the oil with a slotted spoon and transfer to paper towels to drain. Sprinkle lightly with salt and serve hot.

Date K'nafeh

[K'nafeh bil Tamr]

15 SERVINGS

INGREDIENTS

SYRUP:

1½ cups sugar

2 large strips of orange peel

Juice of 1 small orange

FILLING:

1 cup soft pitted dates, chopped

¼ cup raisins

¼ cup shelled pistachios, chopped

¼ cup shredded coconut

1 teaspoon rose water*

1 teaspoon orange blossom water*

K'NAFEH:

4 sticks unsalted butter, melted

1 (1 pound) package *kataifi*, thawed*

My husband remembers his mother making Date K'nafeh during his childhood. We added a few more ingredients and came up with a recipe for this sweet, moist, and delicious version.

Preparation:

Make the syrup: Put sugar, 1 cup of water, orange peel, and orange juice into a medium saucepan. Bring to a boil over medium heat, stirring with a wooden spoon until sugar is dissolved. Stop stirring, reduce heat to low, and simmer approximately 10 to 15 minutes, until syrup thickens. Remove from heat and cool. Remove orange peel from syrup.

Make the filling: Place dates, raisins, pistachios, coconut, rose water, and orange blossom water in a food processor. Pulse on and off until mixture is coarsely ground.

To assemble the *k'nafeh*: Place melted butter in a large, deep bowl. Holding the *kataifi* strands over the butter, pull them apart, allowing them to fall into the butter. Toss them with the butter, using your fingers to combine and continue breaking the strands up until they are each 1 to 2 inches long.

Press half of strands into the bottom of a 9x13-inch baking pan. Spread the filling evenly over the top. Press the remaining *kataifi* strands over the filling to cover. Cover the surface of the *k'nafeh* with tin foil. Place 2 weights (5 pounds each) on top (bags of sugar or cans work fine). Refrigerate 1 hour or up to overnight.

Preheat oven to 350 degrees F. Take weights off and uncover *k'nafeh*. With a sharp, long serrated knife, carefully cut the *k'nafeh* three-quarters of the way through into 30 squares. Place in the oven and bake for 1 hour and 20 minutes, rotating pan every 20 minutes to ensure even baking. The *k'nafeh* is finished when it is golden in color. Remove from the oven and carefully pour the syrup over the *k'nafeh*. Let cool completely and use a spatula to serve.

*See Where to Buy Guide on pages 203–205 for purchasing information. *Kataifi* is sold as "shredded phyllo strands."

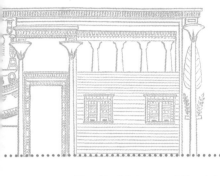

Powdered Orchid Drink

[Sahlab]

Try this drink on a chilly night instead of hot chocolate and you'll have a new favorite! Sahlab *is a smooth, creamy drink, satisfying enough to take the place of dessert. It is made from the starch found in ground orchid bulbs. Instant* sahlab *mixes can be found in Middle Eastern markets. I have seen other recipes that substitute cornstarch for the orchid powder, but I do not recommend it. The unique orchid flavoring is what makes this drink special. Many coffee shops serve* Sahlab *with a topping of chopped roasted peanuts, sliced strawberries, dried coconut, and/or whipped cream.*

INGREDIENTS

4 cups whole milk

¹/₄ cup instant *sahlab* powder*

1 teaspoon orange blossom water*

GARNISHES

4 teaspoons roasted, unsalted peanuts, coarsely chopped

4 strawberries, sliced

2 teaspoons dried coconut, if desired

Whipped cream, if desired

Preparation:

Bring milk to a boil in a medium saucepan over medium heat. Add *sahlab* powder, stir, and reduce heat to low. Add orange blossom water and stir to combine. Pour mixture into serving mugs, tea cups, or clear, heatproof glasses. Sprinkle peanuts evenly on the top of the *sahlab*. Top each with 1 sliced strawberry, ½ teaspoon coconut, and a dot of whipped cream, if desired, and serve hot.

*See Where to Buy Guide on pages 203–205 for purchasing information.

Nile-Style Street Food

Street food is an easy and inexpensive way to experience different cultures. No matter where you go in Egypt, street food will not be far. Walking along the Nile Corniche in Cairo you can sample *Fuul Medammes* (pureed fava beans), freshly roasted nuts, popcorn, roasted corn on the cob. Hot tea, lupine beans, and chickpeas are popular snacks for those strolling along the Mediterranean in Alexandria.

In residential neighborhoods you will find everything from breads to falafel, grilled fish, and kabobs prepared on the streets. In the mornings, you can even find Hot Wheat Berry Cereal sold in bags. Special drinks like licorice root, coconut, and strawberry juice are also sold on the street. Some people set up stands and tables outside of their apartment buildings and prepare food during rush hours when people are coming and going to school and work. This section contains great recipes for whenever you're in the mood for something satisfying and special.

Nile-Style Street Food Menu

▶ Sesame Bread Rings

▶ Lamb Pies

▶ Lamb Rib Kabobs with Arugula and Tahini

▶ Spinach and Meat Triangles

▶ Mixed Nut K'nafeh

▶ Orange, Strawberry, and Mint Cocktail

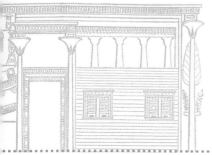

Sesame Bread Rings

[Simit]

Simit *are popular street snacks in both Egypt and Turkey. In Egypt, they are sold at busy traffic intersections throughout the city. Vendors walk back and forth along the medians and sell the* simit *stacked onto dowels sticking out of wooden trays that they carry on their heads. The size of the* simit *range from small, single servings (which is what this recipe makes), to large rings that are meant to be shared. They taste great with tea for a snack, or with jams and cheeses for breakfast. Sesame Bread Rings can be frozen in plastic bags for up to a month. To serve, thaw at room temperature and warm.*

MAKES 4 (4¼-INCH) RINGS

INGREDIENTS

2¼ cups unbleached bread flour

½ teaspoon salt

4 tablespoons unsalted butter, melted

2 teaspoons olive oil

½ cup whole milk

1 egg, lightly beaten

4 tablespoons sesame seeds

Preparation:

Preheat oven to 425 degrees F. Grease 2 baking sheets with unsalted butter and set aside.

Sift flour and salt into a large bowl. Make a crater in the middle and add melted butter, olive oil, 6 tablespoons of water, ¼ cup of the milk, and the egg. Mix well to combine until a dough forms.

On a lightly floured work surface, knead dough for 5 to 10 minutes, until it becomes smooth and elastic. Roll the dough into a 12-inch log and cut it into 4 3-inch-long pieces. Using your hands roll each piece into a 16-inch-long log. Wrap the logs around to form circles and press the ends to seal.

Place rings on a baking sheet and brush with remaining ¼ cup of milk. Sprinkle 1 tablespoon of sesame seeds on the top of each ring and bake, side by side, on the bottom rack of the oven for 20 to 25 minutes or until golden and crispy. Allow to cool and serve.

Lamb Pies

[Howowhsi]

MAKES 10

INGREDIENTS

DOUGH:

1 tablespoon active dry yeast

1 teaspoon salt

2¹/₂ cups unbleached, all-purpose flour

¹/₂ cup whole-wheat pastry flour

¹/₄ cup plus 2 tablespoons olive oil

FILLING:

1 pound ground lamb

1 medium yellow onion, finely chopped

¹/₄ cup plain yogurt, drained in a cheesecloth-lined colander

Juice of 1 lemon

1 teaspoon salt

¹/₄ teaspoon freshly ground black pepper

Lamb pies are a great portable snack and lunch in Egypt. While this recipe includes making the dough from scratch, purchased bread or pizza dough could be used as well. Many Egyptian cooks now buy prepared dough instead of making it themselves but if you have the time, this homemade version is delightful. These pies could also be filled with ground veal, beef, or turkey. Both the filling and dough can be made the night before and stored in the refrigerator, covered, until the next day.

Preparation:

Make dough: Pour 1¹/₄ cups lukewarm water into a bowl. Add yeast and stir to dissolve. Add salt and stir. Add both flours, 1 cup at a time, stirring thoroughly after each addition. Once all of the flour is incorporated, add 1 tablespoon olive oil and mix well. Turn dough out onto a clean, lightly floured surface. Knead dough until it is smooth, approximately 5 to 7 minutes. Place in a large oiled bowl, cover with a clean kitchen towel, and allow to sit in a warm, draft-free place until doubled in size, approximately 1 hour.

In the meantime prepare the filling: Mix the lamb, onion, yogurt, and lemon juice together. Season with salt and freshly ground pepper and stir. Refrigerate until dough has risen.

Preheat the oven to 375 degrees F. Line 3 baking sheets with aluminum foil and grease with 1 tablespoon olive oil. When dough has risen, punch it down and divide it into 10 equal-size balls. Using a rolling pin flatten each ball into a 6-inch circle. Place 1 tablespoon of meat filling in the middle of each circle and fold the sides of the circles over the filling. Place the pies 1-inch apart on the cookie sheets. Brush the tops of the pies with the remaining ¹/₄ cup of olive oil and bake for 30 minutes or until golden and meat is cooked through.

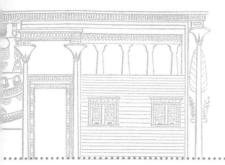

Lamb Ribs with Arugula and Tahini

[Rayesh bil Gargeer wa Tahina]

Driving into the small yet bustling town of Queweisna (pronounced Wesna) *from the highway, the light posts have signs declaring* Allahu Akbar, *"God is Great." Then as you proceed, each of the 99 names of God (in the Muslim tradition) are posted on signs, as are other signs promoting* zikr, *or the remembrance of God.*

The streets are crowded at lunchtime as workers, shopkeepers, and school children make their way back home for lunch. The town butcher is conveniently located next door to the kabob shop that makes perfectly grilled succulent strips of lamb served on a bed of shredded arugula (considered peasant food in Egypt) and tahini sauce with fresh pita bread. Although grilled meat has never been one of my favorite foods, "the kabobs of Queweisna" have caused me to become obsessed with them. I tasted there. I believe that part of their secret is pounding out the lamb meat before putting it on the grill. With this method, you retain all of the flavor that comes from the bone, but the flattened surface cooks more quickly and evenly.

Preparation:

Using a meat pounder, pound the lamb chops until they are about ⅛-inch thick.

Place onion, garlic, lemon juice, lime juice, red pepper flakes, cumin, cinnamon, paprika, coriander, vinegar, corn oil, salt, and pepper in a large shallow bowl. Mix well to combine and place lamb rib chops in mixture, turning to coat. Cover and allow chops to marinate for 2 hours or up to overnight in the refrigerator.

Preheat grill or grill pan on medium-high heat. Drain lamb rib chops and shake off excess marinade. Place chops, fat side up, onto grill or grill pan. Cook for 5 to 7 minutes per side or until desired doneness. Cover chops with tinfoil and allow to rest for 10 minutes before serving.

To serve, place chopped arugula or cilantro on a large platter. Place lamb rib chops on the greens and place warmed pita bread on top of meat. Serve with a bowl of Tahini Sauce.

4 SERVINGS

INGREDIENTS

- 2 pounds lamb rib chops (bone-in)
- 1 yellow onion, coarsely chopped
- 2 cloves garlic, minced
- Juice of 1 lemon
- Juice of 1 lime
- Pinch of dried crushed red pepper flakes
- ½ teaspoon ground cumin
- ½ teaspoon ground cinnamon
- ½ teaspoon paprika
- ½ teaspoon ground coriander
- 1 tablespoon vinegar
- ¼ cup expeller pressed corn oil
- 1 teaspoon salt
- ½ teaspoon freshly ground black pepper
- 1 bunch fresh arugula or cilantro, chopped, for serving
- 4 pita breads, for serving
- 1 recipe Tahini Sauce (page 160), for serving

Spinach and Meat Triangles

[Fatayer bil Sabanikh wa Lahma]

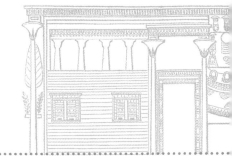

MAKES APPROXIMATELY 2 DOZEN

INGREDIENTS

BREAD:

1 tablespoon active dry yeast

2 cups unbleached, all purpose flour, plus extra for work surface

2 teaspoons extra-virgin olive oil

½ teaspoon salt

FILLING:

2 tablespoons olive oil

1 grated onion, drained well

¼ pound finely ground or minced beef

¾ cup frozen chopped spinach, thawed and squeezed well

Juice of 1 lemon

Salt to taste

Fatayer are tender bread triangles stuffed with a variety of ingredients. They can be found in bread bakeries, at streetside stalls, and in home kitchens. In Egypt, these delightful snacks are usually served at breakfast, but I like to also make them as special appetizers on holidays. Both the filling and the bread dough can be made in advance and stored in the refrigerator. The Spinach and Meat Triangles can also be prepared and frozen for up to a month. Thaw them at room temperature and reheat them in the oven before serving. Be sure to use very finely ground beef or minced meat to achieve the right consistency for the filling.

Preparation:

Make bread dough: Combine yeast with ¼ cup tepid water in a large mixing bowl and let sit for a few minutes to dissolve. Add flour, 1 teaspoon olive oil, and salt. Mix well until blended. Add ⅓ cup water, a little at a time, until dough is smooth. Turn dough out onto a lightly floured work surface and knead until smooth and elastic, from 5 to 10 minutes. Oil another large bowl with remaining teaspoon of olive oil. Place dough in bowl and turn to coat with olive oil. Cover with a kitchen cloth and let rise in a warm place for 1 hour or until doubled in size.

Make the filling: Heat the olive oil in a large frying pan over medium heat. Add the onion and sauté until yellow, about 5 minutes. Break up ground beef with your fingers and add it to the onion. Stir the mixture while cooking until meat is browned. Stir in spinach, lemon juice, and salt to taste. Remove from heat and allow to cool to room temperature before proceeding.

Preheat the oven to 350 degrees F. Line two cookie sheets with parchment paper or grease with butter or oil. Take dough out of the bowl and place on a lightly floured work surface. Lightly dust the top of the dough and a rolling pin with flour. Roll out the dough to approximately ⅛-inch thickness. Cut out 24 (3-inch) circles (the floured rim of a glass works fine).

continued on next page

Place a scant teaspoon of filling in the center of a circle. Fill a small bowl with water and keep it next to the dough. Dip your fingers into the water and wet the outer edges of the dough circle. Bring the bottom half of the circle up to the middle and pinch in the top two sides of the circle and press to seal with the bottom half to form a triangle. If the dough does not seal easily enough, use more water to coat the edges. Repeat process with remaining circles.

Place 12 triangles on each cookie sheet, leaving space between each one. Bake for 20 to 30 minutes, until golden brown, making sure not to open the oven during the first 10 minutes of baking. Serve warm.

Mixed Nut K'nafeh

[K'nafeh bil M'kassarat]

15 SERVINGS

INGREDIENTS

SYRUP:
1½ cups sugar
2 large strips of orange peel
Juice of 1 small orange

FILLING:
½ cup walnuts, chopped
½ cup blanched almonds, chopped
½ cup shelled pistachios, chopped
½ cup roasted, unsalted peanuts, chopped
2 tablespoons sugar
1 teaspoon orange blossom water*

K'NAFEH:
4 sticks unsalted butter, melted
1 (1 pound) package *kataifi*, thawed*

K'nafeh can be filled with nuts, sweet cream, or sweet cheese and stored in the refrigerator for up to 3 days, but it is best eaten the day it is prepared. Keep in mind that this dessert needs to be weighed down in the refrigerator for at least one hour.

Preparation:

Make the syrup: Put sugar, orange peel, orange juice and 1 cup of water into a medium saucepan. Bring to a boil over medium heat, stirring with a wooden spoon until sugar is dissolved. Stop stirring, reduce heat to low, and simmer approximately 10 to 15 minutes, until syrup thickens. Remove from heat and cool. Remove orange peel from syrup, cover and set aside until needed.

Make the filling: Combine walnuts, almonds, pistachios, peanuts, sugar, and orange blossom water in a food processor. Pulse on and off until mixture is coarsely ground.

Assemble the *k'nafeh*: Place melted butter in a large, deep bowl. Holding the *kataifi* strands over the butter, pull them apart and allow to fall into the butter. Toss them with the butter using your fingers and continue breaking the strands up until the strands are 1 to 2 inches long.

Press half of strands into the bottom of a 9x13-inch baking pan. Spread the filling evenly over the top. Press the remaining *kataifi* strands over the filling to cover. Cover the surface of the *k'nafeh* with tin foil. Place 2 weights (5 pounds each) on top (bags of sugar or cans work fine). Refrigerate 1 hour or up to overnight.

Preheat oven to 350 degrees F. Take weights off and uncover *k'nafeh*. With a sharp, long serrated knife, carefully cut 30 squares inside the pan, cutting just three-quarters of the way through. Place in the oven and bake for 1 hour and 20 minutes, rotating pan every 20 minutes to ensure even baking. The *k'nafeh* is finished when it is golden in color. Remove the *k'nafeh* from the oven and carefully pour the syrup over it while still hot. Let cool completely and use a spatula to serve.

TIP ▶ *Make the syrup and filling up to a month ahead of time and store in airtight containers in the refrigerator. Assemble and weigh the k'nafeh the night before serving it. On the day of serving all you'll need to do is cut it, bake it, and pour the syrup on top.*

*See Where to Buy Guide on pages 203–205 for purchasing information. *Kataifi* is sold as "shredded phyllo dough."

Orange, Strawberry, and Mint Cocktail

[Cocktail bil Firwila, Bortuan wa Na'na]

I sampled this delicious cocktail at the Windsor Palace in Alexandria, Egypt, while I was leading an Italian tour group. The children in the group, Gabriele and Erika, were inspired to order the drink because of its bright tri-color presentation. Once the adults got a taste of it, they promptly ordered their own!

Preparation:

Chill 4 clear glasses. Puree strawberries in blender until frothy. Add sugar to taste, and whip until combined. Divide strawberry juice equally among the 4 glasses.

MAKES 4 COCKTAILS

INGREDIENTS

1 pound strawberries, cleaned and trimmed

1/4 cup sugar, or to taste

1 cup orange juice

4 teaspoons mint syrup

4 mint sprigs

Holding the back of a spoon over the strawberry juice (this prevents the two colors from mixing), pour 1/4 cup of orange juice over the top of the spoon. Repeat with the other three glasses. Pour 1 teaspoon of mint syrup into each glass on top of the orange juice and garnish each with a mint sprig. Serve immediately.

Fruit Cocktails, Windsor Palace Hotel, Alexandria, Egypt

Glossary of Ingredients Commonly Used in Egyptian Cuisine

(See Where to Buy Guide on pages 203–205 for purchasing information.)

bulgur Bulgur is a parboiled and dried wheat that is processed into grains.

clarified butter You can clarify butter by melting it and removing the white solids from the top. Clarified butter can also be bought in specialty food markets. Ghee is aged clarified butter sold in Indian and specialty food markets and can be substituted in savory applications.

dried coconut #1 Unsweetened coconut that has been dried and ground.

Egyptian rice Short/medium grain rice produced in Egypt and available in Mediterranean and Middle Eastern markets. Substitute medium grain or Arborio rice if necessary.

expeller pressed oils Expeller pressed refers to the cold extraction of various commercial cooking oils. With the exception of cold-pressed olive oils, vegetable oils that are not expeller pressed are usually extracted using chemicals and heat. It is worth seeking out expeller pressed (organic) vegetable oils for their superior quality.

fuul medammes Broad or fava beans prepared in Egyptian manner.

hulled grains Known as *firikh*, hulled grains are a traditional Middle Eastern ingredient that have a smoky taste and slightly chewy consistency.

kataifi Pastry strands that are sold as "shredded phyllo dough" in English. This is a bit of a misnomer, however, because it implies that phyllo sheets are prepared and then shredded. Actually, the strands are made by brushing batter onto a hot griddle in a circle pattern. The strands are then removed from the griddle and formed into bunches.

maloukhiya Green, leafy herb known as "Jew's Mallow" in English.

orange blossom water Water made from orange blossom oils, this is used as a flavoring for syrups and sweets.

rice flour Flour made from ground rice that is commonly used as a thickening agent in Mediterranean and Asian countries.

rose water Water made from the distillation of rose oil. Used to enhance the flavor of drinks, syrups, and sweets.

semolina Semolina is the heart of durum wheat. It has a yellowish color and is processed to make pasta, couscous, and baked goods in Mediterranean and Middle Eastern cuisine.

sumac Made by grinding the seeds of the sumac plant, which is a member of the cashew family. It produces a beautiful red powder that gives a tangy taste to chicken, eggs, spice mixes, rice, and dips.

tahini A sesame-seed paste referred to as *tahina* in Arabic.

zataar A variety of wild thyme used throughout the Middle East both fresh and dried. There are also various spice mixes called *zataar,* which usually contain *zataar* itself along with sumac, sesame seeds, and salt.

Where To Buy Guide

(See contact information on page 205.)

Arabic Sweet Cheese Aphrodite, Kalustyans

Arabic Tea Aphrodite, Kalustyans, Turkish Taste

Baby Eggplant Kalustyans, Melissas, Whole Foods Markets

Barley Aphrodite, Diamond Organics, Kalustyans, Whole Foods Markets

Bulgur Adriana's Caravan, Aphrodite, Diamond Organics, Kalustyans, Whole Foods Markets

Clarified Butter (*Samn* or *Ghee*) Aphrodite, Kalustyans

Dried Coconut #1 Aphrodite, Whole Foods Markets

Dried Dates Aphrodite, Kalustyans, Turkish Taste, Zabar's

Dried Figs Aphrodite, Kalustyans, Turkish Taste, Zabar's

Egyptian Cheese Aphrodite

Egyptian Pickles Aphrodite, Kalustyans

Egyptian Rice Aphrodite, Kalustyans

Fava Beans (*Fuul Medammes*) (also known as Broad Beans) Adriana's Caravan, Aphrodite, Kalustyans

Hibiscus Leaves/Petals Adriana's Caravan, Aphrodite

Hulled Grains (*Firakh*) Aphrodite, Kalustyans

Kataifi (shredded phyllo strands) Aphrodite, Kalustyans

Labna Aphrodite, Kalustyans, Whole Foods Market

Licorice Root Adriana's Caravan, Aphrodite

Mahlab (ground cherry kernels) Adriana's Caravan, Aphrodite, Kalustyans, Turkish Taste

Maloukhiya (frozen) Aphrodite, Kalustyans

Nigelia Seeds Adriana's Caravan

Nuts Aphrodite, Kalustyans, Turkish Taste, Zabar's, Whole Foods Market

Orange Blossom Water Adriana's Caravan, Aphrodite, Kalustyans

Pomegranate Molasses Adriana's Caravan, Aphrodite, The Spice House

Preserved Lemons Aphrodite, Kalustyans

Rice Flour Aphrodite, Kalustyans, Whole Foods Markets

Rose Water Adriana's Caravan, Aphrodite, Kalustyans, The Spice House

Sahlab Powder Aphrodite, Turkish Taste

Semolina Aphrodite, Diamond Organics, Kalustyans, Turkish Taste

Spices Adriana's Caravan, Aphrodite, Kalustyans, The Spice House, Turkish Taste, Zabar's

Sumac Adriana's Caravan, Aphrodite, Kalustyans, The Spice House

Tamarind Syrup Aphrodite, Kalustyans

Tahini Adriana's Caravan, Aphrodite, Kalustyans, The Spice House, Whole Foods Markets

Turkish Coffee Aphrodite, Kalustyans, Turkish Taste

Turkish Coffee Pots & Cups Aphrodite, Kalustyans, Turkish Taste

Vermicelli Aphrodite, Kalustyans, Turkish Taste

Vine Leaves Adriana's Caravan, Aphrodite, Kalustyans

Whole Wheat Berries Aphrodite, Diamond Organics, Turkish Taste, Whole Foods Markets

Whole-Wheat Pastry Flour Diamond Organics, Kalustyans, Whole Foods Markets

Zataar Adriana's Caravan, Aphrodite, Kalustyans

Contact Information

You can order specialty ingredients from the following sources:

Adriana's Caravan
www.adrianascaravan.com

Aphrodite Greek & Middle Eastern Imports
5886 Leesburg Pike
Falls Church, VA 22041
(703) 931-5055

Diamond Organics
(888) - Organic
www.diamondorganics.com

Elite Naturel
Organic Juice USA, INC
www.organicjuiceusa.com

Kalustyan's
123 Lexington Avenue
New York, NY 10016
(212) 685-3451
www.kalustyans.com

Kamut Association
333 Kamut Lane
Big Sandy, Montana 59250
1-800-644-6450
www.kamut.com

Melissa's/World Variety Produce, Inc.
P.O. Box 21127
Los Angeles, CA 90021
(800) 588-0151
www.melissas.com

The Spice House
1941 Central Street
Evanston, IL 30201
(847) 328-3711

Sur La Table
1765 Sixth Avenue South
Seattle, WA 98134-1608
(866) 328-5412
www.surlatable.com

Turkish Taste
31 Downs Avenue
Greenland, NH 03840
(603) 661-5460
www.turkishtaste.com

Whole Foods Market
www.wholefoodsmarket.com

Zabar's
2245 Broadway
New York, NY 10024
(212) 787-2000
www.zabars.com

Where to Dine in Egypt

The following is a list of restaurants that I enjoy when I am in Egypt.

ALEXANDRIA

Fish Market
Fresh fish and seafood in a beautiful
  setting
El Kashafa el-Bahariya Club
26 Corniche el-Nile
03-480 5114

El Housny Restaurant
Fresh fish, seafood, and Egyptian
  cuisine in a lively neighborhood
Gamal Abd al Nasser Street
Al Mandara
(203) 550 66 55

Pastroudis Café
Coffee and pastries
39 Sharia el-Hurriya

Trianon Café
Coffee and pastries
Midan Zaghloul

Windsor Palace Hotel (Roof Top)
For coffee and tea
17 Shohada Street
El-Ramle Station
Alexandria
(203) 480 82 56

Venous Patisserie
Coffee and pastries
12 Sharia el-Hurriya

ASWAN

Al Masry Restaurant
Kebabs, kofta, and salads
Sharia al-Matar

Medina Restaurant
Inexpensive meal combinations in the
  Souk
Sharia as-Souq (across from the
  Cleopatra Hotel)

Restaurant el-Nil
Fresh fish from Lake Nasser
Corniche el Nile (near Thomas Cook)

CAIRO

Abu el Sid
Traditional Egyptian in an upscale
  Arabesque environment
157 26th of July Street
Zamalek

Abu Shakra
Classic Egyptian & Middle Eastern
  cuisine
17 Gamiat el Dowal el-Arabeya
Mohandiseen

Al Omda – Koushari
Salads, appetizers, and fruit juices
6 Sharia el Gazayer
(off of Gamiat el Dowal el-Arabeya)
02 – 345 2387

At Tahrir – Koushari
19 Abdel Khalek Sarwat
(Off of Talaat Harb Street)

El Abd Pastry
Excellent traditional pastries
Talaat Harb Street
Downtown

El Tabei
Wonderful *Fuul Medammes, Hommos, Sambousak*, appetizers, and salads (eat in and takeout)
Gamiat al Dowal al Arabiyya (just past Midan Mustafa Mahmoud)
Mohandiseen

Felfela
Schwarm and falafel (known as *t'amiya*)
15 Hoda Shawaarawi
Downtown

Gad
A full Egyptian menu in a diner-style setting
Adly Street (across from the synagogue)
Downtown

Kadoura
Fresh seafood and accompaniments
66 Gamiat al Dowal al Arabiyya
Midan Mustafa Mahmoud
335 06 22

Naguib Mahfouz
Great food in an arabesque setting
Khan el Khalili Restaurant
5 Sikket al-Badestan
Khan el Khalili Bazaar
Islamic Cairo

Tebesty
Plain, sweet, and savory *Fateer*
46 Mussdak Street
Dokki
Tebesty has locations all over Cairo and Alexandria. Check *www.otlob.com* for a location near you.

EL FAYOUM OASIS
Café Gabal el Zinah
Lake views and fresh fish
Birket Qarun

New Panorama Village
Shakshuk
Lake Qarun
084- 701 314

LUXOR
El Kebabgy Restaurant
A Luxor landmark serving kabobs, tagins, pizzas, and international favorites
Corniche el Nile
Across the street from the Egyptian National Bank

Metropolitan Café
Drinks, snacks, ice cream with a great Nile view
Corniche el Nile
Opposite Winter Palace and Luxor Temple

Metropolitan Restaurant
Extensive seafood selections with exquisite views
Corniche el Nile
Opposite the Luxor Museum

SINAI REGION

NUWEIBA
Aid Abu Goma
Fresh fish and Bedouin specialties (Further up the sea front from Tarabin)

SHARM EL SHEIKH
Safsafa Restaurant
Excellent Egyptian cuisine; locals
    atmosphere
Old Sharm Market

Tam Tam Oriental Café
Authentic cuisine at great prices
Na'ama Bay

*Author and Baltimore Luxor Alexandria Sister City Committee member Sonal Patel at a
commemorative celebration at the Metropolitan Restaurant in Luxor, Egypt*

Bibliography

BOOKS

Abbas, Jilian. *Festivals of Egypt.* Cairo: Hoopoe Books, 1995.

Al Akili. *Imam Muhammad, Natural Healing With The Medicine Of The Prophet.* Philadelphia: Pearl Publishing House, 1993.

Aldred, Cyril. *The Egyptians,* Third Edition. Thames and Hudson, 1998.

Ali, Abdullah Yusuf (Translator). *The Holy Qu'ran.* New Delhi, India: Kitab Bhavan, 1996.

Bey-Mardam, Farouk Ziryab. *Authentic Arab Cuisine.* Woodbury, CT.: Ici La Press, 2002.

Clark, Jacqueline and Farrow, Joanna. *Mediterranean: A Taste of the Sun in Over 150 Recipes.* London: Hermes House, 2001.

Davidson, Alan. *The Oxford Companion to Food.* New York: The Oxford University Press, 1999.

Epstein, Morris. *All About Jewish Holidays and Customs.* Ktav Publishing House, Inc., 1970.

Green, Gloria Kaufer. *The New Jewish Holiday Cookbook; An International Collection of Recipes and Customs.* New York: Times Books, 1985.

Halici, Nevin. *Sufi Cuisine.* London: Saqi Books, 2005.

Hattstein Markus and Delius, Peter, editors. *Islam; Art and Architecture.* Italy: Konemann, 2004.

Hawass, Zahi. *Curse of the Pharaohs: My Adventures with Mummies.* Washington, DC.: National Geographic Society, 2004
————. *Tutankhamun and The Golden Age of the Pharaohs.* Washington, DC: National Geographic, 2005.

Haykal, Muhammed Husayn. *The Life of Muhammed,* translated by al Faruqi, Isma'il Raji. American Trust Publications, 1976.

Herodotus. *The History Herodotus,* translated by David Green. Chicago: The University of Chicago Press, 1987.

Ilkin, Nur and Kaufman, Sheilah. *A Taste of Turkish Cuisine.* New York: Hippocrene Books, 2002.

Kaufman, Sheilah. *Sephardic Israeli Cuisine; A Mediterranean Mosaic.* New York: Hippocrene Books, 2002.

Quinn, R.M. *Ancient Grain, New Cereal.* Alexandria, VA: ASHS Press, 1999.

Marks, Gil. *The World of Jewish Desserts.* New York: Simon & Schuster, 2000.

Moser, Barry. *The Holy Bible; Containing All the Books Of The Old and New Testaments* (King James version). New York: Viking, 1999.

Muslim Students Association of the United States & Canada. *Muslim Holidays and Ceremonies*; Unit 10, Maryland: International Graphics Printing Service, 1974.

O'Leary, De Lacy. *Islamic Thought and It's Place in History.* New Delhi, India: Goodword Books, 2001.

Pateman, Robert and El-Hamamsy, Salwa. *Cultures of the World: Egypt.* San Jose, CA: Times Media Private Limited, 1993.

Pers, Meijer N. V. *French Cooking.* New York-Toronto: 'Round the World Books, 1972.

Richardson, Dan. *The Rough Guide to Egypt.* London: Rough Guides, Ltd., 2000.

Robertson, Carol. *Turkish Cooking: A Culinary Journey Through Turkey.* Crandall, TX: Frog, Ltd., 1996.

Rodenbeck, Max. *Cairo: The City Victorious.* New York: Knopf, 1999.

Segan, Francine. *The Philosopher's Kitchen: Recipes from Ancient Greece and Rome for The Modern Cook.* New York: Random House, 2004.

Siddiqi, Dr. Muzammil. *Hajj and Umra.* Washington, DC: Islamic Center.

Toussaint-Samat, Maguelonne. *History of Food.* Cambridge, MA: Blackwell Publishers, 1992.

Uddin, Zaheer. *A Handbook of Halaal & Haram Products,* Vol 2, 1st Edition. New York: Center for American Muslim Research and Information, 1997.

Witty, Rabbi Abraham and Rachel J. *Exploring Jewish Tradition: A Transliterated Guide to Everyday Practice and Observance.* Doubleday, 2001.

Zeidler, Judy. *Shavout Food: Turn Torah Fest into a Veggie Feast.* Los Angeles: The Jewish Journal of Greater Los Angeles, 2005-06-10.

NEWSLETTERS & FOLDERS

Egyptian Tourist Authority. *Egypt Folder,* New York.

Jewish Community Council of Cairo (JCC). *Bassatine News,* Issues 1-20, Cairo, Egypt.

National Gallery of Art. *Artistic Exchange: Europe and The Islamic World.* Washington, DC.: July, 2004.

LECTURES

Egypt's Other Pasts; A Pilgrimage Through The Splendors of Coptic, Greco-Roman and Islamic Legacies Symposium, The John F. Kennedy Center for the Performing Arts, Washington, DC: June 2005.

Mack, Rosamond E. Lecture: *Arts of Splendor: Islamic Luxury Goods in Renaissance Italy,* Washington, DC: National Gallery of Art, October 31, 2004.

WEBSITES

Saudi Aramco World 2005, *www.saudiaramcoworld.com*

Index (see also Recipe Index on page 213)

Recipe Index

NUTS. *See also* almonds; peanuts; pistachios; walnuts
Mixed Nut Plate [*Tabaa M'kassarat*], 108

OKRA
Beef and Okra Stew [*Lahma bil Bamya*], 167
Stewed Okra and Tomatoes [*Bamya Matbukh*], 23

ORANGES
Creamy Orange Pudding [*Mahallabayat Bortu'an*], 58
Orange, Strawberry, and Mint Cocktail [*Cocktail bil Firwila, Bortuan wa Na'na*], 200

PASTA
Couscous with Peas, Carrots, and Eggplant [*Couscousi ma Khodar*], 179
Egyptian Rice with Vermicelli [*Roz bil Shareya*], 166
Lentils, Rice, and Pasta with Spicy Tomato Sauce [*Koushari*], 47–48
Macaroni with Meat and Béchamel Sauce [*Macarona Bechamel*], 100–101
Vermicelli, Meat, and Tomato Soup [*Shorbat bil Sharleya, Lahma, wa Tomatum*], 99

PEANUTS
Mixed Nut K'nafeh [*K'nafeh bil M'kassarat*], 199
Peanuts, Coconut, and Raisin Baklava [*Goulash bi Fuul Sudani, wa Zabeeb*], 125–126

PEAS
Chicken, Pea, and Potato Soup [*Shorbat bil Firakh, Bisella, wa Batatis*], 128
Couscous with Peas, Carrots, and Eggplant [*Couscousi ma Khodar*], 179
Pea and Potato Salad [*Salata Batatis wa Bisella*], 147
Pea, Carrot, and Tomato Stew [*Bisella wa Gazar Matboukh*], 158

PEPPERS, BELL
Calf's Liver, Pepper, and Onion Sandwiches [*Sandaweech Kibda bil Filfil*], 137

Mixed Country Salad [*Salata Baladi*], 161

PEPPERS, ROASTED RED
Pomegranate, Walnut, and Red Pepper Puree [*Muhammara*], 178

PHYLLO
Cream-Filled Baklava [*Goulash bil Habib*], 173
Date K'nafeh [*K'nafeh bil Tamr*], 191
Double Chocolate Baklava [*Ba'lawa bil Chokolata*], 182
Mixed Nut K'nafeh [*K'nafeh bil M'kassarat*], 199
Peanuts, Coconut, and Raisin Baklava [*Goulash bi Fuul Sudani, wa Zabeeb*], 125–126
Phyllo Triangles Filled with Lamb [*Sambusak bil Lahma Dani*], 118
Phyllo Triangles with Cheese [*Sambousik bil Gebna*], 46
Savory Cheese Phyllo Pastry [*Goulash bil Gebna*], 132
Savory Phyllo Pastries with Meat [*Goulash bi Lahma*], 81

PISTACHIOS
Egyptian Rice, Apricot, and Pistachio Pudding [*Roz bi Laban bil Amr Din wa Fusdooq*], 175
Mixed Nut K'nafeh [*K'nafeh bil M'kassarat*], 199

POMEGRANATE MOLASSES
Eggplant Salad with Pomegranate Molasses [*Salata Ruman bil Dabs Ruman*], 53
Fattoush Salad [*Salata Fattoush*], 181
Pomegranate, Walnut, and Red Pepper Puree [*Muhammara*], 178

POTATOES
Chicken, Pea, and Potato Soup [*Shorbat bil Firakh, Bisella, wa Batatis*], 128
Egyptian Garlic Aioli [*Salata bil Toum*], 146
Lamb and Potato Stew [*Tagin Lahma Dani bil Batatis*], 131
Pea and Potato Salad [*Salata Batatis wa Bisella*], 147
Roasted Leg of Lamb with Potatoes [*Fakhda Mashwiya bil Batatas*], 79
Veal and Potato Tagin [*Tagin Bitello wa Batatas*], 56

Other Middle Eastern Cookbooks from Hippocrene Books

Egyptian Cooking
Samia Abdennour

From appetizers to desserts, some recipes included are *'Arnabit musa a'a* (Moussaka Cauliflower), *Samak bi-l-tahina* (Fish with Tahina Sauce), *Kosa matbukha bi-l-zabadi* (Zucchini Stewed in Yogurt), and *Lahma mu'assaga* (Savory Minced Beef). The chapters included are Mezze, Breakfast, Main Courses, Sweets and Desserts, Beverages, Kitchen Utensils, and Spices. This classic cookbook also includes a glossary of Arabic terms for ingredients, translated into English, and useful tips on shopping and using traditional cooking utensils.

199 pages · 5½ x 8½ · 0-7818-1643-7 · $12.95pb

The Lebanese Cookbook
Hussien Dekmak

"Some of the finest Lebanese food I have ever tasted."
—Patricia Wells, *International Herald Tribune*

In Lebanon the table is always full. Soups, salads, bread, *mezze*, and entrees are all served at the same time and shared around. The recipes in this book are traditional, home-style cooking prepared with easy-to-get ingredients. You can entertain all tastes by serving a selection of dishes from the various chapters in this wonderful cookbook.

155 pages · 8½ x 9½ · 978-0-7818-1208-5 · 4-color with photos throughout· $29.95hc

The Middle Eastern Kitchen
Ghillie Basan

"An insightful and detailed peek into the kitchens of Iran, Turkey, Syria, Lebanon, Jordan, Egypt, Saudi Arabia, and more. The photos by Jonathan Basan are beautiful, whether of goatherds in Yemen, a Lebanese landscape or of dishes such as *makloub*

(Palestinian rice with chestnuts) or *meghlie* (rice pudding with aniseed)...a fine book to peruse and to cook from when you feel like being transported to a foreign land, but don't have the time or money to leave home."

— New York Daily News

This remarkable and beautifully illustrated book describes more than 75 ingredients used in Middle Eastern cooking. The insightful texts take readers and cooks into the history and diversity of these ancient cultures, while 150 recipes and color photographs allow them to put their knowledge of these ingredients to practical use.

240 pages · 8 x 10 · 0-7818-1023-X · $29.50hc

Mama Nazima's Jewish-Iraqi Cuisine
Rivka Goldman

With Mongolian, Turkish and Indian influences, Jewish-Iraqi cuisine is a special blend—and has never been before documented. Rivka Goldman takes the reader through her memories of an ancient land and culture by means of the culinary heritage passed on to her by her mother.

This insightful cookbook memoir describes the many ways in which the unique sociopolitical history of the Jewish-Iraqi has impacted their foods and the ways in which they are eaten, supplying over 100 healthful family recipes. Hearty stuffed vegetables, meat dishes, refreshing salads and much more accompany tales of friendship loyalty, persecution, escape, exile, and of course, celebration.

192 pages · 6 x 9 · 0-7818-1144-9 · $24.95

Sephardic Israeli Cuisine: A Mediterranean Mosaic
Sheilah Kaufman

Sephardic, derived from the Hebrew word for Spain, defines the Jews of Spain, Portugal, North Africa and the Middle East. The foods of these Mediterranean countries profoundly influenced the Sephardic Israeli cuisine, which abounds with ingredients such as cinnamon, saffron, orange flower water, *tahini* paste, artichokes, fava beans, couscous, bulgur, persimmons, peaches, and limes.

Sephardic Israeli Cuisine offers 120 kosher recipes that celebrate the colorful and delicious culinary mosaic it represents. Using typical Sephardic ingredients, it includes favorites like Yogurt Cheese; Crescent Olive Puffs; Harira: Tamar's Yemenite Chicken Soup; Grilled Fish with Chermoula; Moroccan Cholent; and Moroccan Sweet Potato Pie.

261 pages · 5 ½ x 8 ½ · 0-7818-0926-6 · $24.95hc

Taste of Turkish Cuisine
Nur Ilkin and Sheilah Kaufman

The traditional dishes featured in *A Taste of Turkish Cuisine* make use of a variety of beans, grains, fresh fruits, vegetables, herbs, and, of course, yogurt, one of Turkey's most important contributions to international cuisine. Simple yet rich in flavors, Turkish cuisine resounds of its varied influences, which range from Chinese and Mongolian to Persian and Greek. A history of Turkey's culinary traditions accompanies the 187 recipes, as well as glossaries of commonly used ingredients and Turkish cooking terms.

273 pages · 6 x 9 · 0-7818-0948-7· $24.95hc

A Pied Noir Cookbook French Sephardic Cuisine from Algeria
Chantal Clabrough

This unique cookbook relates the story of the Pied Noir or "Black Feet," Sephardic Jews from the North African nation of Algeria. The cuisine of the Pied Noir reflects a storied history: Expelled from Spain, and later forced to flee Algeria, their cookery was influenced by the nations they inhabited, as well as the trade routes that passed through these areas. Over the centuries, they collected recipes and flavors that came to form a unique and little-known culinary repertoire. The 85 recipes in this fascinating book are accompanied by a history of the Pied Noir and the story of the author's family. A glossary of culinary terms and menus for Pied Noir feasts are also included.

128 pages · 6 x 9 · 0-7818-1082-5 · $24.95hc

The Art of Persian Cooking
Forough Hekmat

The nutritious, easy-to-follow recipes include such traditional Persian dishes as *Abgushte Adas* (Lentil Soup), *Mosamme Khoreshe* (Eggplant Stew), *Lamb Kabob, Cucumber Borani* (Special Cucumber Salad), *Sugar Halva,* and *Gol Moraba* (Flower Preserves).

From creating a holiday menu to determining which utensils to use, this insightful title covers a wide array of practical information to help even the novice chef prepare elaborate Persian dishes. The exotic fare is further enhanced by rich descriptions of the cultural and culinary history of Persian cuisine, without which it cannot be fully appreciated.

190 pages · 5½ x 8½ · 0-7818-0241-5 · $11.95pb